BARKEEP

THE GUIDE
to becoming a professional bartender

Danilo Bozovic • *Andrija Ristic*

Illustrations by Gabriel Lehner

BARKEEP

THE GUIDE
to becoming a professional bartender

HOLLOW POINT
PUBLISHING

HOLLOW POINT
PUBLISHING

63-54 Forest Ave

Queens, NY 11385

By Danilo Božović &

Andrija Ristić

First Edition (2016)

Published by Hollow Point Publishing LLC, New York, New York

www.hollowpointpublishing.net

ISBN: 978-0-9978067-4-8

Illustrations by Gabriel Lehner

DTP/ design by Aleksandar Najdenov

www.evolve.rs

For information about custom editions, special sales, and premium and corporate purchases, please contact Hollow Point Publishing at info@hollowpointpublishing.net

Foreword

I have met Danilo over 6 or 7 years ago when he applied to be an apprentice at Employees Only Restaurant and Bar. His enthusiasm and all around positive outlook immediately struck me. Danilo proved later that besides having a strong work ethic he excelled in his desire to learn and study. He was always the first to come and last to go. Nothing that needed to be done was beneath him and he always went the extra mile for the establishment and his bar team. Today, it makes me really happy to see that Danilo has grown into a true master of his craft and a true lineage holder, someone very much qualified to write such an amazing, modern 21st century bartender's manual.

Although I am sure that many amateur bartenders will love Barkeep it is beyond doubt that the professional bartenders and their apprentices will benefit the most. The huge amount of practical and more importantly very necessary information is laid out in a logical and organic way so that the novice as well as the seasoned veteran can easily find what they are looking for. Barkeep starts with the job description of a Bartender as a professional host and all the challenges that this choice of work brings with itself. Truly a fully developed Bartender has to master both making drinks and serving people. And serving people is a much harder skill to acquire as one's life experiences are crucial to its growth and development. Danilo and Andrija present best practices and beautifully describe the attitudes connected with applied hospitality.

Barkeep has really touched on all elements of proper education of bartenders. My favorite part is certainly the chapter of Food service and the food lexicon. Many bartenders have little to no idea about proper food service and service etiquette. I wish someone taught me proper service when I was starting out as a bar-back. I could have avoided many embarrassing moments in my time.

To what extent the authors have gone to share their knowledge is noticeable in the chapter that describes how to organize work stations, body language and how to move behind the bar. The instructions are easy to grasp, make a lot of sense and are most importantly a very necessary skill to have when working behind the bar with a team.

Naturally the book focuses a great deal on classic and current bar tools and techniques. It goes into depth of the bar set-up, description of various cocktail families, tasting notes and history. And then just when you think that the book couldn't get better the authors present the chapter on Coffee and Tea. In a bartending book! Phenomenal!

I could list a hundred more things that are great about Barkeep and I am certainly very fond of the beautiful illustrations as well but what makes me really happy and proud is to see that one bartender from our lineage has made this amazing effort, combined all the knowledge and finally put it down in a proper educational form. I am positive that Barkeep will be the favorite book for many future generations of bartenders.

Dushan Zaric,
Employees Only NYC, Macao Trading Company NYC and The 86 Co
Los Angeles, February 2016

Contents

PART FIVE - MIXOLOGY

PART SIX - COCKTAIL

PART SEVEN - COCKTAIL PRESENTATION

PART EIGHT ICE

PART NINE - BEER

PART FIFTEEN - WHISKY

PART SIXTEEN - RUM

PART SEVENTEEN - TEQUILA

PART EIGHTEEN - BRANDY

PART NINETEEN - ABSINTHE

PART TWENTY - LIQUEURS

PART TWENTY-ONE - HOUSE-MADE SYRUPS AND INFUSIONS

PART TWENTY-TWO - CLASSIC COCKTAILS

Introduction

This book is dedicated to the just starting apprentice, to the professional bartender, to the cocktail enthusiast and anyone who enjoys a good drink.

- Danilo Božović -

To be a good bartender means to be content, successful and satisfied with one's self. The greater the effort a person is ready to put in working on himself/herself the better, the bartender he/she will become.

Each person has his own reason for entering the bartending profession. Some enter it to finance their studies, earn some pocket money, whereas others truly desire to work at a bar. Some see it as a side job while trying to succeed in other professions. The preparing and serving of cocktails is what mostly attracts people to the bartending profession, but even though it is an appealing part of our craft, it most assuredly is not the only one. Whatever the reason, in order to work behind a bar with ease and quality, one needs a lot of effort, knowledge and experience. Beginnings can be quite difficult and that is why it is imperative to have an experienced and well-intentioned colleague as well as useful literature by one's side. Every bartender about to start working is expected to know the basics of the craft. Although every employer wants a bartender who already has experience, that is not always the case. Like any craft, bartending has its own basics that one needs to master in order to further advance. Bearing that in mind, as an ideal starting position for studying the profession, I recommend the local cafe. Even though this proposition does not seem very appealing, a local cafe will enable the young bartender to offset the lack of experience and gain some beginner confidence necessary for the further development of knowledge and skills. At the local cafe, a young bartender will be able to feel comfort and feel the atmosphere which a bar can provide, the layout of ingredients, as well as develop a sense of routine for making coffee, juice and squeezed juices. While making coffee a bartender will, apart from the basic way the bar operates (hot drinks and non-alcoholic beverages), develop a sense of timing that is, a sense of time required to prepare an order for the waiter or a guest as quickly and efficiently as possible.

Apart from that, he will slowly start learning about serving different kinds of alcohol, working with money and, mostly important, working with people. In the beginning a young bartender will be able to learn a great deal by watching his older and more experienced colleagues, as well as through his beginner's mistakes. Only when he starts feeling comfortable in a crowded bar can a bartender experience working in a night club or cocktail bar. Whichever path a bartender chooses, he should bear in mind that he should not stagnate, and that constant progress and acquisition of new knowledge should become an imperative for him. The time period required for that development is subjective, differs from person to person and depends on the preparedness to work on one's self and his bartending expertise.

A short story about the bar business

The first liquor license in the state of New York was printed, during her short reign, by Queen Anne of Great Britain somewhere in between 1707-1714. Generally, the atmosphere in bars (called salons) at this time, the early 18th century, was drastically different concerning guests as well as the activities that took place inside the bars. The guests of those bars were almost exclusively male, not just sailors, soldiers, politicians but also pirates, gamblers and mercenaries of all kinds. This mix, as well as the fact that people who used to frequent bars drank far more than they do today, led to common disagreements and often physical conflicts inside and outside of bars.

Contrary to today's mostly hedonistic consumption of alcohol, the aim of eighteenth-century bar visitors was to drink as much as they could, without any particular interest in the quality of alcohol consumed. The vast amount of consumed alcohol was not the only matter that complicated the bartenders' job. The standard of living was significantly different than today and bars had to fight for the most necessary provisions such as water. The life of a common man was extraordinarily hard, and the most basic items often presented an unreachable luxury. So bartenders had to, besides tending the bar, maintain order in their establishment. In order to prevent the establishment from plummeting to chaos, the bar room was always separated by bar, while alcohol and other articles were stashed in the rear of the bar, the so called back bar.

Of course, there were people back then who frequented bars in order to relax and enjoy alcohol and company, exchange information and trade. The eighteenth-century will, inter alia, be remembered in the history of mankind by wars between great forces over monopoly on various goods, workforce and natural resources. England and France started one such war, The War of the Spanish Succession (1701–1714). The settlers of the American continent were engaged in similar battles in the eighteenth century with the Native Americans, The Indian Wars East of the Mississippi (1775-1842). Exchange of goods and trade were some of the most profitable forms of business at the time. Tea was imported to the American continent. Profits made by trading, sugar sales and especially the slave trade financed various wars and conquests. Certain strata of the population and the states they lived in grew richer than the rest of the world, gaining in the process the aptitude to influence the historic events in accordance to their own political and economic aspirations.

All this was connected to the rapid advancement of crafts which came as an answer to the constantly developing consumer needs. Spending most of his time in the bar, the bartender possessed the latest news and information. Besides all historic events happening at the time, knowledge and information were considered to be precious, and a good bartender was an informed bartender, which has remained an imperative of the profession to this day. In the nineteenth century entertaining guests by different methods, apart from alcohol, became an important role in bars and saloons, and the owners tried to make the stay in their establishments more memorable and uncommon. Bars started to introduce various aspects of entertainment such as, billiards, stage plays, cock fighting, arm wrestling competitions and so forth. These hospitality establishments merited greater attendance and the entertainment they offered enabled the patron to relax and, at least temporarily, forget all of his troubles. Bars near the gold mines were famous for great changes they brought to the lives of their patrons, mostly miners. People went from poor to extraordinarily rich and each unexpected turning point, whether good or bad, took place at the bar. Elite bars were mostly located in major cities, were better fitted and boasted a wide assortment of goods used to make better cocktails for guests who mostly belonged to the upper layer of society (politicians, nobility, bankers and wealthy merchants).

During this period a bartender retained the role of an intermediary between the drink and the guest. He was still the one to maintain the atmosphere and sell alcoholic beverages at the bar. During the Golden Age of cocktails, between 1830 and 1920, bartender's knowledge and drink mixing expertise comes to the fore.

A good bartender was expected to know how to make a good cocktail, a drink that was becoming ever more popular, so that the art of mixing drinks (mixology) became the crucial component of bar service. Besides his tendency towards mixology, the bartender remained a traditional host, an informed and civil man. Certain bartenders that mastered the theoretical part of bartending, allowed themselves the luxury of doing various bar attractions such as, pouring multiple cocktails at once, flambéing a beverage at the bar and so on. At the time, Vermouth became an important cocktail ingredient and the cocktail culture of the 20th century in general. Unfortunately the Golden Age of cocktails ended when Prohibition came into effect in all US states on the January 16th, 1920. This move by the American government put in jeopardy the bartending profession, making its very existence uncertain. The bartending profession became illegal, so it became reserved to the so-called speak easies, which had to be kept quiet in order not to get discovered by the authorities and closed. Due to these circumstances, bartenders were forced to search for work in other countries or cruiser ships, which were allowed to sell alcohol during certain stages of their voyage. Although some bartenders tried to keep the bar culture at a high standard, the absence of the older, more experienced colleagues took its toll. By the time Prohibition was abolished on December 5th, 1933 the consequences of stagnation of the bar culture were dearly felt. The bartenders who returned to the US were considerably older now and could not do night shifts. One could drink a decent martini in the years following Prohibition exclusively during the day, if one were lucky enough to find an older bartender at the bar.

What would later become one of the most recognizable characteristics of this period was the easy transition of cocktail culture to an era of sweet and multicolored cocktails, which would last until the end of the 20th century. With the help of Dale DeGroff, Gary Regan and other lovers of the forgotten, classic drink, the good old cocktail started to revive in the bar culture and change the wishes and requests of the contemporary guest.

Part one

BARTENDER

"Bartender is a professional host. He is responsible for every guest from the moment they enter the hospitality establishment until the moment they exit. Bartender is, primarily, a master of his trade and the person who possesses immense knowledge, life experience and strong character."

- Danilo Božović -

Bartender, a professional host

The role of the bartender is much more than just making drinks or cocktails, pouring beer or making coffee. As a professional host the bartender is responsible for the whole experience and, at the same time, the well-being of the guest and the establishment. This is accomplished with sincere hospitality and professional service. Although our craft experience different periods the significance of the bartender as a good host remains of the greatest importance till this day. The professional bartender should strive to reach the highest possible personal and professional standards. The best way to learn is from different situations while tending a bar where one should always analyze his performance and work. Realize where the mistakes have been made, correct them and move forward. Nobody can know everything, but what the bartender does not know today, he should know tomorrow. Bartenders, who read books written by greats such as Jerry Thomas or Harry Johnson, recognize the importance of a satisfied guest. For some people, the role of host is more natural because they either grew up next to a person of such behavior and attitude or they innately have the character attributes which allow them to communicate more successfully with people. In order for a bartender to be a good host he needs to understand his guest well enough, to anticipate and satisfy his needs from the moment he enters the bar. For this to be possible it is crucial for a bartender to know and understand his bar (history, drinks, menu, philosophy, etc) if he intends to be a good host to his guest. The tools of our trade can easily be learnt, but to become a good host requires a lot more than that. A bartender's job is to make sure his shift goes smoothly. This is why he should be aware of everything that goes on at the bar. He is the one with control and that is how it should stay until the end of the shift. He should never lose control nor be unpleasant or repulsive towards a guest. All issues that occur during the bartender's shift are his responsibility and up to him to resolve.

While he is in his workplace, a bartender is advised to show confidence and radiate positive energy. No person wants to be in the presence of negativity, wherever he is. A bartender has done his job right if the guest leaves the bar content with service and his experience there. If the guest sits at the bar, the bartender is the one who provides the bar experience, and this is done properly, primarily, by the correct pace and order of service. If the bartender is focused, he will, at crucial moments, approach the guest, prepare a drink, recommend another one, order food, refill the water glass or start and conclude a conversation with guest. Proper order of bartending services includes proper understanding of his guest. Since every guest is different, the relationship, and therefore, the service will differ and adapt to the guest. Some guests are looking for a long conversation, while others do not like to be disturbed. Some guests know what they like to drink, while others do not. Some are looking for specific brands, while others like to try something new. All of these situations affect the flow of service and hospitality. With this being said, a professional host will make it easier to provide good service and hospitality while being in different situations. One needs to keep in mind that the position of a bartender holds so great a responsibility, he greatly affects the success of the whole bar and the establishment. His responsibility is rooted in professionalism, knowledge, experience, organization skill and devotion.

Be true to yourself

In being true to one's self, lies the main source of strength and growth. When one knows himself, he can easily determine which path he wants to take, and which bar best suits his own personal philosophy and beliefs. For every bartender, there is a corresponding bar where he should work. Depending on his temperament and personal propensities, a bartender can choose working in a club, cocktail bar, pub, or coffee bar, the point being that he should feel comfortable and love what he does in order to reach his full working, but also, personal potential. This is why it is important for a bartender to be not only true to himself, for then he will find the perfectly suited bar for him as well as compatible regulars. A bartender should never be a copy of another bartender. We all learn from one another but the point is to listen to that inner voice and guide yourself to become the bartender you are meant to be.

Strict professional

The best way to explain professionalism is through the example of the strict professional. To be a good bartender one needs to be a strict professional. In any work, one should have a professional attitude and serious approach in order to do his job the best he can. It goes without saying, in order to do his job properly, a person should possess the necessary discipline so as to know his function and role in the workplace at every moment. Being a strict professional is, besides being a good host, mindful of your technique and service, which proves a crucial characteristic of every professional bartender. He is aware of his own talents as well as his shortcomings and should strive to better himself. A strict professional is in competition with himself, never with others. There is no place for ego inside of him while working at the bar. Passion, tenacity, confidence, knowledge and love for his job dominate him at work. A bartender who is a strict professional has three clear goals: the welfare of the guest, of the establishment and finally, his own. When a strict professional has clear goals, he easily becomes a good host. By devoting himself to work, he expresses love for his profession and, also, the readiness to constantly better himself and advance. Every person cherishes good service, and there is truth to the fact that it reflects the devotion of the bartender. With this approach to work, a strict professional creates a positive atmosphere in which he can advance professionally and spiritually. Besides devotion, one needs to believe in oneself and his own goals, to trust that everything is possible for this attitude keeps away bad energy and makes the bartender's life easier and more positive. Why is it important to be a strict professional? Ask yourself what kind of world this would be if everybody was a strict professional. Imagine that all people were the best they possibly could be. If a cashier was the best cashier, an accountant the best accountant and a cleaning lady the best possible cleaning lady, the world would be much more beautiful and easier to live in. One does not have to be better than someone else as long as he aims to reach his full potential. To do so, it is important what a person thinks of himself; only then will one improve and grow towards his personal greatness. The strict professional possesses a code which he adheres to. He does not put other people down, but lifts them up. This way he implements his wisdom in a positive way, truly providing growth to the people surrounding him (apprentices, barbacks, colleagues, etc.). When trying someone else's drink, the strict professional does not compete and compare one's self to another. He simply learns from the difference between drinks, improves himself by that much and continues on his path. A strict professional always leaves his personal issues at home, no matter how difficult they are. If they are too difficult to put aside, the bartender should find someone to cover his shift. The strict professional speaks through his actions. If he truly cares about his craft, he will spend time learning, reading and practicing in order to do his job better. He will go that extra mile and only then can one say that he is a strict professional. He not only shows that with words, but most importantly with actions and throughout his work behind the bar. As a strict professional, a bartender has to stand behind his actions. He should always react with a clear mind knowing that he is doing the right thing. The better the bartender does his job the more weight his voice carries, like in any other profession. Everybody recognizes quality work and all efforts will pay off in the end because that is inevitable.

Let the future tell the truth, and evaluate each one according to his work and accomplishments. The present is theirs; the future, for which I have really worked, is mine.

Nikola Tesla

Experience and hospitality

Having experience is mostly referring to two things: life experience and bar experience. Both are very similar to one another and go hand-in-hand. The sum of these two experiences gives the best hospitality possible. In order for the bartender to understand the guest and eventually provide good hospitality, he needs experience. This will benefit him in making the right calls. The bartender should have a good perception of the bar and to know what is going on. He does not only assign seating at the bar but knows in advance when certain actions will take place (when to present menu, remove empty glasses from the bar, offer another round, present the check, etc.). Besides experience, a bartender should have a distinct feel for the bar, how it breathes, the way it works, in order to know how to organize it and maintain the flow of his evening. Each bar has a different tempo; some bars close earlier while others work till late night. When a bartender knows his bar, he knows what music to play at any given time, what the lighting should be, when to do flair, and whether or not he can have a long conversation with a guest. The music played ought to shape the evening and be pleasant to the guests, as well as the bartender. Sometimes, the music played the night before will not be a good fit for the following night. All of these factors contribute towards bad, good or excellent hospitality.

Forefathers of our craft

The three bartenders mentioned in this chapter are perfect examples of probably the first professional bartenders whose work made their names forever present in our craft. We can learn so much from them. I was always fond of the flashy side to Jerry Thomas. His invention of the Blue Blazer opened eyes towards more attractive bar techniques and paved the path for future flair bartenders as well as bartenders who wanted to spice up their flair behind the bar. Attracting guests to the bar is an art, one which he definitely mastered, and something which should be looked upon. Harry Johnson always looked after the guest and his well-being. That is a great lesson for bartenders and definitely other professionals of other crafts. The fact that Harry Craddock never opened his own bar can be a pressure diffuser for many bartenders. One does not necessarily have to open a bar to be a successful bartender. One should listen to himself and do what he sees fit. Had not every generation written down and passed on their knowledge onto the generations that followed, the understanding of this trade and its crafts would not have risen to today's level. The bartenders are burdened with continuing to improve the bartending profession and to conduct it accordingly. The legends of this trade have paved the path upon which the professional bartenders today tread.

Finding a good mentor is very hard but if a young bartender decides to attend bartending courses, he should make sure if the school he plans to attend is indeed worth his time and money. After the finished course, a young bartender has a lot more to learn in order to become a mature and experienced professional, so if he wants to make this job his livelihood it is recommended to find a bar with a good mentor who knows how to shape him and make a quality bartender out of him. Finding a good mentor is a far more important move than finding a bar where he will earn a lot of money. Developing his skills and earning experience will surely yield him money. The ideal situation would be if the young bartender could earn enough money and still learn from an older, more experienced bartender.

Jeremiah (Jerry) P. Thomas

1830 – 1885

Famous bartender, legend of bartending profession, professor Jerry Thomas wrote and published the first bartending cocktails book – *The Bon-Vivant's Companion Or How to Mix Drinks* in 1862. Thomas's book raised awareness of cocktails and cocktail families such as Daisy, Fizz, Flip, Sour, Collins and others. Jerry Thomas was born in 1830 in New York where he learned the bar trade before moving to California during the middle of the 19th century. In 1851 Jerry Thomas decided to return to New York and opened his very first saloon. The time when Jerry Thomas worked differs from today in terms of the fact that the knowledge of the bartending trade was not shared. Information was not accessible at the time as it is today. Jerry wrote a lot and wanted to share his knowledge with other bartenders. Although his first book did not provide advice based on his own experience, the second one was filled with it. It was hard for bartenders of the 19th century to gather materials and information needed for their books because, as we all know, there was no Internet. Today a bartender can access the needed information easily. Jerry's personal life was as interesting as his professional one. He was a respected man, famous for his bar inventory made of silver with various precious gems. He was a man who traveled a large part of the world, but his home remained the Metropolitan bar in New York City. Unfortunately, a bad assessment of shares in the market cost Jerry dearly, and he lost almost everything and had to sell his bar along with most of his property. As a bartender, Thomas possessed a brilliant and creative mind. His approach to the Manhattan, with more vermouth than whisky, opened new horizons when it came to mixing ingredients and the approach to making cocktails. The Blue Blazer cocktail, which attracted the attention of a great number of people, was one of Jerry's cocktail-creations which proved his love towards attractive techniques.

Harry Johnson

1845 – 1933

At the start of the 17th century, German immigrants left their homeland and traveled to America wanting to open their businesses and in search of a better life. During the middle of the 19th century, most German immigrants came to America and, in most cases, opened their pubs or started bartending at local ones. The bartending job fit people who had just arrived to America in need of work and did not require a diploma, but strong character and charisma. Harry Johnson was born on 28th August 1845 in Kaliningrad, Russia. He immigrated to America with his family in 1852 and started his bartending career in San Francisco when he was only fifteen. When he was 23, he started to win competitions and show that his work was of exceptional quality. Harry Johnson published his first bar manual entitled *Bartender's Manual* in 1882. He advised other people how to become better bartenders; his manuals explained how one should act at the bar towards the guests and even how one should be trained. There is no doubt that Harry was a great connoisseur of hospitality and a successful bar owner. His wish was to, besides owning a bar, protect the rights of bartenders by forming a union which enabled bartenders to earn high wages and other benefits. The First World War changed the way Americans viewed German immigrants. This period was not at all easy for a German bartender, nor for Harry and his family. Although Harry led a tumultuous life, he managed to keep it to himself, remaining professional until the end. He continued to travel and sell his books in English, and later in German. He died at the age of 89, a few months before the end of Prohibition, leaving behind his passion and knowledge for generations to come.

Harry Lawson Craddock

1875 – 1963

Harry Lawson Craddock was born on 29th August 1875 in Burleigh, England. Wanting more from life, Harry left his home and large family (he had six siblings), and went to New York where he started to work as a waiter. Covering his colleague's shifts, Harry fell in love with the bartending business and although he wanted to work at the best establishments, his lack of experience prevented him from doing that. He started working at the West End of New York where he managed to keep his job despite his lack of experience. With the ratification of the Volstead Act, he found himself, as many others, in an inconvenient situation. The bartending profession was viewed differently now. The bars kept getting closed, the cocktail culture waned and bartenders were out of a job. Hoping that Prohibition would end soon, Harry went to England with his wife and daughter. The demand for a quality American cocktail was great in London, but there were few bartenders experienced enough, which enabled the American bar to take new life. The Savoy Hotel soon became the home of Harry Craddock, and the extent to which the owner of the hotel was amazed with Harry's work and skill is reflected in the fact that they helped him publish a book entitled *The Savoy Cocktail Book*. After the end of Prohibition, Harry was unwilling to go back to New York because he was satisfied with his life in London, where he would work as a master bartender until the end of his life. He was never interested in owning a bar, but just wanted to work as a bartender who served quality drinks. After nineteen years at the Savoy, Harry decided to leave his workplace and work at the bar called The Dorchester, which was home to many famous politicians such as Winston Churchill and others. Harry died on January 23rd, 1963 at the age of 87. Living the simple life of a true professional, Dr. Manhattan, or Harry Craddock, was one of the best representatives of the American bar and hotel bartending.

Devotion

How does one know if one is devoted enough to his work place? If you approach the bar where you work as if it was your own? Do you take care of it, clean it, treat guests the same as if they were sitting behind your bar? Do you have the same work ethic as you would behind your own bar? If that is the case, rest assured you are devoted. Just alone by being a strict professional, the bartender is already putting in the work and devotion needed. For the bartender to be truly dedicated, he needs to find a bar which he highly respects, and really wants to be a part of.

One should avoid petty people

During one's life, every person will encounter people, schools, organizations or institutions that are not willing to truly teach somebody. Arrogant and conceited behavior is characteristic of a petty person. When you think about it, an individual, who is only starting the bartending trade, cannot know much about it and needs, at least in the beginning, a sure hand to guide him through. Therefore, if a young apprentice is not accepted in the bar he works at or a school he goes to, he should look for a different bar, school or association. Spending time in a counterproductive environment will prevent him from being a successful bartender. In this type of situation, one should always follow his instinct.

Part two

———◆◆◆———

BAR

"A place where people come to relax, have a good time and, even for a short while, forget their troubles. The bar is home to a bartender and a place where he serves people as best he can."

- Danilo Božović -

Bar

The bar is a place of socialization where various drinks are consumed: alcoholic, non-alcoholic, hot, cold, etc. At the bar, people can enjoy good drinks, quality service, live music and relax. The bar is made primarily so a bartender can responsibly handle alcohol. The bar is the workplace of a bartender, so he has to feel free, comfortable, and secure in it, in order for his work to be efficient and of quality. The word bartender signifies a person which tends the bar and keeps everything under control. While the bartender is working, he is also the host, manager, promoter and owner. He is a person responsible for proper functioning of the bar. There are many different bars in the world and each one is specific in its own way. Each bar provides something new and specific, whether it is good service, appearance, location or something else. Every bar has to have a part for waiter service usually at the end of the bar and should be strategically placed so the service is easy to achieve. The surface of the bar reserved for waiter service should be well designed, so the waiter has enough room to take orders, but not so large as to take up too much room designated for bar guests.

Back bar

Most bars have a back bar where the majority of bottles are. They differ from bar to bar and can be high, low, from different materials and different shapes, with its own specific lighting. A mirror on the back bar helps the bartender see what is going on while he has his back turned to the rest of the bar. The back bar gives the first impression when the guest comes in. Wise men say: "Eyes are the mirror of the soul". You could say that the back bar is the mirror of the bar. The back bar should attract the guest's attention and make him want to visit the bar again. The role of the back bar is to transfer the specific energy present at the bar. The quality of establishment, together with professionalism of the bartender is reflected in the quality of drinks and their selection. Material from which the back bar is made, the layout of bottles and lighting are of great significance. When you look towards the bar pourers should be facing left, not only because of consistency, but also functionality. When pouring, if the pourers are facing left, the bartender can fully approach the back bar. That way, he makes room for his colleague to pass behind him and enables the label to be visible to the guest at the same time. The back bar has to be functional. The most frequently used drinks should be on the bottom shelves so it is makes their use easier for the bartender. Bigger and longer bottles can be on the last shelf with more luxurious brands. Tall bottles should not be in front of the frequently used ones because they only hinder the bartender. Drinks of the same category should be kept next to each other.

Example No. 1 – All brands of vodka, gin and tequila should be next to each other. Bottles on the back bar have to be representative and clean. Bottles that attract flies, such as colored alcohol and liqueurs, should be fitted with a screen pourer because they prevent flies from entering. At the end of the shift, pourers should be protected with plastic caps and glasses with a cover to protect them from dust.

The back bar should inspire those behind the bar as well as before it. The visual appearance of the bar is very important. Before opening for public the bartender should check if the bar looks representable. One ought to check if the pourers are clean, aligned, and fit the bottle they are on. Besides that, it is important to make sure bottles are clean and labels are facing the guests. Glasses should be clean and polished, screens and printers checked before opening. The doors of coolers should be clean, and barstools neatly organized. The bartender should check if there is everything in the optimum amounts and refill anything that is missing. If everything is in place, neat and refilled the bar is ready for guests. There are many types of bars and each one of them is different and so is their visual appearance. The type of bar depends on its working hours, drinks selection, food and music offer. A bar's hygiene speaks louder than words. The hygiene of a bar and is one of the first things noticed by guests. A bartender should respect the sanitary rules of the country he is working in and apply them at the bar. He has to take care of noting the perishable products so the whole bar knows when they expire. Fruit files can present a great problem if the bar is not kept clean. As extremely resistant animals, fruit flies can present a lot of troubles for the bartender on summer days. Fruit and fresh ingredients should be kept cold. Before the shift starts, it is highly recommended to taste the products to check if they have expired. Bar equipment has to be kept clean. The state of the bar equipment reflects the attitude of the employees towards the job.

Bar hierarchy

Hierarchy is a great way for one to learn the craft and at the same time, keep the bar system functional. In order to function perfectly, every detail has to be taken into account. Depending on the workload and bar size, the hierarchy usually consists of:

Storage manager is the entry position in the bar business, in case the bar has this position. This is an ideal way for the young apprentice because it can introduce him to the assortment of goods, while he is waiting for a chance to work behind the bar. His job is to note the merchandise entering and exiting the storage space as well as report if some of the goods are depleted during the work shift. The storage manager is responsible for all the goods, its condition and replenishment of its stock.

Fruit preparer is in charge of all garnishes, pressed fruit, orders and maintenance. He should know what amounts should be sliced and juiced for the day. The bar manager should work closely with the fruit preparer so that both sides are familiar with the flow of work. This is a good starting position for people who want to learn the bar business.

Barback is a student of the trade, charged with maintaining the bar and helping the bartender during his shift. He learns by listening to and observing his bartender. In order for a bar to continue to function and operate properly, an experienced bartender should take it upon himself to shape and teach the barback to be even better. Training the barback should be a privilege and a satisfaction for the bartender, not just his responsibility. One day, that barback will pass that knowledge onto his barback. Passing knowledge is not easy. It is up to the bartender to identify the moment when he should correct and constructively criticize his barback. The right word at the right moment is of an incredibly great importance. The less a barback's presence is felt behind the bar the better his movement is. If the barback is in the way of the bartender or is distracting him, he is interfering with the flow of the bar. In order for the bar to provide the best experience possible, the flow should not be interrupted. This is why movement is a crucial part of bartending and of great importance. A barback's movement is of equal importance to the bartender's. Bartender's performance, sale and atmosphere at the bar will depend on the barback's movement and efficiency. In the picture underneath the arrows show the best possible choice of movement for a barback (letter B). The big circles represent "safe zones" or the area where the barback is least likely to collide with the bartender (bartender 1, bartender 2, bartender 3). From the "safe zone," the barback can overlook the bar and see what needs or will need to be restocked. In case the bar is very busy, the barback should know when to enter the bar and to make his time at the bar useful. The barback should use "safe zones" (large drawn circles)– the parts of the bar where the bartenders rarely enter. Those are usually the recesses at the bar which provide easier movement on the one hand, and the opportunity to better perceive the overall state of the bar on the other hand.

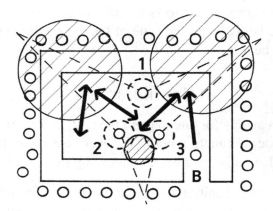

Head barback is the position of the oldest and most responsible barback. His job is to make sure all barback responsibilities are conducted properly. This person is responsible for the barback's schedule and their work in general. He reports directly to the head bartender and bar manager and is first in line to become the bartender.

Bartender is the position which we deal with the most in this book. An individual usually reaches it after a few years as a barback and head barback. Everything the bartender learns during his days as a barback will be useful to him in conducting the job where he will continue his personal and professional advancement.

Head bartender is the leader and the backbone of the bar staff. He should be of strong character, experienced and professional. He is expected to lead and work in the interest of the bar team.

Bar manager is, first and foremost, in charge of accounting and logistics of the bar. That means that he closes the deals with suppliers and brands, promotes the bar, and takes care of the bar functions to the best of his ability. If he wants to keep in touch with current affairs, he can still work behind the bar.

Bar organization skill

A well-organized bar is already 85% of the work done. It requires lots of focus, experience and effort but when done properly, one will enjoy working those busy nights. Before the start of organizing the bar, a bartender should check how many reservations he has for the day, and if there is some kind of a special event in the establishment. Good organization of the bar starts with discipline and coming to work on time. If one comes to work on time, he has all the time he needs to oversee the set up and make sure everything is ready for the shift. Of course, it is normal to occasionally be late but one should not make it a habit. This is one of the ways how the bartender shows his devotion to his establishment. Once behind the bar, the bartender has to organize his work space in order for his job to be performed perfectly. Each bartender has a certain way he likes his set up to be which is totally normal as long as he does not interfere in the general layout of his bar. If he is successful in accomplishing the best organization possible, keeping his drinks coming fast at a high quality will be an easie task. If the set-up is not good, the staff will not work well, service will be of lower standard which will lead to losing guests and lowering the reputation of the bar. On the other hand, if the bar is overcrowded, the bar team will have extra distractions during work. Intuition is very important when it comes to setting up a bar. When it is done, the head bartender should double check if the bar is capable of supporting the workload predicted for the day. Aside from that, the bartender should point out any possible mistakes and oversights to the person who has done the set-up that day in orders to prevent them from happening and to increase the productivity.

It is recommended that bar set-up be conducted according to the bar set up steps in order to easily remember it. Once the steps are learnt, it will become a routine which will enable the employees to better perform their duty. It is highly recommended to set up the front of the bar first because in case the whole set-up is behind schedule, the front will be ready for the first guests. During that time, the barback has to tend to the unfinished part of the bar. Even if the bar is organized in the best manner, the bartender should avoid leaving the bar frequently for two reasons. One is that he will lose his energy presence and the bar will die down. Secondly, one could say all his organization is done in vain because without him to oversee the bar, all his preparation for that shift will be worthless. In order to better organize the bar, the bartender has to imagine the flow of the shift. This kind of preparation is easier for the bartender because it lets him work the shift according to the preconceived plan. If he encounters any issues before opening, he has to resolve them before the shift starts; nothing should be left to chance. Organization is the key element to the shift. The bar should be 100% ready for work, whether a smaller or a greater workload is expected. The approach to organizing a bar ought to be the same. With a serious approach the bartender leads his team towards a good shift. To succeed, each link at the bar should function perfectly, there should be a clear hierarchy structure and equal allocation of responsibilities.

Bar set-up for two bartenders and one barback

Steps a bartender or barback should take the moment they start their shift:

Step No. 1 – Refill the part of the bar that serves food (cutlery and folded napkins)

Step No. 2 – Supplement the plates at the bar.

Step No. 3 – Bring ten bar rags for each workstation.

Step No. 4 - Bring eight bus bins, 4 for each station.

Step No. 5 – Bring additional knife and fork sets (so called roll up sets).

Step No. 7 – Bring enough sugar and salt to each workstation.

Step No. 8 – Bring enough paper rolls and toner for the printer.

Step No. 9 – Set up the cutting board and bar knives, sanitary gloves, tape, and marker for noting the date.

Step No. 10 – Set up the number of rocks glasses needed for the amount of garnish.

Step No. 11 – Place to the side the glasses the barback need to fill, glasses for mint, basil, rosemary, peppermint tops, etc.

Step No. 12 – Check the state of garnishes from the previous night before ones starts preparing new one.

Step No. 13 – After replenishing the garnishes, one should replenish the straws, stirrers, bar napkins, matches and business cards.

Step No. 14 – When one is setting up the bar, one should mind the time. Approximately, this is when the closing bartender comes to work.

Step No. 15 – Refill bottles, dash bottles, clean the pourers and bottles.

Step No. 16 – Set up the bottles and other materials according to the bar standards.

Step No. 17 – At this point one should have an hour and 45 minutes left before the bar opening, which is more than enough to prepare spearmint tops. Depending on the size of the spearmint and other ingredients, the preparation should take around 30 minutes, which leaves something over an hour to the bar opening, and which is enough to spread the garnishes around the workstations and bring the ice.

Step No. 18 – During the shift, should avoid putting the containers with spearmint over the ice bin so as not to fall into the ice.

Step No. 19 – Green garnish (lime, spearmint, cucumber) is recommended to be separated from the red (strawberry, raspberry) or orange ones (oranges), because it will be easier for the bartender to recognize them by color when the bar is crowded and in dark.

Step No. 20 – Place wet paper towels over the spearmint leaves so they do not dry too quickly. Place a big ice cube in the glass with the spearmint and other tops, in order to make them more firm and more presentable.

Step No. 21 – After everything is in place one should double check the whole bar (do the 86 list).

Step No. 22 – Make a list with the following statistics:

- the quantities, especially the articles used greatly over the past few days

- list of things necessary for the bar to function properly

Step No. 23 – Refill the ball point pens, paperclips, etc.

Step No. 24 – Place the water carafes strategically all across the bar. At this point one should have 30 minutes left until opening.

Step No. 25 – Start bringing the ice, take the fresh juices from the fridge and place the white wines on ice.

Step No. 26 – Set up the bar lights according to bar standards.

Step No. 27 – Arrange red wines so they are ready to serve.

Step No. 28 – Finalize cleaning of (printers, computer displays, etc.)

Step No. 29 – Clean the soda gun, let the soda flow through it and the bar is ready to rock.

Private event bar set up

Setting up for private events can be a bit hectic. During organization of private events, the bartender or bar manager ought to pass the following information on to the staff:

No. 1 – The choice of drinks at disposal for the guests of the event.

No. 2 – How many people are attending.

No. 3 – Time of guests' arrival.

No. 4 – Planned service for the day (welcome cocktails, champagne and similar)

No. 5 – Options and prices for extension of the event.

In order to prepare the bar, the bar manager has to foresee and plan the whole flow of events.

Step No. 1 – Six to seven days before the event, the bar manager should order the necessary wares and then, when the wares come in, categorize and label them with the name and date of the event.

Step No. 2 – Five days prior to the event, the host should of the event should be contacted to confirm the number of guests. It is advised to add 20 people to the confirmed number just in case.

Step No. 3 – Product for the event should be delivered at least three day before. When they arrive, the bartender should double check if all drinks have been delivered in the appropriate quantities agreed upon the order.

Step No. 4 – The day before the event, the bar manager should contact all staff attending the event and inform them about any new information.

Step No. 5 – On the day of the event, the staff needs to be briefed. Explain the order or service. Every part of the team should be familiar with its responsibilities.

-Name of the guest and the company organizing the event (i.e. Milan from Barkeep PR)

-Name of person(s) (host) responsible for the event (i.e. Jelena)

-Duration of the event (i.e. 16:00 – 22:00)

-Number of guests (i.e. 250)

-Time of their arrival (i.e. 16:00)

-Order of serving drinks, as well as the drinks on offer.

-Special requests of the organizer.

-End the briefing with questions and open discussion.

-In case of dining at the bar, one ought to have a seating schedule.

-Assignment of staff responsibilities ought to be clear.

-Inform the staff about their party wages.

Part three

BEHIND THE BAR

"When working behind the bar."

- Danilo Božović -

Body language is one more factor which determines the experience and is as equally important as verbal communication. For instance, if the bartender stands with his arms crossed all the time, this usually shows tightness and the absence of desire to communicate. In other words, the bartender does not seem very hospitable. Lowering posture is the best way for the first interaction with the guest in which the bartender and the guest are at the same eye-level, making communication and energy exchange as best possible.

Multitasking is a bartender's best friend

Multitasking while working is bartender's best friend. It makes service much better and easier. It is crucial to maintaining the bar, its atmosphere and service at a high level. Perfect example of multitasking is while the bartender is using one hand to shake the cocktail and uses his free hand to organize his work space or keep the bar clean. A bartender should multitask regardless of what part of the bar he is serving. While he is making a drink, he should have in mind the state of the part of bar in front of him, that is, to clean it if it is dirty, refill the water glass, remove empty glasses, etc. Keeping the bar in good condition reduces the scope of the bartender's work, therefore making him more efficient. It allows the bartender to buy more time for a longer conversation with a guest, to provide better service or to help out a colleague in need. An eye for detail has to be developed early on, as a barback, in order for the bartender to truly develop his multitasking skill. My fellow bartender and old friend, Peca, used to say "There is always something to do behind the bar," and a professional bartender should always have that in mind.

To be in the weeds

If the bar is well organized beforehand, being in the weeds will be easy and fun. To be in the weeds is a part of bar slang which means the bartender is barely keeping up with the workload. At moments like this, the bartender's focus ought to be the strongest. The bar should be organized perfectly and the movement should be synchronized in order to allow everybody to work as efficiently as possible. If the bartender start to panic and go into speeds (speed 6 for example), in which he has no control. He will not help. He will transfer chaos onto his colleagues and guests, and he will just look silly. If ones maximum speed is 4 or 5, one should stay in it, slowly try to get faster through time but keep control always.

Tip No. 1 – A bartender should not be stressed due to great workload or due to fact that some people wait a little before being served. Why should he? This is the time when he makes the greatest amounts of money. Waiting is completely fine, and no one expects to be served immediately in a crowded bar, especially if they see the bartender is giving his best.

Tip No. 2 – A bartender should use peripheral vision to observe who needs to be served next.

Tip No. 3 – A bartender should be happy his shift is busy and that he is "slammed". This means his bar is doing something right. He should embrace it. This is his time to shine the most.

During the rush, a bartender is responsible for the state of morale behind the bar. He should undertake the hardest part of the workload, to direct all guests towards him and to make the job easier for the barback as much as possible. The crowded bar is the perfect time when the bartender can teach his barback efficient work. The most is learned when the whole staff is in the weeds. That is when the human sense is stronger and a person memorizes better because the whole bar staff is focused, fearing failure. It is important that the bar staff makes jokes and enjoys these moments, this contributes to the improving of the atmosphere and makes it easier for the entire team to finish up.

Moving in the weeds

Moving behind the bar can be considered an art form. It takes time to perfect, just like any other bar technique. Good movement behind the bar is of great value for service, hospitality and the establishment's well-being. If the movement is practical and good, the bartender will make more money for himself as well as his bar. For this to be possible, the bar should be well-organized and everything in its place thus moving behind the bar will be so much easier. When it comes to movement, many circumstances influence the way a bartender will work. There are a few points one should pay attention to when moving through the bar:

Tip No. 1 – Directing ones colleague is an effective way to move in the bar. With a well-coordinated team of bartenders, bumping in the bar should be minimal. Tapping the back is the best way to let ones colleague know that one is behind him or are trying to pass. The phrase "behind you" tells ones colleague that one is behind him. Using verbal communication while moving at the bar should be the last resort. This should be a goal for every bar team.

Tip No. 2 – A well-versed bar staff precisely knows how to anticipate the movement of other colleagues, but this kind of understanding takes time in order for the bartenders to know each other.

Tip No. 3 – When leaving the bar, the bartender should notify his colleagues first. Precise movement means that a bartender uses his body language to let his colleagues know where he is intending to move. If the signals are clear enough, the colleague will understand and adjust his movement. There will be no bumping into one another.

Tip No. 4 – When a bartender leaves the bar, regardless of hierarchy, the other bartender should stay at his position while the service bartender or the barback tends to the position of the absent bartender. Why? A bartender creates a specific atmosphere while he is at his station. When he leaves it, he leaves that atmosphere behind. The bartender which stayed behind the bar should maintain his own atmosphere. The service bartender or barback should replace the colleague taking a break. The service bartender has not created his own atmosphere because he works at the service station. It is easy for him to adapt to the existing atmosphere created by the absent bartender. The service bartender should only leave the service station when there is someone else to take his place.

A station is where the bartender makes drinks (Bartender 1 = Station 1; Bartender 2 = Station 2; Bartender 3 = Station 3). They are mostly placed at the optimal distance so the bartenders can monitor and control the part of the bar in front of them. Clearly, the bartender does not offer service exclusively to this part of the bar only. The work stations are placed so that the bartender can focus his energy on the specific part of the bar in front of him. The bartender has to keep control of the bar in front of him and be mindful of his colleague's area as well. The job requires team work because everybody has the same goal – to satisfy the guest, the place they work at and make money. That goal is reachable only if the bar functions flawlessly, and the bar staff work as a team.

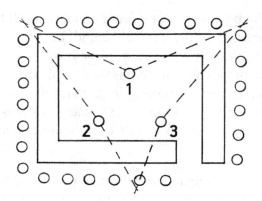

How to balance an overcrowded bar?

In case one of the bartenders is busier, a colleague is expected to help him. This way, the bartender unburdens his colleague, makes service quicker and the bar better. As the example shows, the movement and the positioning of the bartender should have the purpose of the well-being of the bar itself. The upper bartender No. 1 lowers his position and moves closer to the bartender No. 2. The bartender No. 3 comes closer to the bartender No. 2 in order to give the bartender No. 2 better ability to focus on the more crowded area.

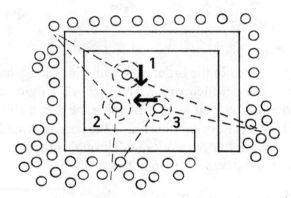

Each bartender is responsible for the area in front of him and his work station, which doesn't mean the area of his colleagues should be neglected. In case the bar is equally busy, bartenders No. 1, No. 2 and No. 3 should be focused on the overall scope of work. Service bartender No. 3 should tend, as time allows him, the part of the bar with less coverage, which is usually the middle part of the bar between bartenders No. 1 and No. 2 (middle of the bar).

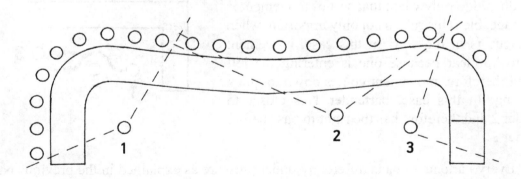

If the bartender No. 2 moves closer to bartender No. 1 in order to help him, the service bartender or barback No. 3 (who does the waiter service) should note the change in positions and take over the part of the bar that the bartender No. 2 left to help the bartender No. 1. Bartender No. 1 should bear in mind that he has left his position unattended, and he should get back to it as soon as possible.

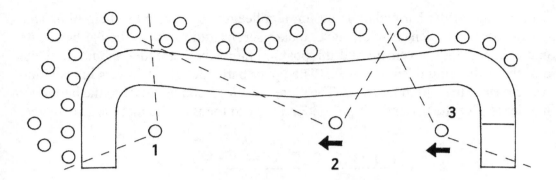

Guests should be served in the order they came in, taking special care of the guests that have been waiting longer for their order. The barback should, at every moment, know the position of his bartenders as well as to anticipate their every move. The barback who goes almost unnoticed in the bar during the shift is the barback that has met his bartenders' expectations and, those of the bar he works at. Through practice, the barback learns the details which will make his movement even better.

The right-hand-side movement rule is the way to go in most cases. What does that mean? In order for the bartenders to move easier and better, the rule of the right hand movement as shown in the picture bellow is crucial. This means each bar member moves to his right side.

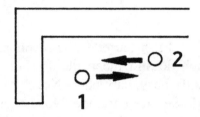

As we know, lots of things are not set in stone in the business. The right-hand-side movement rule is not adhered to only when that sort of movement is not manageable. This rule is not only important when a colleague is in the way. In this case, movement ought to be clear because one is entering the left side and therefore, movement comes down to quick overtaking. In this case, bartender 1 is closer to bartender 2 and therefore has the right to pass before bartender 3.

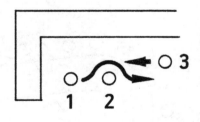

Every bartender reacts differently under pressure as explained in the previous part of the book. Circular movement is mostly done in front of the workstation. While in this work mode the bartender should strive not to pass in front of colleague but behind and around him. Also, the bartender should not spend much time at his workstation allowing other bartenders or barbacks to make use of it as well. Keeping distance from colleagues "zone of reaction" allows for easier circular movement and better anticipation of other's movement as well as better visibility of the bar. How? One should try to understand the "zone of reaction" as a energy-field which pushes other energy-fields.

This means that the movement of bartender No. 2 will influence the movement of bartender No. 3. Not clear? If bartender No. 2 as shown in the picture below moves to the left, his energy-field directs bartender No. 3 to the right. This way a circular motion is formed and if bartender No. 2 wants to go down, bartender No. 3 will go up and this way by making space and avoiding, cause circular motion to come into play. The broken down circle drawn around the bartender No. 2 represent his zone of reaction. In order for him to have enough space to react and maneuver his motions, they should stay as vacant as possible.

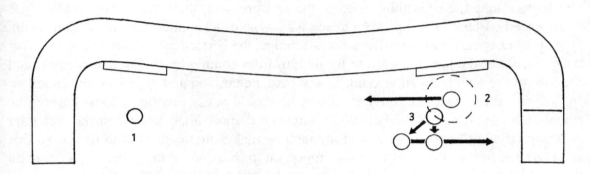

Small advices when moving behind a bar:

Tip 1: Lowering ones shoulder in the intended direction of your movement is a fast 1 second signal in a tight bar environment in which case his colleague should read the intent and make room while still maintaining focus on his job at hand.

Tip 2: When working in a busy bar, moving by keeping only one foot in front will create more open space for movement than by walking normally, one foot at a time.

Problems at the bar

What should one do when having a problem with a guest at the bar? Try not to perceive any situation as a bad one, but look at it as a lesson from which one needs to take out the best. Although the bartender is there to provide good service, he should not tolerate being mistreated and/or malicious comments. The bartender is there to provide service and offer his guest a new and pleasant experience. In case of uncivilized behavior of the guest and absence of a door man, the bartender should walk him out civilly, after he has paid his bill. If he is escorting the guest out, bartender should be of clear mind, confident that he has done the right thing. Before the real problem, there are always subtle signs experienced bartenders can pick up to see what type of a situation they are dealing with. If the misbehaving continues after a few warnings, the bartender has every right to escort the guest out of the bar, and even to forbid him from coming back. The management and security of the establishment should, in any case, be notified and explained the situation. In case the bartender is very busy at the bar, he should notify security who will escort the troublesome guest out of the bar. Body language is most important when the bartender is taking up an order, because at that moment he makes first contact with the guest, that is, leaves the first and usually the most important impression on the guest. Depending on this first impression, a guest's wish to engage the bartender into further conversation will differ. In order for the interaction to be as good as possible, a bartender's eyes should be at the same level as the guest's, and in order to do this, a bartender should lean forward and maintain proper contact. He should not rush guests for the sake of greater profits, nor should he allow them to feel neglected.

Bad actions lead to negative energy

A bartender should never display agitation or repulsiveness, lest he reduces the profit of the bar, and therefore, himself. One should keep in mind that bad actions lead to negative energy and to bad hospitality. The bartender is surrounded by people and his every action, comment, or look influences those around him. He should not do things that could make people in his proximity feel bad. In case of disagreements between colleagues, it is necessary to resolve them in a civilized manner, outside, of course. Work should not suffer due to disagreements. Apart from that, one should bear in mind that by acting reckless, one creates bad energy around him. This will inadvertently drive colleagues and guests away from the establishment. What a guest orders, he should get. Judging his order is unnecessary and unprofessional. A bartender should not delve into what the guest is drinking. He should concentrate on serving the order as best as possible. One should not expect the guest to be familiar with the bar culture and all his potential mistakes in reference to a specific order should not be surprising. It is not recommended to lecture a guest about the quality of drink ordered, unless he is specifically asked. If someone wants a beer with olive juice, he should get beer with olive juice. The bartender's role at the bar is to satisfy the guest by satisfying his whims and wishes, no matter how out of the ordinary they might seem.

Stress and panic

The psychological state of the bartender is crucial when talking about bartending and hospitality. Stress and panic should be avoided. Bartender should use his experience to fight off any unwanted state of mind and be in a Zen state of mind. The psychological state of the bartender is of great importance. It is all in the head. A bad psychological state will result in poor hospitality and discontent. The bartender should be of strong character, confident, and rational at what he does and should not allow for trifles to get to him. He is a person of authority who has to maintain control over himself and his bar. A bartender has to work with enthusiasm, even under great pressure. The key to dealing with pressure is keeping ones composure and being calm. The situations at the bar are always different and the bartender should view each of them as an opportunity to learn something new. After the shift a bartender should think about his work and actions, to spot any possible mistakes and failures in order to make sure they do not occur again. Mistakes are a natural part of our learning, but to make them meaningful, we have to learn something from them. No matter the workload, bartender should make time for each guest. Everything can be done, but focus should not be lost from the job at hand. Confidence is an important trait that a bartender should possess in these stressful situations, as well as in general.

Technique No. 1 – A bartender avoids panic easily if, while taking a large order, he uses his fingers to count the mixed drinks. For example, two vodka and juices, two double vodkas, three gin and tonics and five more drinks. When the bartender is done with taking the order, he should have five outstretched fingers that signify the quantity of mixed drinks he should make. One should serve items such as bottles, beer, cans, etc., first, then unmixed drinks, followed by cocktails served over ice, mixed drinks, and finally straight up cocktails. If the bartender needs more time for a large order, he should add ice at the end (in this case – double vodka).

Technique No. 2 – A bartender can use glasses to memorize the order by putting them in front of him. By putting the garnish on the edge of the glass he will make remembering easier. Guided by personal experience, I recommend the memorizing technique using fingers, sometimes using both hands.

Even though there are a great number of complicated and confusing situations which might occur in our work place, it is important to be fully focused and bear in mind that no problem is unsolvable. This state of mind enables you to become better. A short break gives the bartender a chance to reclaim lost energy necessary to finish his shift. On the other hand, frequent breaks are not good because they take focus off work. Time spent on a break can be used for thoughts about positive things happening or simply for doing something which fulfills the bartender and helps him relax such as coffee, small walk, reading online, texting, checking up Facebook profile, etc.

Fatigue

It is hard to provide good hospitality when one is fatigued and his concentration is down. When this is the case, the stress level is higher and that is definitely not good for providing quality hospitality. If weariness catches up and hours start to seem to go on forever, one should be strict and overcome this. Nobody said the road would be easy, but it will surely be rewarded. The mitigating circumstance is that there is always work at the bar. One can easily fight of fatigue with constant movement and work. Chronic weariness is a totally different subject and to avoid it, a bartender should live a fulfilling life doing what makes one happy. With experience comes the need to look after one's self. Weariness is not the sole concern of the bartender because injuries are also common and a potentially dangerous part of the work. Bartenders constantly use their wrists and therefore, they can hurt themselves while pouring, reaching for ice or mixing drinks. During these actions, a bartender should straighten his wrist without much bending. Sensational pours are beautiful but can injure bartender's hands. A bartender is expected to take care of his whole body since that is the only way he will be fresh and ready for his shift.

Part four

SERVICE

"With good service one shows his passion, knowledge and devotion."

- Danilo Božović -

Service

The more a bartender knows, the better he is, the better his service will be, the more helpful he will be. He will possess more information and, what matters the most, he will do his job better. A bartender's knowledge is greatly reflected in his steps of service. In my opinion, service is the fundamental part of the hospitality and bar business. Apart from the fact that service and hospitality are completely different, they are closely entwined and it is hard to imagine one without the other. Together they provide a unique experience at the bar. The basics of good service will always be a textbook service. You can get the best service possible at a bar or restaurant, but if you just do not feel welcome it will most likely be in vain. Some people do not mind that, but most people do. Either way, the point is to provide as best experience as possible and if one chooses one over the other, he is not doing that. The same goes for hospitality; if people feel welcome but the service is bad, it is still counter productive. In this case one should start with oneself. What do you like?

Bartender should provide the service which:

- Is the establishment standard (the establishment's standard should take precedent)

- He, himself, expects to receive when he frequents a bar as a guest.

A bartender's service is also indicative of his character. A disorderly bar and service present a negative image about the establishment, as well as the bartender. Through good service, one can see the devotion and love for work the bartender possesses, and therefore, the respect for the guest he is serving.

Steps of service

Step 1. Before the start of the shift, a bartender should check the bar in detail to make sure it is completely ready for work. The bartender should check if all the ingredients are fresh and if everything is in appropriate quantities.

Step 2. After greeting the guest, service begins with placing a menu and a glass of water as a clear sign of welcome. The bar napkin should be placed on the bar after the drink order has been received. The bartender should introduce himself only if he is asked to. During the accepting of larger orders it is necessary to repeat it to the guest once more, because it presents an opportunity to double-check the order and affords the guest a chance to change his mind. During the input of the order into the computer, the bartender should double check the order before submitting, especially in case of food. If it comes to an overcrowded situation at the bar, it is up to a bartender to organize seating.

Step 3. Once the guests sit down the bartender should allow them enough time to select food and drinks. Guests should never be rushed when it comes to ordering. When the guests are ready, a bartender should approach and listen to the order with utter focus. During the taking of orders, the bartender should look directly at the guest. The order of serving guests goes from older ladies to younger ones after which gentlemen are served from older to younger ones. If the guests are talking to each other during ordering, one should try not to interrupt their conversation. In order to provide a quality service, the bartender ought to be focused on his work.

Step 4. When serving drinks, the bartender should turn the label on the bottle towards the guest. If the bartender is not satisfied with his drink or cocktail after making it, he should avoid serving it to his guest. When more than 2/3 of the drink is consumed, the bartender should kindly ask if the guest would like his drink to be refreshed. The rule of thumb is that a guest should wait for his cocktail for three minutes after the moment he orders it.

Step 5. Cocktails are recommended to be made in front of the guests. All the cocktail garnishes, bitters or other ingredients. This way the bartender saves time and provides a unique experience for his guests.

Step 6. While working with food, the thumb should not be in contact with the food on the plate. Once the plate is presented, it should be clean. The protein plate should be served directly in front of the guest. Bartender should state the name of the food and drink while presenting it to the guest.

Step 7. When refilling water, the bartender should make sure that ice is in the glass and not the carafe; in order to prevent unnecessary spilling. When handling glasses, he should try to take them by the bottom, not by the top. Whatever the manner of bartender's refilling, his service should be clean and dry.

Working with food

The part of the book is written with the help of Živko Radojčić, a friend and talented New York chef. At the end of the book, there is a small chapter called, "Food lexicon", in which Živko talks about food terminology. This is very beneficial to know. Working with people is one of the most demanding and, sometimes, thankless jobs. On the other hand, the bartending profession can be easy, interesting, and dynamic if you can use your knowledge and personality to satisfy the guest. In every establishment, it is important the hall and bar staff know the ingredients from the menu, as well as terminology used to write the menu in order to be able to answer all questions and requests of the guest professionally. Educating the staff is the responsibility of the kitchen chef and maître d'. The chef writes the menu and gives it to the maître d' along with the detailed description of all courses and existing allergies each time the menu is written, or changed, in order to educate the staff. The Maître d', besides educating the staff, also has to check the knowledge of all employees with various tests, before service, in order to keep the level of quality constant. In every restaurant, pre-meal meetings are organized just before the start of service, where the chef explains the specials of the day, points out the possible changes to the menu, and answers all the questions in reference to the menu. The Maître d' is charged with reading the list of all reservations and pointing out the potential regulars and/or VIP guests. This way, the staff performance is elevated and the service of the establishment improves. In most restaurants, if a guest wishes to alter a dish, the change should be consulted with the chef before it is approved, unless it is a common change which the chef has no issue with.

Before the food ordering takes place, one should make sure there are no dietary restrictions. Food service always starts with an appetizer, unless requested otherwise. Family style restaurants usually serve food as it comes, or as the chef fires (sends it), because everything is being shared. As the food is served, the bartender or barback should warn the guest if there is a higher temperature item or a warm plate. As a rule, the protein should always be directly in front of the guest. As the dishes are being served, the name of the dish should be pronounced with a short description. In the case of a steak, pork chop, etc., the guest should be given a steak knife. Sharing a spoon is highly recommended when serving a couple or a family style dinner. The biggest mistake that one can make is to put the thumb too deep in the dish and even dip the finger into the food. This is a big no-no. If possible, after each course, the plates should be switched. At the end the guest should be offered an option of coffee or dessert.

Signals made by positioning silverware on the plate after the meal are very important.

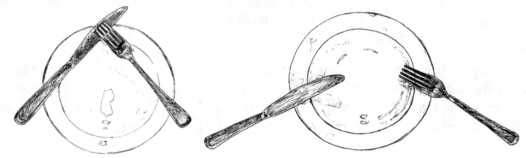

If the knife and fork are crossed, facing each other, it means that the guest has not finished his meal.

If the knife and fork are parallel to each other, it means the guest has finished his meal.

The guest will not always signal that he is done with his meal in this fashion, but the bartender should be familiar with this way of communication in case he comes across a person who uses it. The plates should be removed only when all the guests at the table have finished eating. If there is any food left on the plate after the meal, the guest should be asked if he would like to have it packed to-go. When removing the plate off the bar a bartender should clean the plate using his right hand (in case he is right-handed). Place the plates below the one that contains the remains of food (held in your left hand). Place the spoon and fork over the knives with the fork into the spoon to avoid the possibility of cutlery sliding off the plates.

At the end of the course, the guest should be offered an option of coffee or a dessert.

Before presenting the bill, the area in front of the guest should be cleaned. When presenting the bill, the bartender should discreetly ask the host if he is paying for everything. One should keep in mind that the service is not complete the moment a guest pays his bill, but only when he, satisfied with the service provided, leaves the establishment.

Tips of service

Advice No. 1 – One should use a single short straw when serving a drink on the rocks (whiskey, vodka, rum, etc.) and two short straws when serving a cocktail on the rocks.

Advice No. 2 – If the guest at the bar spills his drink unintentionally, it is up to the bartender whether he should make a new one and replace the spilt drink free of charge. If the drink was full or half full, the bartender should replace the drink with a new one without charging the guest.

Advice No. 3 – The bartender who receives the order from the guests should provide service from start to the end, unless the guest or guests come particularly because of a specific bartender in mind. In that case, the colleague should take over if he wants to. If a bartender has already started to make certain drinks for a guest, he should continue making those drinks throughout the course of the night.

Advice No. 4 – If the bartender performs the pour with two or more bottles, he should make sure that all the pourers are identical and clean so the alcohol from both bottles flows with equal intensity. This technique is strongly advised if free pouring a Negroni.

Advice No. 5 - During service, hot drinks and food should be a priority because when they are served cold, they lose their purpose and testify to the bad quality of service.

Advice No. 6 – A bartender should avoid interrupting guests while eating or while having a conversation.

Advice No. 7 – When a new product arrives to the bar, the bartender is advised to try it. That is one of the best ways he will understand the flavor profile.

Let us summarize the path of service in a shorter way: Greet the guest when he enters the restaurant as well as when he exits. In case the guest chooses to sit at the bar, a bartender should serve him a glass of water and menu. A bartender should look straight at the guests and firstly take orders from ladies and then gentlemen. After he takes the orders, napkins should be placed in front of the guests so the fellow colleague bartender or a barback can see the guests have been served. If the guests have ordered cocktails the ingredients for garnishing should be placed in front of them. During service the bartender has to balance his presence, to allow room for guests to experience the atmosphere of the restaurant and to communicate uninterruptedly. As long as there are guests present, a bartender has to keep the part of the bar in front of them clean. Water should be replenished while the guests are at the bar. When guests are ready to pay, the bartender should discreetly inquire about the manner of payment. During the presenting of the bill, the bartender should hand the bill with order details so the guest can inspect what they are paying and thank the guests. Service is not complete until the guests leave the bar.

Tipping

The end result of service and hospitality is tip. Will tipping always be adequate? It will not, but this does not always mean that service was bad. Some people just leave smaller tips. One should accept that as reality and continue to do his job in the best manner possible. In the US bartenders live on the profit they make from tips; that is our bread. In Europe, bartenders have fixed salaries and therefore, the tip-leaving customs are lower. Of course, tips are not something that is implicitly understood, but depend on the good faith of the guest and on the service provided. While a smaller tip (one dollar per a drink) is expected when serving simple drinks (bottled beverages, juice, coffee), the tip amount will vary depending on the quality when serving cocktails. Even so, one should try to tip based on his feel. Rule of thumb when leaving a tip:

10 % and lower – bad service and hospitality

18 % - satisfactory service and hospitality

20 % and more – outstanding service and hospitality

Part five

MIXOLOGY

"The art of mixing drinks."

- Danilo Božović, Andrija Ristić -

Mixology

The art of mixing drinks is an integral part of the bar craft. In order for a bar to be more successful, bartenders have to mix drinks well. Without the proper literature, one can only master his techniques through practice. To be able to mix drinks, a bartender should understand the ingredients he deals with, possess experience in liquor handling, know how they interact with one another and the best ways of their mixing. This demands that a bartender constantly try out cocktails, alcohol, spices and juices. With constant practice, the bartender will gain experience which will enable him to build his taste for the cocktail and his own mixing technique. In order to achieve this goal, one needs time, persistence and the will to learn. Mixology is, in that sense, a demanding technique because it requires a bartender's full concentration and focus on the cocktail preparation. As every good cook displays love and passion for his job through food, so the bartender shows his emotions and character through the drinks he makes.

1780 – 1830

This period in the history of bartending is marked with the minimal number of ingredients. Bar equipment was almost not present, and bartenders were forced to compromise. On the other hand, lemon and lime juice were of great benefit, as well as toddy sticks used to crush sugar and mix drinks. Punch bowls were also popular at most bars. Ingredients mostly used during this time period were: red wine, champagne, sherry, Jamaican and Virgin Isles rum, cognac, Dutch gin, whisky (mostly unmatured), apple brandy and apple schnapps. Non-alcoholic ingredients were mostly milk, eggs and hot water, nutmeg, lemon and lime, orange, pineapple, sugar, honey and maple syrup. Drinks were mostly made similarly to punches. Therefore, we can say that this technique presented a foundation of the later mixing techniques. At the end of the 18th century, drinks with their separate names emerged. After a long battle over sugar, sugarcane and rum monopoly, bourbon started gaining popularity as a drink while the demand for rum declined. Punches and shrubs were made in great amounts, and were the most popular drinks of the time. After the publishing of the definition for the cocktail in 1806, people started regarding this drink differently. The demand for cocktails rose, and bartenders become more inspired to create new drinks for their regular guests. Every good bartender used to have a couple of his own creations up his sleeve for every guest that came to drink something different.

1830 – 1920

This period is often referred to as the golden age of the bar profession. The cocktail demand was becoming increasingly larger and the craft gained popularity. This was the time when classic cocktails that opposed global trends of the time were made, and forever remained present in bar culture. Besides that, the classic cocktails set the criteria for future generations. Introducing ice as a commercial good made the job easier and popularized the cocktail as a drink. Before that, ice was available only to the wealthy. Back then, it was delivered to bars in the form of big blocks. Soon enough, there were tools on the market for ice chipping which made its everyday use even easier. Straws also appeared on the market at this point, mostly in order for the guests' teeth not to come in contact with ice. Sugar and other syrups were starting to be used as ingredients in cocktails, and with the invention of shakers, drinks started to be shaken and mixed with more quality ice. Modern bar equipment was becoming ever more available to bartenders so new mixing techniques also emerged. Drinks could be cooled more easily, which meant they no longer had to be served exclusively with ice. During this period, strainers became an integral part of bar equipment since guests could ask for their drinks without ice – straight up. The garnish gained an ever more important role in mixology and fruit was massively used in decorative cocktails. Bitters became the secret weapon of bartenders, enabling them to make more beautiful, elegant and balanced drinks.

This period was also marked by the appearance of the first manuals about the bartending profession, and the art of mixing cocktails, in which bartenders started revealing their long guarded secrets. These books became very popular, and their topics raised awareness of the cocktail culture, work principles and codes of conduct at the bar. What followed this written expansion were the competition during which bartenders, competing against other colleagues, could show their skill and knowledge, learn new things, and improve their craft. The golden age of cocktails is characterized by some of the most famous cocktails and cocktail families: Crusta, Gimlet, Smash, Sour, Collins, Julep, Rickey, Manhattan, Aviation, Americano, Sherry Cobbler and so on.

1920 – 1991

Although this period is famous for the creation of the Margarita, Side Car, French 75, and Mai Tai, it will always be remembered as a period of stagnation in the bartending profession. Between 1920 and 1933, Prohibition was in effect in America, which considerably stalled the progress of the bartending profession and bar business in general. Criminalization of bartending left great consequences on the further development of cocktails, and this was best reflected in the exodus of bartenders from America to Europe, the Caribbean or transoceanic ships. Hidden bars had secret names like Blind Pig or Speak Easy and only a handful of people knew their exact locations. During Prohibition, bars were a public secret. With the repeal of the Eighteenth Amendment, bartenders who decided to come back to American cities found great changes. The bar scene was no longer the same. The recipes used by the older bartenders were almost completely forgotten and the bartenders who worked before Prohibition aged and could no longer do night shifts. Lovers of a good cocktail could drink a good martini only in morning shifts or during brunches, when the older colleagues worked at the bar. It cannot be said that the creative process of bartenders stopped during this period but it surely stagnated.

The bartenders who left for the Caribbean or Europe continued to make drinks and kept the standard services and the craft at a high level. At the time, Tiki and cocktail culture based on tropical drinks and Polynesian style gained popularity. Bartenders such as Trader Vic Bergeron and Ernest Raymond Beaumont Gantt, commonly known as "Don the Beachcomber", became legends. This period proved very turbulent and left behind cocktails such as Blood and Sand, Clover Club, Brandy Alexander, Black Russian, Corpse Reviver #2, Bloody Mary, French 75, Side Car and Mai Tai which are consumed to this very day. The "dark period" managed to overshadow the cocktail culture of the nineties when various colored liqueurs with flavors and sweet cocktails with artificial aromas were popularized. At the end of the 20th century it was not cool to drink a martini or a Manhattan, because "old guys" drank that. Trends imposed sweet cocktails with multiple flavors and colors. The end of this dark age is noted by a period of reigniting cocktail culture and old customs, that is, the classic approach which Dale DeGroff would restore at the Rainbow Room in 1987 in New York. Dale DeGroff, one of the most influential and respected bartenders of the modern era, restored classic cocktails with fresh ingredients as well as the passion, approach, and hope that a cocktail could regain its former, well-deserved glory once again.

1991 – 2016

During this period cocktails started to change their form and reappear on the gastronomic scene. Bartenders began to avoid using vodka and some bars chose not to serve it at all. They decided that vodka cannot come to the fore in a cocktail and expressed revolt towards the whole vodka movement that had led to the creation of sweet and multicolored cocktails. The early 1990's showed a growth in the popularity of gin and whiskey cocktails. A lot of time would pass until bartenders accepted vodka again as an ingredient and a part of bar culture. Thanks to enthusiastic bartenders, people started to order classic cocktails and neglect the ones from the previous era. The approach to bartending techniques found inspirations in classic techniques. Bartenders make laboratories out of their old workstations where they test their drinks daily, mix ingredients, and experiment. This kind of approach has resulted in reviving the old glory of cocktails. Cocktail bars have become an integral part of every city. Restaurants now include various cocktail programs and this was led to a great bartender demand. Experienced bartenders have managed to rise to enviable levels of knowledge during this professional expansion and then pass it onto their younger colleagues. In this sense, passing the knowledge from generation to generation has become a continuous way of maintaining the bartending profession. The bartenders of today should be proud because they live in an age when bar knowledge is at its high again and classic cocktails are at the peak of their popularity.

What is better, mixology or flair?

Flair bartending is fun. It takes a long time to learn and master but it is fun. The wish for attractive bar work has existed since the beginning of bar culture. Harry Johnson and Jerry Thomas are among the first to use attractive moves during drink serving in order to get guests' attention. Harry's simultaneous pouring into separate glasses, Jerry's Blue Blazer cocktail which demands flaming technique, and the beautiful and attractive bar tools that Jerry possessed are just some of the things that paved the way for bar techniques, mixology and flair bartending. Certain people would try to undermine flair and call it a gimmick or not "real bartending". Everyone has the right to their own opinion but I think that flair is equally important to our craft as mixology and vice versa. How can one undermine something which requires 3-4 hours of practice a day at least? The right answer to this question 'What is better, mixology or flair?" does not exist, for both disciplines are equally useful for the craft as long as they do not lead to the neglecting of guests. A bad example of flair would be when a bartender concentrates exclusively on flair and neglects the guests and leads to the lowering of service. If a guests waits for fifteen minutes for their drinks, that is bad flair and counterproductive service. Flair bartending was mostly celebrated in a 1988 movie "Cocktail" where Tom Cruise portrays the role of a young flair bartender who tries to make it in life. Many bartenders learned their first flair moves directly from this movie.

Flair bartending consists of two categories: exhibition and working flair. Exhibition flair mostly concentrates on the technique of a very demanding nature which is mostly used in competitions or when there is scarcely any liquid left in a bottle at the bar. Working flair, on the other hand, does not depend on the remaining volume of liquid in the bottle and can be used in every day work at the bar. Flair bartending is divided in two styles: European and Latin American. The difference is that the European style possesses various exchanges of bottles during work, whereas the Latin American approach is mostly based on juggling of bar elements. People often mistake flair for a five element exhibition, which is wrong. Flair does not need to be a series of stunts lasting five minutes. Flair can be an attractive pour, glass throw, spoon tumbling, etc. The definition of flair bartending in short is: "Flair is an attractive drink preparing bar technique". Flair bartending and mixology are equally important disciplines. According to the learning order, a bartender should study mixology first which will help learn how mixing drinks works and then move over to attractiveness of his bartending approach.

Note 1 – While using mixology, one should not neglect his guest.

Note 2 – While using flair, the cocktail should not be neglected (balance, visual presentation, flavor, etc.) Flair bartending and mixology make work at the bar more interesting, more fun and diverse. It is up to each bartender to decide how much of each style he wants to learn and how to mix them up. Keep in mind, the more one knows the more one is worth.

Find yourself in every cocktail

Cocktail making techniques are vital if the bartender wishes to make a good drink. Eventually the aim is that the bartender finds himself in every cocktail. What does this mean? The bartender ought to learn the history of the drink, which recipe works best for him, as well as what the cocktail is about. In doing so, one can use that knowledge and give his personality to the drink itself. The cocktail has to tell its story and show the passion one has. In order to achieve this, one should first understand the cocktail (its ingredients and history) and to know in what light one wants to present ones cocktail (original, dry, more refreshing, etc.). To understand the cocktail means to know how it is formed, what is the goal of the cocktail itself, what is the proportion of ingredients, how long should it be shaken/stirred, etc. It is up to the bartender to present his cocktail to a guest. One should always try to make the cocktail in front of the guest. His character is of deciding importance in that moment for it will determine the end result and with it the taste of ones cocktail.

Example 1 – If a bartender prefers a drier Negroni, he will increase the quantity of gin by 1/4 oz.

Example 2 – If a bartender prefers a refreshing Cosmopolitan he will add ¼ oz. to ½ oz. of cranberry juice more.

Example 3 – If a bartender likes a more prominent Corpse Reviver No. 2, he will not use the recipe with an equal proportion of ingredients but will decrease the quantity of lemon by half.

Example 4 – If a bartender wants to intensify the maple flavor in a Hot Toddy, he will use agave instead of honey.

Had Jerry Thomas not found himself in his cocktails, the Jerry Thomas Manhattan would not exist. This principle of work is applied when a bartender works on increasing his knowledge and changing of the cocktail menu. At the bar, recipes are known and the procedures are advised to be followed. If a bartender thinks a certain recipe or approach is better, he should certainly inform the bar team so that they can make the decision together whether to change the bar standard. Some classic cocktail mixing techniques are already standardized, leaving no room for change.

Cocktail code

As previously mentioned, to every cocktail there is a personal approach. Every cocktail has a specific code that each bartender sees differently. The bartender implements this code while choosing his way of making the drink. Some bartenders like to pour in modifiers first and then the base. Others like to pour in the base first and then the rest. Some bartenders like to measure with jiggers while they make a cocktail while other like to measure it visually while free-pouring. All of these are specific parts of approach to making cocktails. None of the mentioned ways is wrong as long as the result is a good drink. By making good drinks bartender gives meaning to his technique. All discussions about cocktail making techniques are needless because the end result is the only thing that counts. How good the drink is. Will the guest be satisfied and order another cocktail? That is the true test to one's bartending technique and recipe approach.

Free pour or jiggers

In order for a bartender to crack the code of the cocktail, he should try his drinks every time he makes it in order to understand its true meaning, behavior and to envision the best technique for that certain drink. Before the bartender understands what approach suits him best, to start, he should see if he wants to use the free pour or jigger method. Although counting measurement is a useful technique, it has its drawbacks. For example, clean alcohol, liqueur and syrups possess different densities. Therefore, the measurement cannot be the same. Visual measurement is, on the other hand, the safest option because it leaves little to chance. A bartender should practice his free pour every day in order to be sure while determining measurements. In order to use the free pour method correctly one should take into account the size of the glass used in the cocktail preparation.

It is important for a bartender to feel comfortable while making a cocktail, no matter the approach to making. Through the process of determining his own style and constant experimenting, the bartender will develop his own approach to work. The aim of using jiggers is to minimize the potential for error and maximize consistency, but even when using jiggers, the same cocktail made by two different bartenders can taste different. One bartender can shake longer than the other, a cocktail glass can be more chilled than the other and pouring from one jigger can be more precise than the other. All of these factors mixology, flair, free pour, jigger measuring are equally important as long as they enable the bartender to shine and make the best possible drink he can.

When is a cocktail poorly made? Before serving the cocktail the bartender should taste his drink in order to check its quality. If the bartender does not like the taste, he ought to make a new one and discard the poorly made one.

Bar techniques

Building method

The building method entails direct pouring of alcohol into the glass where the drink will be served. Depending on technique, first add alcohol, measure it visually, then add ice in order to slow down the dilution of drink and fill the glass with juice. The building method is mainly used with highball drinks (mixed drinks) like Cuba Libre, Screwdriver, Gin & Tonic, etc.

Shaking

During shaking, the drink is cooled while water and air are added. Cocktails need to be shaken vigorously for eight seconds. Of course, the bartender should use his intuition when shaking certain drinks. Drinks with milk, eggs, juice and different kinds of mashes and cordials are shaken in order to merge the ingredients better. Drinks (Gimlets, Margaritas, Sours, Daiquiris, etc.) which contain enriched syrup, agave, etc. require a vigorous and a touch longer shake for all the ingredients to combine together properly. Shaking a cocktail with both hands is more effective, and therefore recommended. While holding the shaker, a bartender has to feel the temperature and feel how diluted the drink is becoming. The misting/ perspiring of the shaker is a sign that a cocktail is cooled. Dry shaking is a special kind of shaking without ice which is used when a bartender wants to get a creamy and foamy texture of a cocktail containing egg. During dry shaking, cover the shaker with a mixing glass at straight angle in order to avoid unnecessary spilling of protein. After the shake, one should add ice and repeat the whole process in order to cool down the cocktail.

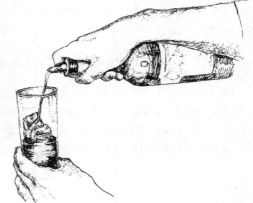

Stirring

Stirring is a technique used when working with alcohol. Drinks made strictly of alcohol are stirred in order to be less diluted, to let the character of the alcohol used come to the fore (Gin Martini, Negroni, Manhattan). Stirring takes 40 revolutions with a bar spoon.

Muddling

Muddling is a technique where bartenders get juices from fruit, open up aromas of herbs such as mint, dissolve sugar with bitters, etc. By muddling spearmint and sugar, the bartender opens up aromas of mint leaves by slowly scratching the surface of the spearmint with the muddler and sugar. Muddling can be done in a mixing glass or directly in the serving glass (Mint Julep, Mojito, Old Fashioned, etc.). One should be careful when muddling spearmint and similar plants so as not to make a puree, but only free the aroma of the plant. During muddling, oil molecules found in leaves are freed and the cocktail becomes more aromatic and pleasant. A muddler is an exceptional bar element for flair, especially during making of an Old Fashioned. There are muddlers of different shapes and sizes on the market and it is up to the bartender to decide which one suits him the best.

Layering

This technique requires the knowledge of spirits, liqueurs and their densities, sugar and alcohol content. Liqueurs branded as crème (Crème de cassis, crème de banana, etc.) have higher sugar content, therefore are denser and have a heavier body. If a bartender does not know the sugar content of a liqueur, he should check the label on the bottle because the lower the alcohol content, the greater the sugar content.

Layering is done in three ways:

1. Textbook layering over the body of bar spoon. The spiral shape of the spoon makes layering easier.

2. Layering over the bottom of the spoon. The bar spoon should be clean.

3. This method does not require a bar spoon, but a cocktail is layered by tipping the glass and slowly pouring next to the inner side of the glass. The same part of glass should not be used for pouring all ingredients because the cocktail will mix. Pousse-cafe is, for example, the kind of drink built by layering. It remains one of the rarely ordered cocktails.

Blending

The first blenders were made in the beginning of the 20th century. Blended or frozen cocktails joined the cocktail culture only later. During blending, fresh fruit and crushed ice is recommended because that way the blades of the blender are preserved. Depending on the ingredients in the blender and the ice used, blending should last for 15 – 20 seconds. When making frozen cocktails, one should feel free to use drinks of greater alcohol content in order for a cocktail to retain its character.

Rolling

The rolling technique (circular motion) is used when a cocktail contains thicker juices as is the case with a Bloody Mary. It contains tomato juice which loses its body and flavor if diluted too much. In order to avoid losing the characteristics of the juice, bartenders use the rolling technique, which means easy motion of juice from the cap shaker to the glass. This way, the bartender preserves the body of the cocktail and allows its taste to come to the fore.

Swizzling

The first swizzle sticks were used in the Caribbean islands in the 17th century for stirring elixirs rich in rum. The Swizzle is a very old "Caribbean blender". When and how is it used? When making cocktails that need to be diluted, its aromas open up without adding air. Similar to stirring, swizzling is mostly used with tall glasses. Swizzling is done by using ones palms to rotate the stick quickly and it resembles lighting a campfire. The bartender should mind the glass temperature he achieves by swizzling.

Bar equipment

Bar equipment enables the bartender to apply his techniques easier and better. It is essential to have good bar equipment behind the bar, for in order to be a good craftsman, one should have good quality tools as Dushan Zaric would say. It is very important a bartender maintains his equipment so it is clean and ready to use at every moment. Mixture of vinegar and water is perfect for maintaining the shine of the bar equipment. The popular proportion is 2 oz. or 6 cl of vinegar to 16 oz. or 5 dl of water.

Boston shaker

A Boston shaker is an integral piece of equipment of a bar and it consist of a glass part (mixing glass) and a metal shaker. The volume of the mixing glass is 16 oz. or 48 cl whereas the metal shaker is 22 oz. or 66 cl. Some bars use a completely metal shaker but the problem with this kind of shaker is that free pour is impossible if measuring visually.

Cap Shaker

Shaking cup is used for shaking drinks done directly in a Collins glass.

Mixing glass

Mixing glass is an important bar element and since it is made of glass a bartender can see everything that is going on inside it.

Hawthorne strainer

A Hawthorne strainer strains the drink as well as keeps the ice in the shaker. It is recognizable by the long spring which adjusts the grip and regulates the strain of cocktail.

Julep strainer

A Julep strainer is a type of strainer which holds the ice in the mixing glass and sometimes the shaker during straining. The Julep strainer fits the mixing glass perfectly and strains the cooled cocktail efficiently while holding the ice in the glass.

Bar spoon

A Bar spoon is used during the bar technique called stirring. Bartenders use the spoon to stir the cocktail with ice.

Muddler

Muddler can be made of different materials but in the bar trade, wooden muddlers are most widely used.

Boston shaker   *Mixing glass*

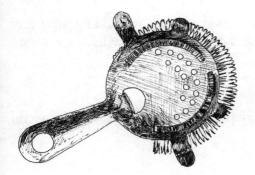
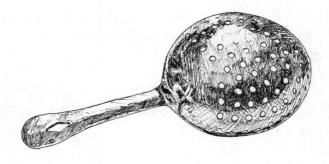

Hawthorne strainer   *Julep strainer*

Bar spoon

Bar knife

A Knife (pairing knife) is used during preparation of garnish, fruit and vegetables. Its flexibility makes the bartender's job easier during garnish preparation (especially with twists).

Jigger

It is used during the measuring of the amount of liquid needed for a cocktail. Since there are various shapes of jiggers, it is up to a bartender to decide which one suits his style and techniques best.

Bar opener

Bar opener for bottles can be found in different shapes, colors and materials. Although extremely easy to use in practice, a wine corkscrew with a bottle opener part is recommended.

Wine corkscrew

Used for opening wine and sometimes, depending on the corkscrew type, for opening beer as well.

Grater

Used during preparation of zests (grated lime, lemon or orange peel) or grating any dry ingredient. Grater should be clean because it easily mixes flavors with other grated ingredients.

Fine sieve

It is used when separating pulp, pit, and fleshy parts of fruit and vegetables we do not want in a cocktail.

Funnel

Very useful tool that every bar needs to have.

Tong

A necessary element of every bar. Mostly used when handling garnish.

Champagne stopper

Prolongs the lifespan of an open bottle of champagne or sparkling wine. The stopper helps Champagne last for two to three days, respectively.

Jigger

Bar opener

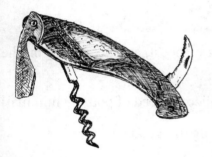

Wine corkscrew

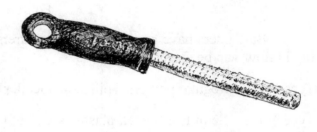

Grater

Fine sieve

Funnel

Tong

Champagne stopper

Bar mallet

This is very useful behind the bar, especially if a bar sells a lot of cocktails with crushed ice. A Bar mallet can replace an ice crushing machine but requires hard labor.

Atomizer

It is used to add a small amount of aroma to a cocktail.

Dropper

It is used when a cocktail need a minimal amount of an ingredient (in drops).

Dash bottle

Usually a smaller shaped bottle used to add small quantities or a dash (1/8 of a teaspoon) of liquid to a drink.

Pourers

Bartenders have a great choice of pourers at their disposal, and depending on the liquid flow, can be categorized as:

Type No. 1 – Regular pourers (spill stop, metal, plastic, silicon; speed of pouring minimal)

Type No. 2 – Semi fast (metal, plastic, speed of pouring slightly greater)

Type No. 3 – Fast (metal, have the greatest speed of pouring and mostly used for thicker drinks like Baileys and Kahlua)

Screen pourers are particular pourers that protect the alcohol from flies. The plastic caps used to cover pourers provide similar protection. The body of the pourer is made from rubber, is corrugated and adaptable to diverse types of bottles. When the corrugated part becomes too narrow due to prolonged use, you should soak it in hot water in order to get his shape back. With cheaper pourers, soaking them in hot water will not return them to their previous shape. Those pourers are for single use only.

Atomizer

Dropper

Dash bottle

Pourers

Part six

COCKTAIL

"A cocktail is a drink that should make the moment more pleasurable and provide a perfect sense of fulfillment."

- Danilo Božović, Andrija Ristić -

Cocktail

On May 13th, 1806 the first definition of cocktail was published in the New York newspapers *Balance and Columbian Repository* and it read: "Stimulating liquor, composed of spirits of any kind, sugar, water and bitters", simply put a "bittered sling." This newspaper could not have described the cocktail any better. Although the etymology of the word cocktail remains unknown, there are numerous legends and stories that speak of the creation of the word cocktail. One of the more beautiful legends is the one about the French apothecary Antoine Amedie Peychaud, the creator of Peychaud's bitters. In 1795, he opened a pharmacy in New Orleans where he served the drink in a glass for serving boiled eggs. He used this glass to serve his famous Sazerac, and the legend says that the word cocktail stems precisely from the French word "coquetier" which referred to the glass bowl for serving eggs at the time. One of the more interesting stories about the etymology of the word cocktail is linked to the period of American – Mexican wars. During the negotiations about the cessation of hostilities, King Axolotl VIII offered the American general a drink and he accepted. Out of nowhere, came the king's daughter carrying a tray. The king introduced his lovely daughter: "This is my daughter and her name is Coctel", to which the general responded, charmed by her beauty, that he will make sure her name lives on. One other story tells about cockfighting. As legend has it, the owner of the winning rooster would take the defeated rooster's tail feathers and stir his drink as a sign of victory. Due to this legend, people believe the word cocktail to originate exactly from the phrase rooster's tail (cock's tail). Legends are mostly interesting stories worth telling no matter their probable inaccuracy.

What is a cocktail?

It is believed the first mixed drinks were made due to the fact that alcohol was of such poor quality it was hard to consume unmixed. By mixing it with various drinks, alcohol would gain flavor, but a lot of time passed before the cocktail became a gastronomic sensation. A well-made cocktail should offer a symphony of flavors and each sip should unveil a new aroma. The taste of cocktail should not disappear quickly but present an unending journey through which each sip one discovers something new. Every cocktail is different and special in its own way; therefore, there is no best cocktail, only the one which suits the right moment. In order for a cocktail to be better, it should be made from fresh ingredients. Cocktails should be served cold, unless the recipe states otherwise (i.e. Hot Toddy, Irish coffee, etc.). Cocktail should not be a shortcut to drunkenness, but a new and different way to enjoy alcohol.

The base

The base of a cocktail is its foundation. Cocktails do not have to have just one base, this depends on the type of cocktail. Manifestation of the base depends on the secondary ingredients as well as their reaction with the base. Usually spirits like gin, whiskey, rum, brandy, vodka, tequila and so on are used for the base. The mixer binds the ingredients and gives meaning to the cocktail, and it is usually an ingredient such as aromatic bitters or other ingredients of stronger aroma. Although mixers are found in small quantities in a cocktail, they fully open up the cocktail aroma, bind the tastes, give depth to the drink and fulfill the gastronomic pleasure.

The balance

In order for a cocktail to meet the expectations of the guest, it has to be made with balance from start to end. To discover the right recipe is far more complex than mixing the ingredients that are compatible. The right recipe requires the bartender to show his character throughout the cocktail. He has to show the cocktail in the best light, as he sees fit. This requires a lot of experience and attention to detail. Eventually, through lots of thinking, the bartender will come up with the best recipe/approach to every cocktail. When we test a specific combination of flavors, we should first decide what kind of spirit will complement the flavors we are experimenting with, as well as if the drink will be short or long, aperitif or digestive (after dinner drink). When preparing a cocktail it is important to take into account:

- intensity of aroma and flavor

- balance

- does the cocktail have stratification

- the way flavor changes in the mouth

A good cocktail should have an intense taste, but one should carefully mind the extent of that intensity. It depends on the type of cocktail we want to make. For instance, an intense Manhattan should be stirred exactly 40 revolutions and there is a thin line between perfect dilution, and watered down and flat. Whereas, a good Negroni ought to be stirred a bit more than 40 revolutions. A good Margarita, ought to be shaken a bit longer than 8 seconds. With this approach, the statement of these three cocktails is the strongest. There are lots of factors that influence the flavor intensity of the cocktail and all should be taken into account before we come to a final recipe. The level of alcohol that specific ingredient possess is of great importance when determining the intensity. Besides that, the creator of the cocktail should bear in mind the history of alcohol used, that is, for how long it was matured in casks, how dry/sweet it is and so on. The technique of mixing a cocktail is as important as the ingredients. The manner in which we apply each mixing technique when making a cocktail is of paramount importance because each cocktail demands a different mixing approach. Here is where we notice that in the bartending craft, things are not set in stone.

Before we continue with defining taste we have to pay attention to components that make the flavor special: Flavor, aroma and, in no way less important, body and texture. Taste consists of five senses. Using those senses one can decide whether the drink is: sweet, sour, salty, bitter or umami (savory taste). The upper surface of tongue is covered in small buds called *papillae*. Those buds retain liquid and parts of food in the mouth so during chewing or tasting food and/or drink various parts of the tongue react to different flavors: sweet, salty, sour, bitter and umami. Tasting drinks or food should resemble a movie, which means that each tasting should have a beginning, middle and end. The beginning of the movie introduces us to its purpose. The middle presents a further development of the theme which directs us, as actors, in the right direction, coordinates acting and determines the genre of the movie. The end usually gives meaning to the whole movie, changing the point of every scene we have seen so far. The sweeter the cocktail is the more intense the flavors will be. Sugar also helps with dampening strong sour or bitter flavors found in citrus peels and certain spices. If we know this, we cannot simply add sugar to a cocktail because we will make it weak and too intense, but we should stick to the optimal point, no more than ¾ oz of simple syrup especially when working with an enriched simple syrup (2:1, sugar to water).

Example No. 1 – A short drink with a base spirit, sugar and citrus peel does not require much sugar. If we start making an Old Fashioned with more sugar we will have to finish it with more bourbon and a longer stir in order to reduce the level of sweetness. On the other hand, a long drink prepared in a blender with lots of ice and cream will need sugar added. The melting of ice, cream and the outside temperature will have great effect on reducing the flavor intensity so we need to add extra sugar.

Sour is a sensation caused by an ingredient of certain sourness, no matter if it is citrus, dairy or acetic. Sour does not increase the flavor intensity, but appeals to certain flavors. Mild flavors as citrus, fruit, floral or herbal will be brought to surface by sourness. Warmer flavors such as certain spices, vanilla and lime go very well together, but lime does not intensify the taste of vanilla. If we compare this to rose, elder flower, or strawberry we will notice that lime accents their taste. The most important effect of sour is accentuating the rest of ingredients in a way that gives a cocktail a refreshing quality. Of course, we should bear in mind all the time that sugar is an important ingredient of the sour cocktails because without it cocktails are too strong and aggressive. Dry ingredients like wine or cider are, technically, also sour so they are used in aperitif cocktails because they create cocktails with a refreshing finish. When working with fresh juices pressed before the shift, bear in mind the transformation they go through. If you do not use up a bottle of freshly pressed lemon before the end of shift, it will oxidize and turn extremely sour. In these situations a bartender has to adjust the amount of citrus used in making of a cocktail, in order to balance the taste. There are pain receptors in our mouth which are a part of the trigeminal nerve and react to alcohol, capsaicin, the ingredient responsible for hotness in chilies and isothiocyanates which is responsible for pungency in horseradish and mustard, as well as gingerols in ginger.

When these elements stimulate the pain receptors in our mouth, they stimulate the taste receptors at the same time so we feel a taste of increased intensity in our mouths. Of course, chilies are not the only one that increase taste intensity; we experience spiciness as a secondary aroma such as floral, herbal or spicy aromatic which gives the cocktail an additional level of complexity. In smaller amounts, chilies trigger salivation and have an appetizing effect therefore, if used correctly, can turn a less round cocktail into something you would like to drink over and over again. Isothiocyanates, found in horseradish and mustard, are easy to evaporate and that is why we feel a burning sensation in the nose while we consume it. Capsaicin does not evaporate easily and does not dissolve in water so it remains in mouth considerably longer. Milk helps to neutralize the spiciness because *capsaicin* dissolves in milk fat. The level of spice, or should I say too spicy is different with everyone, so what is too spicy for me might be a touch spicy to someone else. Tolerance of spiciness should be kept in mind when making a drink. The bartender should ask or estimate the level of spicy tolerance his guest has and is looking for in his drink. This is crucial in balancing out a spicy drink while behind the bar.

How do you know when a cocktail is well balanced?

The cocktail balance is crucial to its good taste. A cocktail is balanced when it does not possess any single accentuated taste but all the ingredients are unified into one dominant taste with different secondary aromas. In order to achieve balance in a cocktail one should be fully focused and motivated; each step in the process should have its purpose, and the goal is a tasty and unforgettable cocktail. A good cocktail should have a ratio in respect to sourness/sweetness, as well as aroma and taste, which should be in accordance with the cocktail's style. Each time one adds sugar, sour or a bitter ingredient, he should have the drinks balance in mind. Sour and bitter ingredients have unpleasant tastes, so they have to be mitigated with something sweet. A margarita is, for example, tastefully sour. But if we do not add any sugar it will be unpleasantly sour. Similar to that, if you take sugar out of an Old Fashioned, its alcohol and bitterness will prevail. On the other hand, sweet ingredients can be too simple and oversaturated on their own, so this needs to be mitigated with sour, or dry ingredients which will make a cocktail refreshing, or with aromatic bitters in order to give them complexity and tenderness. A margarita without lime would be oversaturated and not refreshing in the aftertaste. An Old Fashioned without an orange/lemon twist or aromatic bitters would be chilled bourbon without any structure. Balance is the reason why so many recipes are alike when it comes to ingredients. Only the proper approach and quality mixing guarantees a good and tasty cocktail. A cocktail should not be only sweet or sour, nor just strong or spicy. A cocktail should have strength, but it should be elegantly manifested through balance with other ingredients.

Gin has less intense flavor than bourbon, basically it is extremely sophisticated vodka with aroma, and with only 20 grams of juniper per liter of neutral alcohol. When combining different flavors it is important to try and understand the character of each one. We can divide them into categories such as: wooden (from a cask), fruity, spicy, herbal and floral. Fruity flavors and their combinations make up just the background of a cocktail. Therefore, we will not discuss them further here. Yes, apple and pear go nicely together, but a lot more is needed to make them exquisitely tasty. Vanilla and cinnamon can be used to make the flavor more pleasant, cardamom and anise can make them more exotic, and lemongrass more refreshing. Raspberry gives a lot more sourness, so it is a better starting combination than pear, because it accentuates the flavor with its sourness. The true potential of the 21st century of mixing drinks lies in the shades offered by these herbs and spices. In the case of free pouring, each bartender develops his own approach to mixing cocktails. Some bartenders pour the base first, others the mixer, where some start with the sweeteners. Each bartender should find the appropriate mixing order so as to master the technique of cocktail making. Or he should have a suitable pouring order for each drink specifically. The colder the cocktail, the more the intensity of aromas and flavors will be lessened and will make the cocktail seem less sweet. This happens because cold affects our receptors as an anesthetic, making them inactive.

When we consume a cold drink, it is warmed up as it progresses towards the throat and the cold reduces sweetness more than sourness and bitterness. Therefore, frozen drinks should have a strong taste or more sugar in order to gain full flavor intensity. This especially refers to cocktails, rather than liqueurs consumed with ice. The final amount of sugar in a cocktail is not too high; in any case it does not exceed 100 g per liter. Liqueurs are mostly drinks with large amounts of sugar (200g/l), which leads to increased viscosity in lower temperatures and makes the alcohol seem extra sweet. Believe it or not color affects our perception of sweetness of a drink. Therefore affects its intensity. If we take three, colored sugar-syrups, red, green and colorless, the red one will seem the sweetest and the green one least sweet. However, we should take care for our brain is playing tricks on us. In nature, green signifies immaturity and our brain is conditioned to recognize it. The point of tasting is to evaluate the spirit and form an impression. Smoking is very detrimental to palate sensors. During tasting, do not wear strong perfumes in order not to distract the senses and allow the taster to enjoy the aroma fully. You should start tasting with of lighter aromas and gradually go to alcoholic drinks of stronger aromas. The taster should consume water in between different tastings in order to refresh and rest the palate. The sensors should be aware of the changes happening at every moment. Tasting should be conducted using a glass designed for it, that is, a snifter glass. These glasses are pear-shaped. Thanks to that, they excel at providing different aromas of alcohol in question. During tasting, hold the glass at a 45 degree angle. Do not swirl the glass because it makes the alcohol "wake up" and makes it unpleasant.

However, this is not the case when tasting wine, during which the taster can manipulate the glass freely. Tears, or drops, of alcohol can often be seen dripping down the glass during tasting. The size of these drops depicts the alcoholic content of the spirit. If the drop is small and narrow, that means the alcohol concentration is greater. The longer the drop takes to slide to the bottom of the glass, the sweeter the spirit. When the person tasting finishes smelling the spirit, he can take a small sip. The liquid should be "chewed" and should not be swallowed immediately, because the point of the sip is to fully activate the sensors in the mouth by completely covering them with the consumed spirit. After "chewing" one should let the spirit slide down the throat and concentrate on the taste that remains in the mouth. The aroma we get during tasting consists of oils, alcohol, sugar and fat. The longer the alcohol stays in wooden casks, the higher the intensity. Also, the climate where the maturing is done influences the intensity and aroma of the spirit. It is known that maturing is considerably quicker in areas of warmer climates. The age of the barrel where the spirit is stored is also of note because profusely aged casks can stop increasing the intensity of aromas in alcohol.

Let us take American whiskies for example, for they are usually aged in new casks. Manhattan is made with rye whiskey mostly aged for six years or less - Wild Turkey rye,

Pikesville, Rittenhouse or Sazerac 6 years old. Older examples would be Van Winkle 13, Sazarac 18 and different extremely old cask strength examples. The greater the amount of alcohol the more intense the aroma. Therefore, the rules of adding a proper dosage are not clear, similar to the case with sugar. A good Martinez for instance requires a stronger gin, for the complexity of flavors to come out as well as to achieve the drier flavor. The higher percentage of alcohol will activate a greater number of pain receptors in the mouth, and will also influence the aromas. Let us compare two glasses of gin, one diluted with water, the other straight. The diluted one will, of course, be of lower intensity but its taste will be considerably different because it will open up aromas and flavors not felt in the undiluted gin. It is good to know that what we perceive as taste is in fact linked to smell. Alcohol easily binds with taste molecules and is a better solvent than water. That is why when we macerate fruit in alcohol, it absorbs all the fruit flavors. In the water solution, the taste molecules are not that bound and a great deal of them can evaporate so that we can smell and taste them. If we add more water, we allow these molecules to escape, increasing the intensity of aromas and therefore, the perception of taste. However, if we dilute the cocktail too much we reduce the intensity of flavor. Most aromas and flavors in cocktails are formed by combining simpler compounds. If you have ever had the opportunity to see the wine set of aromas, with all the different types that can appear in a cup of wine, you will understand what we are talking about. All these numerous molecules have different binding characteristics related to alcohol, and will be released in specific proportions depending on the alcohol percentage. It is necessary to find an optimal amount of alcohol for a good cocktail, high enough to manifest a clear gustative intensity in the cocktail, but not so high so as to violate the aroma and flavor.

Tasting glasses have to be colorless and clean in order for a spirit color to come to the fore. The bottom of the glass should be wider than the top. A professional taster uses sherry *copita* glasses. They should have a lid in order to save the aroma during the whole process. There are various and mostly divided opinions when it comes to the use of water in consuming whiskies and alcohol in general. Although in Scotland, for example, "a half and half" ratio is very popular, these matters are highly subjective. Alcohol, and of course whisky, should be consumed as one prefers. The rest is immaterial. During tasting, the glass should be placed against white paper or a wall in order to better accentuate the color of the spirit. Darker colors mean the spirit spent more years in a cask. During tasting, the sensors in our nose are active. The sense of smell is around ten thousand times stronger than the sense of taste. It is recommended the mouth stay open during tasting so alcoholic fumes do not get inhaled directly.

Example No. 1 – A light, golden color may point to the fact that the spirit was matured in bourbon casks or in some cases caramel coloring.

Example No. 2 - Darker colors mean that the spirit spent longer in contact with wood.

In order for a bartender to master different flavors and recognize quality combinations of aromas, he should play with ingredients and constantly experiment with their flavors. The result of the attempt to make a cocktail is as important as the experience a bartender earns while making a new cocktail. Each new cocktail will add to the bartender's experience and personal advancement. The forefathers of the bartending craft have played with ingredients and recipes, and kept experimenting. Had it not been for their desire to experiment with flavors, we would not have so many excellent classic cocktails today.

Cocktail families

Cocktail families are designed for a bartender to identify the drink in question with ease, its ingredients, garnish and the glass it should be served in. Without categorizing cocktails by families it would be hard to remember every drink. Before a bartender starts memorizing recipes he should learn the cocktail families and their ingredients because that is the basic knowledge.

Highball

The Esquire Magazine's 1949 *Handbook for Hosts* claimed that the Highball was invented around 1890 by Patrick Gavin Duffy, the bartender at Manhattan's Ashland House on Fourth Avenue. Highball came to be as a whiskey drink and after the First World War, there was a shortage of aged whiskey in the world so people started making highballs with blended whiskey. After the Second World War vodka became a very popular ingredient in the highball. A classic highball consists of 2 oz. of alcohol and 4-6 oz. of club soda, ginger ale, etc. A highball or mixed drink, in most cases, is called after the alcohol used (gin-tonic, juice –vodka, rum and coke). Vodka juice is known as a Screwdriver. Seagrams 7 and Seven Up is knows as Seven and Seven, and vodka and cranberry juice as a Cape Codder.

Juice-vodka or Screwdriver – slice of orange

Vodka-cranberry or Cape Codder – lime wedge

Vodka-grapefruit or Greyhound – no garnish

Vodka/gin/other alcohol with tonic – lime wedge

Vodka/gin/other alcohol with soda – lemon wedge

Vodka/gin/whiskey/other spirit with sprite – lemon wedge

Vodka/gin/whiskey/other spirit with ginger ale – lime wedge

Vodka/gin/whiskey/other spirit with coke – no garnish

Rum with coke – lime wedge (exception)

Martini

The Martini is the king of cocktails and a prime example of a minimal number of ingredients having an excellent flavor profile. No cocktail has as many stories built around it as the Martini. What gin is best to use, whether to use gin or vodka, if it should be garnished with a twist or olives, what kind of olives, and whether to cool gin, vodka or the vermouth are just some of the numerous questions that a Martini lover can ask. One thing remains certain: if a guest orders a Martini he probably knows the way he likes it. The rule of serving olives with a potato vodka Martini is correct in theory, but not in practice. It is advised to shake a Vodka Martini and stir a Gin Martini. The earliest known Martini recipe appears in Harry Johnson's 1888 book, *New and Improved Bartender's Manual*.

The amount of vermouth in a Martini will depend on what kind of Martini a bartender wants to make wet, regular, dry, very dry, extra dry, perfect, in and out or bone dry.

Wet Martini – 1 oz. or 3 cl of dry vermouth
Martini – ¾ oz. or 2.25 cl of dry vermouth
Dry Martini – ½ oz. or 1.5 cl of dry vermouth
Very Dry Martini – splash 1/8 oz. or 0.4 cl of dry vermouth

Extra Dry Martini – no dry vermouth

In and Out Martini – cover the inner part of mixing glass with dry vermouth. The point of an In and Out Martini is to possess minimal flavor of vermouth.

Perfect Martini – equal proportions of dry and sweet vermouth.

The deciding factor when it comes to the quality of a Martini is its temperature and dilution. Stirring melts the ice, adds water and cools the cocktail. The state of ice used is very important, which should result in the body of the Martini to be full and oily. In order for it to be oily, the cocktail has to be cooled properly. It is recommended that bartender uses cooled vermouth. Alcohol used should not be cooled in order to not slow down the dilution of ice needed. When shaking, one should add ice into the mixing glass. Add two thirds of the shaker with ice. The bartender should place the shaker onto the mixing glass and mind that no ice falls out. A properly assembled shaker will be full of ice and will, with strong shaking, make the Vodka Martini very cool. The martini will get an oily structure and keep the characteristics of the vodka. A flavored Martini has nothing in common with the original martini. The Classic Martini represented the glamorous era of Sinatra, fancy suits, gangsters and dames. Younger generations wanted to bring back the old times of consuming Martini, but without its strong taste, so martini with different flavors were created and became popular in the 1990's.

Note No. 1 – In order to secure additionally low temperature of the Martini, the bartender should shake ice in order to additionally cool the shaker.

Note No. 2 – A good Martini, needs time and patience.

Sour

Sour is one of the oldest families of cocktails. It is made with a base alcohol, lemon juice and sugar syrup. Base spirit is always found in the name of the cocktail. The whiskey sour was first published in Jerry Thomas' *How to Mix Drinks, or the Bon Vivant's Companion* (1862) and later republished in his famous *The Bar-Tenders Guide*. Seltzer was originally used, but neglected over time. The egg white, as an option, was later added as a creamy element to the cocktail. Sour cocktails nowadays are served in an old fashioned/low tumbler glass. It is garnished with an orange flag.

Cobbler

The first Cobblers were made with wine or spirit, consumed over crushed ice with a very large quantity of fresh fruit. This is one of the refreshing families where citrus fruit provides freshness and balance between sugar and alcohol. The existence of this cocktail was first noted in 1830 and its first representative was Sherry Cobbler. Harry Johnson observed in 1882, "without doubt the most popular beverage in the country, with ladies as well as with gentlemen." It is served with all ingredients shaken (base alcohol, fruit and sugar) and poured into a tall glass without straining. Although orange is very popular in making cobblers, other fruit like lemon, pineapple, raspberry and blackberry are used in making this cocktail as well.

Collins

At the start of the 17th century, it is believed that a waiter by the name of John Collins created this drink at the Limmer's Hotel in London. Traditionally, Collins were made with sweetened gin (Old Tom) so the recipe at the time needed less sugar. Today, this cocktail is made from a spirit, sugar, lemon juice and sparkling water (club soda or seltzer). Pour all the ingredients into the mixing glass, apart from sparkling water. Add ice and shake the cocktail vigorously. Add soda or sparkling water. The Collins is served over fresh ice in a Collins glass. The first recorded Tom Collins recipe was mentioned in the second edition of Jerry Thomas book, "The Bartender's Guide", published in 1876.

Tom Collins – made with gin

Jose Collins – made with tequila

John Collins – made with bourbon

Michael Collins – made with Irish whiskey

Fizz

Traditional Fizz cocktails were made with alcohol, lemon juice, sugar, sparkling water (club soda or seltzer) and egg white. A Fizz had to be shaken for a long time in order to mix the egg white properly and to get a nice foamy structure. Traditional Fizzes were served without ice. One of the most famous cocktails belonging to this family is the Ramos Gin Fizz. Ramos Gin Fizz was created by Henry Charles Ramos in 1888. It was a huge success and it required 35 "shaker boys", bar staff who was in charge of only shaking Ramos Gin Fizzes 12 minutes per a drink.

Info 1 – The rich foam was the garnish of the Fizz.

Info 2 – As with previous cocktails, Fizzes are known by the name of the alcohol used (gin-fizz, vodka-fizz, rum-fizz)

Julep

Julep is a drink which became popular in the South of United States where the elderly would claim that whiskey is drunk like water and that it tastes like honey. The name originates from the Arabic *juleb*, which is a herbal-infused sweet water. The most famous juleps are: Mint Julep (bourbon base), Brandy Julep and Champagne Julep. Mojito is a cocktail which belongs in the the Julep family. The Julep cocktails are made with alcohol, mint, sugar, little soda or mineral water, while aromatic bitters are optional. Mint Juleps were known to be made with brandy (peach) and cognac, and it was not until later that whiskey was used as a standard ingredient. Mint Julep was popular enough to become a 1938 Kentucky Derby official cocktail, and the secret to its success since the 19th century is the quality of mint, to which can testify all the lovers of this cocktail. There are more than twenty different sorts of mint but the spearmint is the sort recommended for the Julep.

Champagne Cocktail

Champagne Cocktails are made with champagne or sparkling wine, no matter the amount. The Original Champagne Cocktail was always made with a sugar cube soaked with bitters. Examples of Champagne Cocktails are: Champagne Cocktail, French 75, Bellini, Kir Royal, Old Cuban, Mimosa, etc.

Punch

Punch was made in India and Indonesia in the early 1600s, after which it was brought to England. Punch is derived from a Hindu word पञ्च (*pañc*), which means "five," therefore every punch should consist of five ingredients: alcohol, water (wine), spice (tea), sugar and fresh juice. The complex style behind the making of punch had a bearing on the later development of preparation methods and various cocktail techniques. It can be said that people consumed punch long before the creation of column made spirits, which means that the alcohol used in punch preparation was of very strong and full flavor, so the ingredients had to be mixed carefully in order to give it a pleasant flavor. Traditional punches require strong spirits that have a recognizable taste.

Toddy

The modern Toddy is one of the rare cocktail families consumed warm. Therefore, they are mostly consumed during winter. *The American Herbal,* published in 1801, describing the Toddy as a "salutary liquor". It contains alcohol, sugar, lemon juice and hot water. Sugar used in making a Toddy may be in the form of honey, agave syrup, etc.

Rickey

Rickey belongs to the highball cocktail family. It consists of alcohol, sparkling water (club soda or seltzer) and lime juice. A very refreshing drink in the summer time. It is believed that the Rickey cocktail family was invented thanks to a democrat lobbyist, Colonel Joe Rickey, who liked to drink whiskey with club soda in the Shoemaker's restaurant in Washington. At the beginning of the 19th century, a bartender added a bit of lime in Joe's whiskey soda in order to fresh it up and the result was today's Joe Rickey. Gin-Rickey is another traditional cocktail from the Rickey cocktail family which is exceedingly popular, perhaps the most popular cocktail from this family.

Crusta

Crusta is a creation of Mister Joseph Santino, celebrated Spanish caterer. The first Crusta cocktail was made in the middle of the 19th century in his Santina's Saloon bar in New Orleans. This cocktail category got its name from the sugary rim with which it is served. Brandy Crusta is the most popular member of this family. The ingredients of every Crusta, no matter the alcohol used are: base alcohol, citrus liqueur (Cointreau, Triple Sec), lemon juice, sugar rim and long lemon or orange peel (the length of glass circumference). There are various variations of a Crusta. Orange bitters are an incredible ingredient in a Crusta cocktail.

Daisy

The Daisy cocktail family is similar to a Sour cocktail family. Tequila Daisy which dates back to 1936 contains orange liqueur. At the beginning of the 20th century, grenadine syrup replaced the orange liqueur. It is prepared by shaking the base alcohol (mostly rum or gin), sugar, lemon juice and fruit syrup. The cocktail is then topped up with club soda or seltzer and consumed over crushed ice in a rock glass. Traditional Daisies were made with orange liqueur. Jerry Thomas served his Daisies over crushed ice, whereas Harry Craddock served it over broken ice.

Shrub

Even before Shrub became popular, Romans had used vinegar in their beverages. A Shrub was also consumed on boats in order to prevent scurvy. The traditional ingredients were usually: rum or brandy, fresh lemon, lime or orange juice and a sweet mix of vinegar with spices, roots and various fresh fruit juice. Shrubs ingredients depend on the season of the year. When making a Shrub use the same amount of vinegar and sugar with twice that amount of mixing fruit.

Gimlet

The Gimlet is named after a Navy surgeon from England by the name of Sir Thomas D. Gimlette who was making this drink in order to stop the scurvy among sailors. The traditional ingredients include: alcohol (gin) and Rose's Lime juice or alcohol (gin, vodka, etc.), fresh lime juice and sugar syrup.

Flip

Flips are mixed drinks made from alcohol or wine, a whole egg (or just the yolk) and sugar. By the 19th century, Flip was established as a popular drink. Sherry and brandy flips are among the most popular mixes from this cocktail family. A Flip needs to be shaken vigorously in order to get the desired texture and dissolve the egg. It is served in a smaller goblet and usually garnished with grated nutmeg.

Egg Nogg

Egg Nogg is a type of drink very popular around winter holidays and is prepared by mixing alcohol (brandy, rum, whiskey, Madeira, sherry, etc) with a whole egg, sugar, rich milk (milk, cream, etc). Egg Nogg can be made as a single drink or as punch. Traditionally, it is served in punch glasses and it was consumed mostly by the upper classes. How to Mix Drinks or or Bon Vivant's Companion by Jerry Thomas (1862), included six recipes for Egg Noggs: Egg Nogg, Hot Egg Nogg, Sherry Egg Nogg, General Harrison's Egg Nogg and Baltimore Egg Nogg.

Pousse Cafe

Pousse Cafe is a layered drink, known to be a after dinner drink or drink consumed after coffee. It is prepared by layering liqueurs in the drink which enhances its exotic appeal. Liqueurs tend to be heavier than spirits due to a higher level of sugar content. The B-52 is one of more famous drinks from the Pousse Cafe family.

Sling

The first Sling printed was in the book called Cocktails: How to Mix Them (1922) by Robert Vermeire was made with Gin, Benedictine, Dry Cherry Brandy, lemon juice, Orange and Angostura bitters and soda water. The most famous sling is the Gin Singapore Sling created by Mr. Ngiam Tong Boon somewhere around 1915 in the Raffles Hotel, Singapore made with Gin, Cherry Heering liqueur, Cointreau triple sec, Benedictine, Pineapple juice, lime juice, Grenadine and Angostura bitters.

Smash

This type of drink is made from base alcohol, sugar and mint. This family belongs to the Julep cocktail family. Whiskey smash is a cocktail which first appears in Jerry Thomas' *How to Mix Drinks* or *The Bon Vivant's Companion* (1862). Harry Johnson's 1888 *Bartender's Manual* presents a recipe for an Old Style Whiskey Smash made with sugar, water, mint, whiskey, and a garnish of seasonal fruit. Over time fruit such as peaches, pineapple, pears and ginger would come to replace mint as an ingredient. Fruit used in preparing smash is muddled, the rest of the ingredients are added and then vigorously shaken in the next eight seconds and poured, along with the used ice, in a rock glass.

Swizzle

Swizzle is a family of tropical cocktails consumed (with only booze, with or without citrus, with or without soda) over crushed ice. They are made by swizzling which demands the use of the Jamaican swizzle stick (which is native to the Caribbean). It is a great show and everyone at the bar enjoys watching the bartender making a Swizzle. Swizzling is done by spinning the stick between your palms, just like making camp fire. Doing so the Swizzle becomes cool and ready to be served.

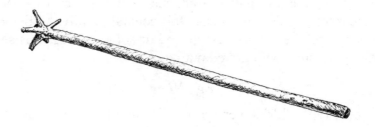

Part seven

COCKTAIL PRESENTATION

"The presentation is as equally important as the taste."

- Danilo Božović -

Garnish

The visual presentation of a cocktail should not be neglected; a good garnish is one of the key elements for providing the complete pleasure of a drink. A garnish should correspond to the cocktail and present its personality the right way. Aside from the fact that a garnish needs to be creatively arranged, there are certain rules a bartender should to adhere to. A bartender should use logic when garnishing his cocktail. It should have meaning, and the cocktail ingredients should be visible through the garnish.

Example No. 1 – If the cocktail contains lime juice, it should not be garnished with lemon.

Example No. 2 – If the cocktail consists of different types of alcohol, being "boozy", there is no point in garnishing it with pineapple, an umbrella or something else that will present it inappropriately.

Garnish is not just a decoration but greatly affect the taste. Manhattan, Martini, Cosmopolitan and Old Fashioned, with or without a twist, taste completely differently. Classic cocktails have already-determined garnishes that should not be changed unless the guest asks for it.

Example No. 1 – Martini is garnished with a lemon twist.

Example No. 2 – Jerry Thomas Manhattan is garnished with a lemon twist.

Example No. 3 – Dirty Martini is garnished with olives.

Example No. 4 – Sour cocktails are garnished with an orange flag (slice of orange with a brandied cherry).

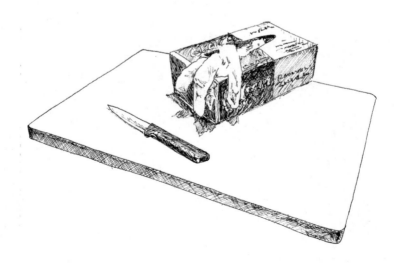

Garnish preparation

Wedges

The preparation of wedges requires fresh fruit (lemon, lime, orange) from which you need to cut off the ends. If during the preparation of wedges the ends are not cut off, they will release bitter, unpleasant flavor while making a cocktail with it. Cut the fruit from inside out. If necessary to split the fruit, turn it over so the peel is touching the cutting board and cut a line down the side of the fruit. After that, cut the half into three identical pieces. Wedges are used for highballs and similar.

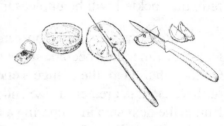

Slices

Start the preparation by cutting off the ends of the fruit. Then, split the fruit in half and turn the fleshy part facing down on the cutting board. From one half of the fruit, depending on its size, a bartender can make six to eight slices. This garnish is usually used for highballs, mixed drinks and other cocktails. Try to make sure the slices are placed in the glass and not on its edge. The cocktail will seem more elegant and attractive if the garnish is not "protruding" from the edge of the glass.

Wheels

Start with cutting off the ends of the fruit. Then, cut the fruit across in order to get thin circles. Depending on its size, a bartender can make five to seven wheels from one fruit. As with slices, it is good to place the wheel inside the glass when presenting the drink to a guest.

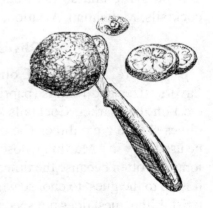

Twists

If a bartender is not using a knife while preparing twists he should make sure that he does not cut into the flesh or pith (the white layer of citrus fruits).

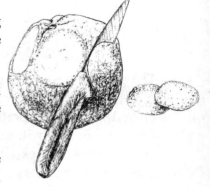

Reason No. 1 – If the flesh is cut into, the twist will add fruit flavor to the cocktail aroma, and in the case of the pith, the cocktail will be unpleasantly bitter.

Reason No. 2 – Upon removing the ends of the lemon or lime, they become more stable and easier to cut. On the other hand, the orange's ends do not need to be cut off because it is greater in size and, therefore, more stable than lemon or lime. Turning the fruit is the next step in preparing a twist and since the fruit now has a support on the cut off part, it will minimize its movement during cutting. Lemon and lime twists are cut from top to bottom. It is recommended that lemon and lime twist be cut in a straight line. Orange twist, on the other hand, should be circular. Twists are usually used with drinks that require a citrus aroma (Martini, Manhattan, Old Fashioned Martinez and Cosmopolitan).

Flags

A flag is a garnish made from two parts: fruit and maraschino cherry. Place the cherry in the middle of the wheel/slice, fold it over the cherry and pierce it with a toothpick or a bar sword.

Brandied cherries

Homemade brandied cherries are a great ingredient in cocktails and there are endless possibilities when it comes to playing with them. Avoid artificial cherries and serve exclusively homemade ones. Sour cherries can be macerated in cognac, brandy, chocolate, almond syrup and so on. Sour cherries as a garnish are mostly found in the following cocktails: Manhattan, Aviation, Rob Roy, Old Fashioned, Collins, Pina Coladas and so on.

Olives

There are a lot of olives of different origins, flavors, sizes and fillings (paprika, peppers, blue cheese, etc.) on the market. Cocktails which are decorated with olives should have three. The old rule that olives should be used only in a Martini, whose base is potato vodka, was long forgotten because the times changed and, nowadays, it is up to the guest to choose whether he wants olives or a twist. If the guest does not specify anything about garnish and the bartender forgets to ask, olives, in the case of a Dirty Martini, are the best option. In the case of a Martini, lemon twist is the best option.

Dry fruits and herbs

There are many choices of fresh and dry fruits as well as a most diverse selection of herbs and spices that can be used when preparing garnishes. The garnish chosen for a cocktail should be edible and if it is not, the guest should be notified.

Sugar and other rims

Sugar edges, rims of salt, cinnamon or chocolate are a part of décor the garnish provides and which, apart from seeming attractive, provide additional flavor. If the recipe itself does not include this, this kind of décor may or may not end up on a cocktail. This depends entirely on the bartender's will and desire for creativity. A Margarita can be served with a rim of salt. A Side Car can be served with a rim of sugar. A Salty Dog is served with a rim of salt, while the family of cocktails named Crusta is made with a sugar rim.

Dust

Dust is an oxidized liqueur turned into a powder. Leave a choice liqueur (Benedictine, Campari, Grand Marnier, Chartreuse) to oxidize in open air, on a flat plate, for about ten days. After some time, the liqueur will crystallize owing to the combination of sugar, alcohol and air. Once it is crystallized, it can easily be turned into dust by crushing the hard matter.

Eggs

Eggs represent an everyday ingredient in cocktails, responsible for their structure and full body.

How to make foam from egg whites?

During the beating of egg whites, the main protein, ovalbumin, expands and opens up turning into foam. Lemon acid mixed with sugar syrup has the role of stabilizing the foam and maintaining its texture. With some cocktails, creamy foam formed on the top of the glass is used as garnish. Egg as an ingredient is used in: traditional Sours, Fizzes, Flips and Nogs. The coffee cocktail is one of the more famous classic in which the key ingredient is a whole egg.

Tops

The tops of basil or mint are usually used in order to enhance the visual presentation of a cocktail. The leaves release oil essence and enhance the cocktail experience with its aroma. The tops of the stalks should not be too lush. They should not contain less than three or more than five leaves.

Glassware

Glasses are a part of every establishment. Their shape and presentation equally represent an establishment as the rest of the interior. It is very important to have enough usable glasses at every moment. If the bar runs out of a certain type of glass, the establishment leaves the impression of irresponsibility and not being serious. So, the bar should have backup glasses. Glasses should be clean and polished at every moment. Glasses are polished using warm water steam with two clean towels in order to avoid contact with hands. The glass body consists of three parts: the bowl is the part holding alcohol, the foot or base is the part on which the glass stands and the stem is the glass's neck. Glasses are divided into four main types:

1. **Tumbler** (low, high)

2. **Footed ware**

3. **Stemware**

4. **Mug**

Tumblers are glasses without a neck. They exist in different sizes and their sides can be straight or slant. It depends on the cocktail which tumbler will be used. Types of tumblers:

Collins, Highball – high tumblers

Rock, Old Fashioned – low tumblers

Footed ware is a glass without the neck

Brandy snifter, Hurricane

Stemware is a glass that possesses all three parts (bowl, foot and stem)

Coupe glass, Cocktail glass, Champagne flute

Mug is actually a tumbler with a handle, possesses thicker glass and is an outstanding glass for serving beer.

Old Fashioned glass/ low tumbler

"On the rocks" is a term usually linked to an Old Fashioned glass, and the drink served this way is usually a cocktail or alcohol. Old Fashioned glass is famous as a low tumbler or a rock glass. Double Old Fashioned signifies the glass where a double dosage of alcohol is served and its volume is usually 5 – 8 oz or 18 – 24 cl.

Highball glass

It is used for mixed drinks and fizz cocktails. Mixed drinks are traditionally served in highball glasses of 8 - 9 oz. (juice-vodka, whiskey-soda, etc.). Highball glass is 24 – 36 cl in volume and is longer than an Old Fashioned glass and wider than a Collins glass.

Cocktail or Martini glass

The cocktail glass was traditionally made in order to serve martini and cocktails without ice. The rule of thumb states that a cocktail glass should not contain ice, that is, that a drink should not be consumed using a straw (today it is up to the subjective feeling of the guest).

Coupe glass

A coupe glass is used to serve "up" cocktails and this glass is usually around 8 oz. in size.

Snifter glass

Type of glass reserved for serving drinks without ice. This type of glass is mostly used while serving brandy, cognac and some liqueurs. Mixed drinks are not served in a snifter glass.

Hurricane glass

It is used in consuming tropical and frozen cocktails. This type of glass is popular in tropical lands and bars that like to accentuate tropical decor.

Tiki glass

Ceramic glasses used in serving Tiki cocktails and drinks inspired by Polynesian culture.

Shot glass

Used in fast consumption of alcohol, cocktails and mixed drinks.

Sherry Glass, Port Glass, Taster or Pony Glass

Sherry and port glasses are of specific design in order to better manifest aromas during consumption. Most restaurants use, to make things easier, one type of glass for serving port and sherry. A pony glass is used when serving dessert wines.

Mugs and beer glass

Glasses used for beer are important when it comes to regulating temperature. Lots of breweries have experts who decide what shape and glass thickness will present a beer best.

Wine glass

Red wine demands a wider and larger glass in order for its aromas to open up. On the other hand, white and rose wines are served in smaller and narrower glasses. The most widely known wine glasses are the representatives of the Bordeaux and Bourgogne region. If a bar serves water in wine glasses, there should be a distinction between wine and water glasses. Wine glasses are positioned on the right, and water glasses on the left part of table. In case food is served, the arrangement of glasses should go from right to left in the following order: champagne, white wine, red wine and then water. In case champagne is not consumed, the arrangement stays the same.

Part eight

ICE

"The key ingredient to a good drink."

- Danilo Božović, Andrija Ristić -

Ice

People always longed for cold beverages. India, China and Egypt are but a few countries that started to use ice in gastronomy. In India, for example, ice was produced by boiling water (releasing air) and then filling cone shaped holes in the earth with it. The boiled water would spend a night under the earth. Cold wind would freeze the surface of water creating necessary quantities of ice. It is interesting that this way of producing ice is still used in Bengal. One of the traditional ways of making ice was the one where a glass bottle was filled with water, wrapped in a wet cloth and left in a cool and dark place. The Romans saved ice for the summer by putting snow in a cone-shaped hole in the ground of 7.62 m in diameter and 15.24 m deep at almost 1000 m above sea level. Another method which the Romans used was to make the ice in the desert, and harvest it early in the morning when the desert was at its coldest, and there was enough time to take it to the ice house to be stored. Ice was brought in large quantities from Scandinavia. That ice was of suspicious quality due to snow, parts of frozen lakes and artificially made ice were subjected to exterior influences. The deliveries of ice were mostly done across the ocean and would reach their destination halved due to warm wind and climate so the ice was available only to upper social classes. Before the 1830's, food was preserved through salting, spicing, pickling or smoking. Butchers slaughtered meat only for the day's trade, as preservation for longer periods was not practical. Dairy products and fresh fruits and vegetables subject to spoilage were sold in local markets since storage and shipping farm produce over any significant distance or time was not practical. Milk was often hauled to city markets at night when temperatures were cooler. Ale and beer making required cool temperatures, and its manufacture was limited to the cooler months. The solution to these problems was found in the harvesting of natural ice. Before the invention of artificial refrigeration in the early twentieth century, ice was harvested every winter and stored in large ice houses, the proprietors of which sold ice to shippers of fresh fish, waterfowl, and produce for train deliveries to large cities. Commercial sales of ice were started in the beginning of 19th century by a few innovative people. Ice demand was large. People wanted to savor cold drinks and it was a matter of time when someone started mass distribution of ice. That person was Frederic Tudor from Boston. He is credited for the beginning of ice distribution in North America.

The appearance of ice led to a revolution in the banking industry and Frederic Tudor, called King of Ice, held monopoly over the ice business for many years. He was an extremely good and smart businessman. Although very profitable in the beginning, the offer and demand for ice dwindled with the invention of the refrigerator, and this tendency would carry on with the beginning of production of freezers and ice machines in the middle of the 20th century. Today we have a growing number of bars who taking their ice very seriously. Cracked, carved, shaved, flavored and imported there is now ice out there for every palate, and even among those bars that aren't in a position to stock six type of ice on nightly basis, the simple cube has undergone a transformation, mainly thanks to better equipment, improved water and a greater appreciation of the science bit behind the cooling and dilution of cocktails. You should treat your ice like you would any other ingredient. What's the point of making your own syrups and juices and making and using the best spirits, only to then use dirty ice, or ice that's half melted in it? The biggest mistake bars tend to make when buying an ice machine is trying to save the money. Cheapest ice machines makes bad ice and usually need replacing sooner than expected, when in fact, good quality machine might cost more, but make excellent ice and can last over ten years or even longer if you look after it properly.

The most basic types of ice are: powdered, shaved, block, ice ball, ice cube, crushed, ground and pellet:

Shaved ice is scraped directly off the bar-top block. Shaved ice differs from powdered ice by being less like a snowball and more like a mass of snowflakes.

Block of ice are the first form of ice available behind a bar. Bartenders needed a lot of effort to get a desired amount of ice from blocks. In order to handle it you, needed a lot of knowledge and attention.

Ice ball is a subgroup of ice block because it is made from it. The advantage of this ice is its slower melting.

Ice cube is mostly used in bars. Ideal for stirring, shaking and serving drinks. Good ice cube dimensions are 3.2 by 3.2 by 3.2 cm. It needs to be firm, fresh and dry.

Crushed ice can be made by crushing with an ice knife or a mallet. It is diluted and as such it is ideal for making frozen (blended) drinks. These drinks are blended for about 20 seconds. This kind of ice is used in blending because it is easier to get the desired form of puree and damages the blades considerably less.

Pellet ice is similar to crushed ice, but it is cube shaped and is perfect for swizzle, tropical and frozen cocktails.

Part nine

---◆◆▮◆◆---

BEER

„Nothing like a cold one"

- Danilo Božović, Andrija Ristić -

Fermentation

The fermentation is a natural process during which sugar turns into alcohol and carbon dioxide under influence of yeast. Specifically, fermentation is a process during which sugar (glucose, fructose, sucrose), is turned into ethyl alcohol, CO_2, heat and water. In the process of fermentation, the type of yeast used is an important factor.

The difference between fermentation and distillation.

Wine is fermented grape juice.

Beer is fermented grain wort.

Vodka is a spirit made from distillation of fermented grain wort.

The fermentation process can be stopped in several ways:

• By lowering atmospheric temperature so low yeast cannot ferment.

• By removing yeast and filtering the fermented mass.

• By destroying yeast with fortification by adding alcohol.

Everything that contains sugar can be fermented. Most types of grain turn to ethyl alcohol. The rest of the process can be used in animal feed. Beer is fermented barley juice and other types of grain and hop. Water makes up to 95% of beer. Beer, besides wine, holds the longest consuming tradition on the planet. The Egyptians made beer and taught the ancient Greeks beer making techniques. Barley started to be used in beer making culture only later. Egyptians considered beer to be very nutritious and gave it to their workers in order to give them strength to endure hard physical labor. Beer production was a noble and respected profession in ancient Egypt and beer makers were closely linked to religion and the reigning class. Beer was used in religious ceremonies during which priests would offer it to Egyptian gods as a sign of respect, good will, and loyalty. Ale was one of the first beers. It existed long before the coming of lighter beers. On the American continent, ale was consumed long before the migration of German immigrants who brought the technique of making lager beers with them.

The role of yeast plays a decisive part in fermentation process, therefore the knowledge of its behavior and reaction with other ingredients is of paramount importance for production of quality alcoholic drinks. Monitoring yeast can help the manufacturer a lot because he can measure the time of fermentation and see if the yeast is effective or not. A yeast with a lot of pores is of a sweeter taste, arid smell and lighter in color can be described as good. If the yeast is "dead", floats or is bluish in color with sour taste and smell, it can be said that it is bad and not fit to use in fermentation. The role of yeast in wine production is great because, due to oxygen deprivation, it turns sugar into ethyl alcohol, carbon dioxide, heat and water. The more sugar there is in wine the greater the percent of alcohol in the final product. Sometimes, master distillers interrupt the fermentation process in order to preserve a part of sugar and make the fermented juice (wine, beer) sweeter. This process is used in dessert wine and porto production. Unfiltered beer is distilled, and the remains of the process, called the backset, are put back into the fermenter. Backset maintains the PH value that the master wants in the distiller which means that the sour mash process uses the fermented mash from the previous fermentation.

Beer production

The first step in beer making is formation of grain malt. In order for starch to ferment it has to be placed into warm water in order to germinate and become ready for fermentation. By putting starch into warm water an enzyme, Amylase, is created which changes the molecular structure of starch and makes it easier for yeast to make alcohol. The malt is dried and roasted in order to get the desired color and aroma of beer. Dried grain malt or grist is mixed with warm water and this process is called mashing. By mixing grist and water a thick liquid called wort is formed. Then hop is added and everything is cooked for an hour or two. After cooking, the barley that provided color and bitterness is removed from the wort. Wort is cooled and ready for fermentation which is done in a barrel, to which, besides wort, one liter of yeast is added for every 140 liters of beer. By feeding on the maltose sugar, yeast releases carbon dioxide and alcohol. Fermentation takes from five to ten days depending on the type of yeast and temperature of fermentation. After that, beer is filtered in order to clear all impurities and surplus of yeast left after fermentation. Depending on beer style, the maturation period can last from several weeks (ale) to several months (lager).

Beer service

One should make sure the beer served is cold (around 5 C or 41 F). Ales are on the other hand served at a warmer temperature. Beer should be served in a glass, unless the guest wants different. By pouring it in a glass beer is allowed to open up its aroma and form a foam. Some guests like to pour their beer on their own. The label should face the guest and beer should be on his right side, whereas the glass should be on the left. The foam helps maintain the temperature of the beer. Glass used for service should be clean and in certain situations, cooled. The thickness of glass plays an important role in maintaining beer temperature.

Whats the difference between ale and lager?

Traditionally, beers are divided into ales and lagers. Lager is a beer of lighter color and body whereas ale is mostly darker and of heavier body.

Ales and Lagers

Ales & Lagers are two main groups in beer classification. Ales are traditional beers, predating lagers by thousands of years. Lagers are relatively modern creations and are less than two hundred years old. The type of yeast that we use determines the style of beer we make, and the types of yeast dictate the temperature of the fermentation. Ales are traditionally fermented at a higher temperature, at 12-21 C (55-70 F). Lagers are typically fermented at a lower temperature, at 3-10 C (38-50 F). Colder fermentation slows the yeast activity requires longer storing time. Cool surroundings enables the development of fruity aromas (esters) and other fermentation by-products more characteristic of ales. This process is responsible for the purer flavor of lagers, and longer storing (lagering) makes the beer smoother.

Ale

Ale is of heavier body with bitterer flavor than other beers. They are of a more robust flavor and can be fruity and aromatic. Ales are generally served warmer 7-12 C or 45 – 55 F. The following ales belong to the group of famous ales: English Pale Ales, Scottish and Irish Ales, American Ales, English Brown Ales, Porters, Stouts, Indian Pale Ales, Belgian and French Ales, Sour Ales, Belgian Strong Ales, Strong Ales. A few examples:

Northern English Brown Ale (English Brown Ale) – light, hop aroma and nutty.

Belgian Dubbel (Belgian Strong Ale) – strong and complex.

Belgian Pale Ale (Belgian and French Ale) – fruity, spicy and bronze colored.

Berliner Weisse (Sour Ale) – refreshing wheat beer of sour taste.

Biere de Garde (Belgian and French Ale) – an ale from villages of northern France with complex flavor and copper color.

Irish Red Ale (Scottish and Irish Ale) – light hop aroma.

American Amber Ale (American Ale) – malt flavor with medium hop aroma.

American Stout (Stout) – dark and bitter with a creamy flavor.

Gueuze (Sour Ale) – Belgian beer of sour flavor.

American Indian Pale Ale (Indian Pale Ale) – complex with golden-copper color. Full flavor and sour-fruity aroma with enough bitterness.

Standard Ordinary Bitter (English Pale Ale) – light to medium body with malt aroma.

Old Ale (Strong Ale) – of buttery, toasty and rich flavor.

Brown Porter (Porter) – mild with medium body. Low to medium malt flavor.

Oatmeal Stout (Stout) – heavy body and grainy flavor.

Russian Imperial Stout (Stout) – dark with a heavy body with aromas of cocoa and coffee.

Lager

A lager is a light refreshing beer of subtle body; its name originates from the German word "lagern" which means to stockpile. They have a crisp and In the group of famous ales belong: Light Lager, Pilsner, European Amber Lager, Dark Lager, Bock. They are served cooler 3-7 C (38-45 F).

Premium American Lager (Light Lager) – Crisp with low malt and hop notes.

Vienna Lager (European Amber Lager) – Crisp with subtle hops.

Dark American Lager (Dark Lager) – Light to medium body with low malt presence.

German Pilsner / Pils (Pilsner) – general light beer of subtle body; the original pilsner is Pilsner Urquell from the Czech town of the same name.

Traditional Bock (Bock)– a dark and malty lager beer.

Doppelbock (Bock) – a dark lager with rich aroma.

Beers which don't belong in the category of ales or lagers but in a category of their own: Kölsch, Cream Ale, Weizen/Weiss bier, Smoked Beer, Wood Aged Beer, etc.

Cider

Cider or "sidra" (in Spanish) comes from a Hebrew word "shekhar" meaning "strong drink". Cider is fermented apple juice. Perry (cider's cousin) is fermented pear juice mostly produced in southern part of Normandy. Percentage of alcohol in ciders can vary between two and eight percent but there are cider with more than 12 percent of alcohol. Ciders also range from dry to sweet and apples that are sweeter and tastier to eat produce cider of lower quality. Normandy is a part of the region famous for quality of its apples and produces the best ciders whereas in America ciders are mostly produced in Massachusetts and Pennsylvania. The history of cider in America is deeply connected with the coming of European settlers from Great Britain in 17th and 18th century. Standard ciders and perries: English Cider, French Cider, Common Perry and Traditional Perry. Specialty ciders and perries: New England Cider, Fruit Cider, Apple Wine and Other Specialty Cider and Perry.

Part ten

WINE

„Hard to imagine without.“

- Danilo Božović, Uroš Đukić, Stefan Stojanović -

Wine

Wine was consumed by ancient nations such as Egyptians, Romans and Greeks. Romans spread their love of grapes and wine making throughout Europe. Proof that wine was consumed in the Far East goes back almost eight thousand years BC in regions of today's Iran, Syria, Lebanon and the Caucasus. Wine was regarded as very valuable goods and Greeks and Romans used it as means of payment. It is not known who started making wine. What we know for sure is that Christianity had a lot to do with popularizing wine because it was used during religious rites, so Christians regarded it as food, not alcohol. Church made wine for its own use and Pope Clement V raised the vineyards Chateauneuf du Pape in 15th century which are well-known for their quality even today. Wine underwent a revolution during the 1960's, because Loius Pasteur revealed and explained in detail the fermentation process. With this move he opened the door for industry to make wine with technology instead of naturally, by hand. Wine is fermented grape juice. It is made by plucking ripe grapes, putting it in a container, pressing the juice, fermenting and filtering. Yeast found in grapes turns sugar from its juice into alcohol and CO_2. The result of fermentation is wine. The temperature during fermentation is very important because it influences the final result. White wines are fermented at lower temperatures than red wines. Wine producer decides what kind of container he will use for fermentation. They are mostly made of oak or stainless steel. Dead yeast (lees) can stay in fermented wine juice longer in order to provide richer texture. Fermentation usually takes from three days to three months. After fermentation, wine should be matured for some time which depends on the manufacturer. After maturing, wine is filtered in order to stabilize it and clear it of possible impurities. Different wines can be blended or mixed in order to get the desired wine and to cut costs.

Wine service

When a guest is choosing a wine, one should try and recommend the best wine within the price range the guest intends to pay for it. One should not hesitate to inquire about how much is the guest planning to spend on the wine because this way, by reducing the frame of possibilities, service is made easier. One should offer three options closest to the price range of his guest. Before the wine is brought for presentation it is necessary to have polished glasses ready in front of the guest. During presentation, the bartender should mention the name of the wine, year of production, it classification, as well as the manufacturer's name while holding the bottle so that the label faces the guest both during presentation and when pouring. With two precise moves the bartender should slice open the foil. The foil should not be thrown away. When opening (sparkling) wine the bartender should try to get the cork out gently, without loud opening of the bottle. Cork is the best indicator of the state of wine served. Serving can be done in several ways. After determining the quality of wine and getting approval from the host, the wine is served for younger ladies firstly and then for gentleman (host should be served the last). No matter how many guests there are, one should try to evenly distribute the wine.

Light dry white wines, rosés, champagne, sparkling wines are usually served at 4 - 10 C or 40 - 50 F. Full-bodied white wines and light, fruity reds are usually served at 10 - 15 C or 50 - 60 F. Full-bodied red wines and Ports tend to be served at 15 - 18 C or 60 - 65 F. If there are too many guest the host should be advised to order two bottles instead of one. The bottle should be left on the bar so that the label faces the host. Apart from that, it is important to place the wine near the guests so it is not out of their reach. Evening is usually started with a champagne or sparkling wine. White wines are usually consumed before red ones and lighter and drier wines before sweeter and heavier wines. Sparkling wine should be on ice. For larger groups, a Magnum bottle (size of two bottles) can be recommended. Splits (375 ml) are sparkling bottles used in cocktail bars where they are also served per glass. A corkage fee is a fee charged to a guest who brings his own wine to the restaurant/ bar. According to etiquette, wine brought into restaurant/bar should not be one of the wines on offer in the establishment unless it is a very rare and special year. Corkage fee is two times larger for the Magnum bottles, in most cases.

Decanting

Wine decanting is a process where wine sediment are removed and the wine is exposed to oxygen. Decanting is done at a "gueridon" or a small (assistance) or at the bar. In order to decant wine one needs: carafe (glass container), candle (used to identify sediment through bottle), wine cradle, corkscrew, two napkins, two little plates, matches or a lighter. Depending on one's height, candle should be adjusted. One should avoid placing the bottle too near the candle in order not to warm up the wine. It is important to concentrate on the pour, and to pay attention to the bottle neck. When the sediment starts seeping into the carafe the decanting should stop.

Wine tasting

One should enjoy the wine, therefore slowly taste it. Before tasting he should look at the wine because color can tell a lot. He should rotate the wine in glass three to four times and then place his nose above the glass in order to better sense the aroma. By smelling the wine with the mouth open, the bartender will sense the finer aromas and alcohol will not attack the sense of smell aggressively. One should take a moderate sip of wine, hold it in his mouth and then inhale little air over the wine. The mouth should move similarly to chewing and before drinking. The whole process of wine tasting should not last for more than a few seconds. Aromas that can easily be noticed in wine are: fruity, floral, vanilla, herbal, earthy, tobacco, coffee, chocolate. Wine sweetness is explained through its dryness: the drier the wine the less sweet it is. Most wines have a certain dose of sourness, white wines more so than reds. Wine body is very important and during tasting one should feel if the body is light, medium or heavy. In case the wine is spoiled the aromas felt will be unpleasant: yeast, vinegar, chemical aroma, sweat aroma, cardboard or as if the wine was boiled.

Old and new world

In order for wine world to divide wines into styles and traditions that countries have in wine making, a division into the old and new world was made. Old world encompasses all countries that have had wine making cultures for centuries: France, Italy, Spain, Portugal, Greece and Germany. The new world entails all countries that started to produce high quality wines later on: Australia, New Zealand, Chile, Argentina, South Africa, USA...

White grape varieties

Pinot Grigio – Pinot gris, Grauer Monch, Grey Pinot

Country of origin: France

Cultivation: France, Italy, Germany, Serbia, Croatia

USA, Chile, Argentina, South Africa, Australia and New Zealand

Color: Pale yellow

Aroma: lemon, grapefruit, Williams pear

Flavor: granny smith apple, lemon, pear

Body: light

New World (fruit) VS Old World (earth)

Albarino – Alvarinho, Cainho Branco

Country of origin: Spain

Cultivation: Spain, Portugal, USA, Chile, Argentina

Color: light yellow

Aroma: ripe pear, apricot, lemon peel

Flavor: apple, citrus, pear

Body: medium to heavy

Riesling – Rauschling, Johannisberger

Country of origin – Germany

Cultivation: Germany, Austria, Serbia, Italy, France, USA, Australia, New Zealand, South Africa

Riesling is one of the most popular white grape varieties around the world. The reason it is widespread is the possibility to make different types of wine out of it. Riesling is a sort whose palette of flavors goes from bone dry to different levels of sweet. Riesling is also one of rare white wines that is suitable for aging.

Color: yellow with green notes

Aroma: peach, lemon peel, melon

Flavor: dry, mineral, biting, refreshing or sweet with great balance of sweet and sour

Body: medium

Gewürztraminer – Gewurtz, Traminer Mosque, Hot Traminer

Country of origin: France

Cultivation: France, Germany, Switzerland, Italy, USA, South Africa, Canada, New Zealand

Gewürztraminer is a grape sort from the family of Rieslings, has similar characteristics and aromas but also one thing that differentiates it which is gewurtz – spiciness.

Pinot Blanc – Pinot Bianco, Feher Burgundy, White Pinot

Country of origin: France (Alsace)

Cultivation: France, Italy, Hungary, Croatia, Serbia, USA, Australia, South Africa

Color: pale yellow

Aroma: tropical fruit, pineapple, flowers

Flavor: dry, refreshing, mineral

Body: heavy

Viogner – Picotin Blanc, Barbin, Rebolot

Country of origin: France (Rhone Valley)

Cultivation: France, USA, Argentina, Australia, Chile

Color: golden yellow

Aroma: citrus, peach, apricot

Flavor: semi-dry, oily

Body: medium to heavy

Trebbiano – *Ugni Blanc, St Emilion, White Hermitage*

Country of origin: Italy

Cultivation: Italy, France, USA, Australia

Trebbiano is a grape sort mostly grown in the northern part of Italy and is the fifth most grown sort in the world. Trebbiano or Ugni Blanc are sorts of grape used to make Cognac and Armagnac.

Color: old gold

Aroma: herbal, spicy

Flavor: refreshing, rosemary, sour

Body: medium

Grenache Blanc – *Garnacha Blanca*

Country of origin: France (South Rhone Valley)

Cultivation: France

Grenache Blanc is a white grape varieties which is a symbol of the south part of river Rhone in France. Grenache Blanc is rarely found as 100% wine but it gives flavor to most white and rose blends produced in this part of France.

Color: yellow

Aroma: thyme, sage, citrus

Flavor: dry wine with green olives flavor and notes of sea salt

Body: medium

Roussanne – *Roussanne Blanc, Barbine, Picotine Blanc*

Country of origin: France (South Rhone Valley)

Cultivation: France, USA

Roussanne is a grape sort grown in the French region of South Rhone and is mostly found in blend with Marsanne.

Color: dark yellow

Aroma: spices, roasted hazelnuts, pear

Flavor: oily texture and exotic fruit

Body: medium to heavy

Sauvignon Blanc – *Fume Blanc, Muscat-Sylvaner*

Country of origin: France (*Loire Valley*)

Cultivation: France, Italy, Spain, New Zealand, Chile, USA, South Africa

Sauvignon Blanc is a grape sort very popular among wine connoisseurs. Aromas that Sauvignon Blanc possesses are remembered forever. Sauvignon Blanc is the grape sort that shows people its best characteristics at a young age (1 – 3 years). French wines made in Sancerre and Pouilly Fume appellations are made of 100% Sauvignon Blanc as well as

Fume Blanc by Robert Mondavy (one of rare Sauvignon Blancs which is left to mature in oak casks.)

Color: pale yellow

Aroma: citrus, mown grass

Flavor: dry wine of fruity aromas and very sour

Body: medium

Malvasia – Malvazia

Country of origin: Greece

Cultivation: Mediterranean belt of Europe and USA

Malvasia is white grape sort and widely spread in Mediterranean countries.

Color: amber

Aroma: flower, caramel

Prosecco – Glera, Bianchetta Trevigiana

Country of origin: Italy (Tree Venice)

Cultivation: Italy

Prosecco is a white wine sort coming from northeastern Italy. Prosecco is a grape sort as well as region in Italy. Prosecco is frequently used in semi-sparkling (frizzante) and sparkling (spoumantte) wines.

Color: straw yellow

Aroma: rising dough, green apples, basil

Flavor: dry wine of balanced bubbles

Body: medium

Cortese

Country of origin: northern part of Italy

Cultivation: Italy

Cortese is a grape sort which is grown in northern part of Italy, in Piedmont and Lombardy regions. The most famous wine made of Cortese is Gavi and Gavi di Gavi.

Melon de Bourgogne – Muscadet, Melon

Country of origin: France (Loire Valley)

Cultivation: France, USA

Every wine that has Muscadet on its label, under French law, has to be made from Melon de Bourgogne grape sort.

Color: gold

Aroma: grapefruit, melon, minerals

Flavor: dry wine with accentuated notes of green plums

Body: medium to heavy

Semillon – Colombier, Blanc Doux, Wyndruif

Country of origin: France (Bordeaoux)

Cultivation: France, Germany, USA, Australia, Chile, Argentina, South Africa

Semillon is a white grape sort which is, apart from Sauvignon Blanc, one of two main sorts in the very famous white wine Sauterenes.

Aroma: apple, pear, vanilla

Flavor: dry wine of moderate sourness and oily structure

Body: medium

Sylvaner – Gruner Silvaner, Johannisberger, Sylvaner Verde

Country of origin: Austria

Cultivation: France, Austria, Germany, USA

Sylvaner is a white grape sort that is mostly grown in the French region Alsace, which is famous as one of four primary sorts that give quality to wines of Alsace.

Color: yellow

Aroma: citrus, melon, smoke

Flavor: dry wine with mineral finish and moderate sourness

Body: medium

Muller-Thurgau – Sylvaner-Riesling

Country of origin: Switzerland (Thurgau)

Cultivation: France, Germany, Austria, Croatia, Czech Republic, Australia, New Zealand, USA

Muller-Thurgau is a white wine sort created in 19th century in a Swiss town Thurgau by crossing Sylvaner and Riesling and all praises for this revolutionary wine discovery goes to Dr. Muller.

Aroma: white peaches, pears and meadow flowers

Flavor: dry wine with flavor of peach and stronger finish

Body: medium

Chardonnay – Chablis, White Burgundy

Country of origin: France (Burgundy)

Cultivation: Almost every country that grows grapes has a Chardonnay

Chardonnay is the most famous white grape sort in the world. Almost every inhabitant of Earth, when asked what wine he would like to drink, (level of knowledge of wines not important) would answer – Chardonnay. A small number of people know that this grape sort makes two different types of wine, depending on the geographic region; In France (old world) or California (new world).

Chardonnay (old world) / Burgundy style

Fermentation is done in stainless steel containers at a controlled temperature, in order for wine to keep all the fruity aromas that Chardonnay as a sort possesses. Wine is not left to mature in oak barrels and contact with wood is avoided altogether.

Color: golden yellow

Aroma: green apples, yeast

Flavor: dry wine of oily texture with refreshing notes

Body: medium

Chardonnay (new world) style

Fermentation is done in stainless steel containers but when the process of malolactic fermentation (process where at a certain temperature fruit acids turn into dairy) is done, it is left to mature in oak casks.

Color: old gold

Aroma: vanilla, burre, ripe apples

Flavor: dry wine of accentuated sourness of creamy structure

Body: heavy

Vermentino – Agostenga, Vermentino Bianco, Favorita

Country of origin: Italy (Corcica)

Cultivation: Italy, France, USA

Vermentino is a white grape sort that is mostly grown on Mediterranean islands like Sardinia (Italy) and Corsica (France) but can be found in California (USA).

Color: light yellow

Aroma: peach, lemon peel, dry herbs

Flavor: dry wine with lemon peel flavor and a mineral finish

Body: medium

Red grape varieties

Pinot Noir - Blaufrankisch, Spatburgunder

Country of origin: France (Burgundy)

Cultivation: France, Italy, Austria, Germany, Serbia, USA, New Zealand

Pinot Noir is red grape sort that is grown all over the world. It is very hard and demanding to grow (even the slightest illness can ruin it) both in a vineyard as well as later during wine production. This sort is very famous for giving extremely quality and expensive wines that rise to the highest prices in auctions.

Color: pale red

Aroma: sour cherry, rose petals, cinnamon

Flavor: silky – velvety, soft and fine tannins

Body: medium

Cabernet Franc – Bouchet, Breton

Country of origin: France (Bordeaux)

Cultivation: France, USA, South Africa

Cabarnet Franc is a red grape sort mostly grown in French region of Bordeaux, almost exclusively for blending with other sorts.

Bordeaux blend (Cabernet Sauvignon, Merlot, Cabernet Franc, Petit Verdot, Malbec)

Aroma: black currant, violet, asparagus

Flavor: black currant, distinctive tannins and high level of sourness

Body: medium to heavy

Cabernet Sauvignon – Petit Bouchet, Vidure, Sauvignon Rouge

Country of origin: France (Bordeaux)

Cultivation: France, Italy, Spain, Serbia, Croatia, USA, Australia, south Africa, Argentina, Chile

Cabernet Sauvignon is a red grape sort mostly grown in Bordeaux region and is the main ingredient in Bordeaux wines (right bank of river Gironde). Besides France, it is grown all over the world and is the most cultivated red grape variety in the world.

Color: dark red

Aroma: blueberry, green olives, pepper

Flavor: blueberry, thick textures and distinctive tannins

Body: heavy

Malbec – *Auxerrois in Cahoirs, Pressac*

Country of origin: France (Bordeaux)

Cultivation: France, Argentina, Chile

Malbec is a grape sort which originated in France but in time spread to Argentina which is the greatest producer of this sort in the world currently.

Color: purple

Aroma: dry plum, violet, forest fruit jam

Flavor: berries, moderate tannins with basil notes

Body: medium to heavy

Petit Verdot – Verdot

Country of origin: France (Bordeaux)

Cultivation: France, Argentina, Australia, USA

Petit Verdot is a red grape sort that is grown in Bordeaux and provides a minor percentage as part of wines from that region.

Color: dark red

Aroma: banana, sawdust

Grenache – Garnacha, Alicanite, Cannonau

Country of origin: Spain (Rioja)

Cultivation: Spain, France, Italy, Argentina. Chile

Grenache (France) or Garnacha (Spain) is a red grape sort which is mostly grown in Europe. Most famous wines made from this sort are from Rhone Valley and they are: Gigondas and Chateauneuf du Pape.

Color: ruby

Aroma: black currant, thyme, orange flower

Flavor: fleshy, moderate tannins and extra sourness

Body: medium to heavy

Sangiovese – Brunello, Nielluccio

Country of origin: Italy (Toscana)

Cultivation: Italy

Sangiovese is a red grape sort mostly used as one of the main ingredients of some famous wines such as Chianti, Brunello di Montalcino, Rosso di Montalcino, Super Tuscans.

Color: purple

Aroma: strawberry, plum, violet

Flavor: sour cherry, distinctive tannins

Body: medium

Nebbiolo

Country of origin: Italy (Piedmont)

Cultivation: Italy, Austria, Australia, Chile

Nebbiolo is a red grape sort that is mostly grown and gives best results in Italian region of Piedmont. This sort is used for production of Barollo and Barbaresco, two of the most renowned and globally accepted wines.

Color: bright purple

Aroma: raspberry, truffles, tobacco

Flavor: sour cherry, spices, distinctive tannins

Body: heavy

Merlot

Country of origin: France (Bordeaux)

Cultivation: France, Italy, Australia, Chile, USA

Merlot is a red grape sort mostly grown in Bordeaux (typically on the left bank of Gironde), but around the globe as well. Besides Cabarnet Sauvignon, Merlot is the most important sort of grape among the famous Chateau Bordeaux wines.

Color: purple

Aroma: ripe strawberry, plum, tobacco

Flavor: black cherry, plum, silky tannins

Body: medium

Syrah – Shiraz

Country of origin: France (Rhone Valley)

Cultivation: France, Australia (Shiraz), South Africa, USA

Syrah is a red grape sort mostly grown in France and Australia which is known for being used in production of sparkling wines of high quality.

Australia – Shiraz

France – Syrah

Color: distinctly purple

Aroma: blueberry, smoked meat, eucalyptus

Flavor: blueberry, white pepper, distinctive tannins and sourness

Body: medium to heavy

Pinotage – Perold's Hermitage x Pinot

Country of origin: South Africa

Cultivation: South Africa, USA, New Zealand

Pinotage is a red grape sort mostly grown in South Africa. It was made by crossing Pinot Noir and Cinsault (Hermitage) in South Africa during Apartheid in 1925.

Color: bright purple

Aroma: plum, licorice, smoked meat

Flavor: pancetta, sweet tobacco

Body: medium to heavy

Cinsaut – Hermitage

Country of origin: France

Cultivation: France, Lebanon

Cinsault is a grape sort mostly grown in the Mediterranean part of France. This grape sort is famous for being a frequent guest in wines of the southern France.

Color: garnet

Aroma: sour cherry, nicoise olive

Flavor: spicy flavor and delicate tannins

Body: light to medium

Mourvedre – Mataro, Monastrell

Country of origin: Spain

Cultivation: Spain, France, Australia, USA

Mourvedre is a red grape sort mostly grown in the south of France. This sort is famous for its unbelievably dry rose wines – Bandol.

Aroma: wild game, earthy notes, overripe red fruit

Flavor: raspberry, distinctive tannins, high percentage of alcohol

Body: medium

Primitivo – Zinfandel, Crljenak Kastelanski

Country of origin: Croatia

Cultivation: Italy, Croatia, USA, South Africa

Primitivo is a red grape sort which is very interesting because of the dispute between Croatian and Italy about whether Primitivo, that is Crljenak Kastelanski, is the ancestor of the Californian Zinfandel.

Color: ruby red

Aroma: blueberry, anise, pepper

Flavor: dray wine, distinctive and well concentrated tannins

Body: medium to heavy

Barbera – Barbera

Country of origin: Italy (Monferato)

Cultivation: Italy, Austrlia, Argentina, USA

Barbera is red grape sort mostly grown in the north of Italy. This sort is mostly present in three villages in Piedmont and it is named after them - Barbera D'Asti, Barbera D'Alba i Barbera del Monferrato.

Color: dusky purple

Aroma: cherry, raspberry, blackberry

Flavor: dry wine with distinctive ripe fruit flavor

Body: medium

Gamay – Gamay

Country of origin: France (Burgundy – Beaujolais)

Cultivation: France, USA

Gamay is a grape sort mostly grown in the French region of Burgundy and it is used in production of some famous Beaujolais wines - *Beaujolais Nuevo, Beaujolais Villages, Beaujolais Cru.*

Color: purple

Aroma: wild strawberry, sour cherry, pepper

Flavor: dry wine of great sourness and delicate tannin structure

Body: light to medium

Dolcetto – Dolisn, Ormeasco

Country of origin: Italy

Cultivation: Italy, USA

Dolcetto is a red grape sort mostly grow in Italy (Piedmont) and is third in importance in the region, right after Nebbiolo and Barbera.

Aroma: black cherry, dry plum

Flavor: dry wine of fruity characteristics with distinctive tannins and low level of sourness

Body: medium

Lambrusco

Country of origin: Italy (Emilia Romagna)

Cultivation: Italy

Aroma: black cherry, blueberry, cinnamon

Flavor: dry wine, of high sourness with stone fruit flavors

Body: medium

Pinot Meunier – Miller's Burgunder, Schwartzriesling

Country of origin: France (Bordeaux)

Cultivation: France, Germany, USA

Pinot Meunier is a red grape sort mostly grown in France and is one of three ingredients in Champagne blend.

Color: pale ruby

Aroma: candied fruit, smoked meat, tobacco

Flavor: Dry wine, low in sourness with delicate tannins

Body: light

Rose wine

Rose wine is extremely popular during summer, but true lovers consume it throughout the year. It is consumed cooled (10 – 13 C or 50 – 55 F) and can be consumed with almost all food, but is mostly served with cheese, light salads, fish, olives, crackers and different desserts. Unfortunately, rose, despite its quality, has a reputation of being too sweet and cheap wine. Rose is an exceptionally subtle wine of light body. It is made of red grape sorts. Wine color is acquired from the skin of red grapes. During rose wine production, grape skin is in contact considerably less than in red wine production. Red grape is pressed and its skin is left in the juice (several hours up to three days) in order for wine to get that red that is pink color, which can vary from lighter to darker shades of pink. Apart from production, sort of grapes influences the color.

Sparkling wine

Sparkling wines are a different sort; they contain carbon dioxide which is responsible for the sparkling. Most of sparkling wines undergo two processes of fermentation. The first process produces the wine, whereas the second provides it with sparkling feature. The second fermentation can be done using "charmat" method which is adding sugar and yeast in order to quickly get great amounts of wine in a short period of time. The traditional (champagne) method is the one that is conducted in each bottle separately. This kind of fermentation takes between twelve months and three years and every bottle in this process ferments on its own, therefore is unique. Champagne is the most famous sparkling wine from France. It is regulated by EU law that only sparkling wines from the Champagne region can be called champagne. Champagne is, as the word suggests, made by the champagne method. Champagne is made from three grape sorts:

Pinot Noir which gives champagne body and structure

Pinot Menuir which provides it with fruity and floral aromas

Chardonnay which gives is freshness.

There are three methods of production of sparkling wines

Traditional method or "methode champenoise" (only method allowed in champagne production). Champenoise method originates from France. Oldest method of highest quality in sparkling wine production. Sparkling wines were originally as any other (without bubbles). Then, how do the bubbles appear? Fermentation is responsible which can happen in two ways:

1 – Spontaneous fermentation is a process where grape juice, with some help from wild yeasts and high temperature, turns sugar into alcohol. This method of fermentation is outdated because the winemaker cannot influence the process and the quality of wine, which is why today's winemakers mostly avoid it.

2 – Controlled fermentation is a process where grape juice is under the influence of cultivated yeasts and controlled temperature depending on what the winemaker wants to get and what characteristics he wants to accentuate.

Sparkling wines undergo first fermentation as all other wines, except that sparkling wines fermented using champenoise method undergo the second fermentation in the bottle. During the second fermentation in the bottle gas and CO_2 are created. After the second fermentation is complete, the wine possesses bubbles and is ready to bottle. Dead yeast removal is done by rotating the bottle 180 degrees and immersing only the bottle's neck in a liquid which will freeze the neck and the remaining yeast in it. After that, the bottle is placed back into normal position and by removing the metal cork from the bottle the dead yeast is removed. The whole process leads to a small loss of liquid easily compensated with new wine (the same brand if possible). This process is called dosage. After the dosage a regular champagne cork is placed on the bottle and it is put back to rest which takes as long as every individual winemaker deems fit.

Transfer or "Charmat" method is similar to the traditional method of production of sparkling wines and is used to produce wines such as Prosecco. Wine is put into huge, stainless steel containers where cultivated yeasts are added and where second fermentation takes place. When it is finished, wine is filtered (dead yeasts are removed) and bottled. When bottled wine is left to rest and then is ready for distribution and consuming.

Carbonization is the method of carbonization is the same method used in soft carbonated drinks. This method excludes the use of cultivated yeast, wine is put into containers and CO_2 is directly injected which produces bubbles. Although efficient, this method produces wines of inferior quality.

A small number of champagnes are made exclusively from chardonnay sort and that kind of champagne is known as blanc de blanc. Blanc de noir is champagne made from pure Pinot Noir. Rose champagne is made through short maceration of red grapes or mixing of white and red wine. Cremant is a very confusing term that signifies wine that has an atmospheric pressure of 3 – 4 millibars in the bottle, therefore less bubbles. This kind of wine was introduced in Cremant village in the Champagne region. Cremant is also used in other regions of France but in that case falls under sparkling wine category. The term Vintage Champagne refers to special vintages/years which the manufacturer wants to point out. Vintage Champagne makes up around 15% of the whole wine market. As Vintage, champagne is matured 3 – 6 years. Cuvee Prestige or Tete du Cuvee represents champagne of highest quality and a hallmark of the house, and usually, it is produced three times in a decade and reaches exuberant prices. Categorization of champagne according to level of sugar in it is:

Brut Nature – dry 0 - 5g/l of sugar (0.0 - 0.5%)

Extra brut – very dry

Brut - dry 5 - 15g/l (0.5 - 1.5%)

Extra Sec – semi-dry 12 - 20g/l of sugar (1.2 - 2.0%)

Sec – mildly sweet 17 - 35g/l of sugar (1.7 - 3.5%)

Demi-sec – moderately sweet 33 - 50g/l of sugar (3.3 - 5.0%)

Doux – very sweet 50 - more g/l (5.0 % and more)

Prosecco is the most popular sparkling wine from Italy, suitable for any occasion. Prosecco can be made in one of the nine provinces of Veneto and Friuli Venezia Giulia regions. It varies from dry to sweet. Terminology which can sometimes confuse when it comes to prosecco is the sparkling level it possesses. Frizzante is less sparkling while spumante is an extremely sparkling prosecco. Cava is a sparkling wine from Spain, made using the traditional method with the second fermentation inside the bottle. The most famous cava is Freixenet. Grape sorts used in making cavas are: Macabeo, Parelada, Xarello. Franciacorta is a small appellation in Lombardi. Italy sports marvelous sparkling wines made using champoneise method. Champagne originates in French Champagne region which is near the city of Rem and Prosecco from an Italian region Veneto or Friuli. Basic champagnes are three to four times more expensive than Prosecco. Champagne is matured longer in the presence of yeast and therefore has a different aroma from Prosecco. Apart from the difference in flavor and production champagne is more expensive due to its prestige.

Part eleven

FORTIFIED WINE

„Extra strength."

- Danilo Božović, Andrija Ristić -

Fortified wine

Alcohol used in fortification of wine and extraction of plants by immersing or redistilling should be of agricultural origin, mostly grape spirits or a neutral alcohol. During the 17th century, wine was transported in casks and so, exposed to oxygen it would go bad. The fortification of wine with (brandy) was a traditional way of preserving the wine, during long sea voyages.

Dessert wines belong to a group of fortified wines, to which alcohol was added, most often in form of brandy. They usually have between 16 -24% ABV, and depending on when alcohol was added the wine can be drier or sweeter. If alcohol is added during the fermentation process, fortified wine will, due to interrupted fermentation, be sweeter. If the alcohol is added after the fermentation the wine will be drier. Dessert wines are mostly of sweet aromas but there are, of course, exceptions. Dry sherry is one of the examples that dessert wines do not have to be sweet. Sherry is a dessert wine coming from Spain and is divided into "fino" (light body) and "oloroso" (heavy body). Sherry is made in the Solera system, by adding sugar sherry becomes sweeter. We will talk more about the Solera system in the upcoming brandy chapter. Malaga is basically made the same way as sherry but does not possess so distinctive a character, therefore is less popular. Porto is a fortified wine from the Portuguese city of Douro. This wine was created by accident. Namely, the British added brandy to Portuguese wine during transport in order to stabilize it. Porto became a sensation and has been consumed in large quantities since. It is served at room temperature (18 C or 64 F). It is made out of six types of grapes: Touriga Nacional, Tinta Cao, Tinta Baroca, Tinta Amarela, Touriga Francesca, Tinta Roriz. Types of Porto:

Ruby Port is a very popular style of Porto, aged for about three years.

Vintage character (Reserve) is a middle class of Porto.

Late bottled vintage (lvb) was made from one year's harvest which matures for two years.

Crusted or **crusting port** is not filtered and is of different ages.

Vintage port is made from on year's harvest and is matured up to ten years.

Single Quinta is produced from individual vineyards ("quintas").

Tawny port is mostly of full flavor and is matured for at least five years.

Aged Tawny is a Porto matured for ten, twenty and even forty years. Colheita Tawny is the hallmark of Porto from a very good year.

Madeira is a fortified wine which got the name after the mountainous island of Madeira. Madeira sports different styles, from dry to sweet and it is said that it is the oldest sort in the world. In 16th century Dutch traded Madeira through their Dutch East India Company in Asia. British and Americans soon realized the value of Madeira. Madeira was one of the few wines that George Washington and Benjamin Franklin simply adored. There is even a legend according to which Thomas Jefferson used this wine to toast the Declaration of Independence.

There are four sorts of Madeira:

Sercial (Riesling) – dry

Verdelho – semi-dry

Bual – semi-sweet

Malmsey (Malvasia) – sweet

Marsala is a fortified wine originating from Sicily, which is produced by post-fermentation fortification (adding brandy). Solera system is used. Due to the volcanic ground on which it grows it is mostly resinous. Marsala is produced using the following sorts: *Catarratto*, *Grillo* i *Inzolia*. Marsala is considered one of fortified wines of best quality. It is made in three colors, depending on the quantity of Moscato syrup added: Oro (golden), Ambra (amber) and Rubino (ruby). Every color is made in dry, semi-dry and sweet style. The level of quality depends on the time spent in the cask:

1 year - *Fino*

2 years - *Superiore*

4 years - *Superiore Riserva*

5 years - *Vergine*

10 yeasr - *Stravecchio*

Vermouth

Vermouths are flavored, fortified wines. Before bartenders started using Vermouth in mixing drinks it was used in medicinal purposes. Vermouth is a French word derived from the German word "wermut" which means wormwood. Throughout history, Vermouth was classified as dry and sweet. Sweet vermouth contains 16 – 18 % ABV and 10 – 15 % of sugar, whereas dry vermouth has no more than 5% of sugar. Dry ingredients used in flavoring vermouth are: clove, cinnamon, quinine, peels of lemon and other citrus fruit, orange peel, pepper, cardamom, marjoram, chamomile, coriander, juniper, ginger, hyssop. Vermouths are a part of fortified wines family, enriched with aromatic herbs and spices. What differentiates them from other aromatized wine is the plant *Artemisia Absinthium*, for which absinthe is also known. In word of Giuseppe Gallo, the global ambassador for martini-vermouth: "Vermouth without wormwood is like "limoncello" without lemon." Vermouth is an important ingredient of classic but also modern cocktails.

History of vermouth

There is no exact date of the "birth" of vermouth but is believed that Hippocrates invented it. He macerated wormwood and ash flowers in a strong and sweet Greek wine making a so called Hippocrates' wine or *vinum absinthianum* which he prescribed for rheumatism, anemia and pain. In Roman times, aromatic wine recipes contained even more exotic plants that were available to herbalists at the time. Romans mixed wine with aromatic Mediterranean herbs and honey that was highly valued for its healing properties. The most famous parts of vermouth production were, one in Piedmont below the Alps which meant that the producers had all kinds of herbs growing practically on their doorstep and the other center in the southeast near today's French border. Merchants from Venice brought new herbs such as cardamom, ginger, cinnamon, clove, sandalwood, rhubarb which inspired new recipes of vermouth. In 1563, Emanuel the Third, king of Savoy, due to pressure of French and Spanish toward his territories, proclaimed Turin his capital instead of today's Chambray. The king and his supporters accept the Piedmont tradition in making aromatic wines and in 1768 create a wine called Aperitivo de Corte. The new method was spread across pharmacies where wormwood concentrates were sold and mixed with wine and in 1786 the first commercial brand of vermouth appeared on shelves of a pharmacy on Piazza della Fiera square (today's Piazza Castelo) made by a gentlemen named Antonio Benetto Carpano. Namely, he used high quality wine made from Muscat grapes and aromatized it with a mixture made by local monks and fortified it with alcohol creating the final recipe. He was not the first to create vermouth but the first one to commercialize it. He named it "Wermut". Carpano's vermouth became very popular among the high class led by Count of Savoy, Amadeus III, who suspended the production of the popular Rosolio liqueur (rose and spices) and ordered Carpano's Wermut. As French was the official language of Savoy at the time the German term Wermut was replaced by the French vermouth. Joseph Noilly, herbalist from Lyon, discovered, during a sea voyage, that salty air improves the taste of vermouth so he moved to Marseille in 1813, and aromatized his wine with herbs such as wormwood, chamomile and bitter orange creating a dry and aromatic vermouth we know today as Noilly Prat.

Vermouth styles

Apart from difference between dry and sweet vermouths, obvious differences in vermouth start with wine used in their production, as well as combination of herbs. There is a popular belief that Italian vermouths are sweeter and made of red wine whereas French ones came later and are made out of dry white wines. The truth is that there are differences in styles even though these two regions have never been clearly defined and today they both use dry and sweet vermouths. Although, initially, red vermouths were made of red wine, today they are mostly made of white wine with added caramel which gives them copper red color. Some French manufacturers reveal that after fortification and maturing in oak casks, vermouth of considerably higher quality is produced. Besides that, French producers found that by leaving the barrels in the open where they are subjected to weather and atmospheric changes, the maturing process is quickened and improved. Generally speaking, it can be said that the French vermouths have the tendency to be matured in oak barrels and usually have spicy aroma and are drier (the most famous ones are Noilly Prat and Chambery). On the other hand, Italian vermouths have a wider pallet of styles (the most famous ones are Cinzano and Martini) produced near Turin, which have a tendency to be a touch sweeter and more floral. In the end, with many brands rising, every brand of vermouth brings something unique to the table.

Styles of vermouth categorized by sugar content:

Extra dry - less than 30 g of sugar per liter and minimum 15% ABV

Dry - less than 50 g of sugar per liter and minimum 16% ABV

Semi dry - between 50- 90 g of sugar per liter

Semi sweet - between 90- 130 g of sugar per liter

Sweet - 130 g or more of sugar per liter (usually 150 g)

Main ingredient is wine and its content should be at least 75% in the final product so the quality of wine drastically affects the quality of vermouth. Generally, neutral white wine resistant to oxidation is preferred in vermouth production. Besides that, it is important that the wine used contains low levels of tannin in order to avoid madérisation and darkening over time. Plants (leaves, flowers, fruit, seeds, roots and peel) are natural aromatics that determine the character of vermouth. A very wide spectrum of plants is used in vermouth production: angelica, laurel, chamomile, cardamom, cinnamon, sage, clove, coriander, ginger, hop, juniper, balm, lemon peel, licorice, marjoram, nutmeg, orange peel, iris, raspberry, rhubarb, rose, saffron, star anise, thyme, vanilla and other. As it was mentioned earlier, vermouth should contain Artemisia which, in almost all variants, contains thujone in different quantities. Thujone is characterized as a bad ingredient of wormwood and is credited with symptoms such as hallucinations, facial tics, dementia, etc. This, of course, is not true because thujone is found in far greater quantities in cooking ingredients (sage is a culinary plant that contains thujone and is synonymous with healthy food). Sugar is crucial both for balancing bitter herbs and forming the body and texture of vermouth. "Mistelle" or dessert wine can be base sweeteners with the addition of white sugar from sugar cane or beet. Caramel is used for coloring red vermouths but also influences its body and texture.

How is Vermouth made?

Every product based on wine, strengthened with alcohol, aromatic herbs and spices is an aromatized wine, but according to EEC (European Economic Community) regulation 1601/91 and the amendment 251/2014, there are three main features that differentiate vermouth from the rest of aromatized wines:

1. It has to be aromatized with at least one herb from the family Artemisia wormwood – whereas quantity and type are not clarified.

2. At least 75% of the final product should be wine made by EU laws.

3. Has to contain at least 14.5 % ABV to a maximum of 22% ABV.

Wine prepared to be the base for vermouth undergoes the process ordinary for all wines and wine products. Although the alcohol is generally added later, base wine for some types of vermouth can be fortified during the beginning stages of the process, especially in France. Herbs and spices are added in different ways, most commonly as concentrated extracts made by maceration of herbs in a neutral alcohol or by distillation of herbs with alcohol after they have spent a certain amount of time in it. Vermouth is usually sweetened, some by adding sugar and others with the natural grape sugar by stopping the fermentation process by adding alcohol and killing the yeast before it turns all the sugar into alcohol. This low alcohol and sweet wine is known as Mistelle. Mistelle wine is mainly mixed in the base wine which is in turn mixed with alcohol, water, plant extracts and caramel in mixing containers. After homogenization, vermouth is left to mature for a few weeks. After clarification and stabilization, it is a practice to cool the vermouth for a few days at a temperature of -8 C or -46 F close to its freezing point and only then is the vermouth ready to be bottled.

Part twelve

---◆◆━◆◆---

DISTILLATION AND DIFFERENT SPIRITS

"Extracting the soul."

- Danilo Božović, Andrija Ristić -

124   BARKEEP: THE GUIDE to becoming a professional bartender

Distillation

is a process of extracting alcohol from a fermented mash with a long history and records that can be tracked back to ancient Egyptians as well as Alexandria and the Far East. Materials such as wood, clay and glass were used in first distillations and copper stills came into use only later. Alcohol was primarily used in medicinal purposes as well as in perfume production. Distillation is a process during which by heating the fermented juice we extract the alcohol which evaporates at a considerably lower temperature than water (minimum 78.5 C or 173 F). After the first distillation the alcohol will, due to condensation, hold a lot of impurities as well as a certain amount of water steam, so fermented mashes are distilled several times in order to get the most and the purest alcohol out of it. Water amounts to 30 – 40% of the final distillation product.

90 proof = 45% ABV or alcohol by volume, 80 proof = 40% ABV

distillation in chemistry and medicine led to alcohol being used in consumption purposes. The phrase "aqua vitae" (water of life) is one of the terms used for describing and naming alcohol. Vodka is an old Slavic word meaning "holy, dear water" and the phrase "eau de vie" means water of life. Despite the limitations of technology, people have strived to implore different ways of making good-flavored alcohol. The French added apples and pears into their brandy while other countries added anise, juniper, wormwood and so on.

Pot-still

the process of distillation the fermented juice is distilled two to three times. Pot still was invented by the Dutch in the 16th century. Copper is, according to many, the best metal for distillation because it is a good heat conductor and is easy to shape.

** – heating the fermented wort (dried barley, mixed with hot water which is then cooled and filtered)

** – The place where alcohol is transformed from gas to liquid.

is done twice, the first one in the wash and the second one in the low wine still. Traditional rums were made this way. Great copper still are used for pot still distillation. After the first distillation the result is around 23% ABV. Since the first distillation provides low alcohol content, it is the second one that extracts the "heart" of the spirit and the alcohol content of 72% ABV. The longer the distillation the stronger aromas start to emerge (oily, leathery), however, one should be careful because these aromas can become unpleasant. They are called "fusel oils." Master distiller is in charge of the whole process of distillation. If he wants his spirit to contain stronger and heavier aromas he will precisely know to what extent he should allow the more pleasant fusel oil aromas to come to the fore. If, on the other hand, he wants a lighter spirit, he will avoid fusel oils in his aromas. Alcohol made by pot method has its own specificity. The pot still is the type of still used in producing whisky, brandy, some tequilas, some vodkas and the rest of colored spirits. By using this still, the spirit will keep most of its aroma.

Column-still

In the 19th century distillers started to devise ways of producing maximized quantities of alcohol of lighter aromas. Scottish distiller Robert Stein made a first step towards this kind of production in 1827. Three years later his design was improved by the genius of an Irishman, Aeneas Coffey. Coffey's (continuous) still got the name after him and is still in use today. The result was a still cheaper than a pot still which produced a light spirit with a small quantity of fusel oils. Column still consist of two columns (parts). Wash, or "beer", enters the rectificator, and then the bottom of wash is heated in order to isolate the alcohol from the fermented juice. Heavier ingredients do not undergo the following steps of this kind of distillation so lighter elements and aromas prevail and form the final product which results in 90 – 95% ABV. Multiple column-still is the result of master distiller's devotion to distillation technologies with the aim of producing more neutral spirits. Distillation done in this way is of repetitive character. In case of uninterrupted distillation the whole process is continuously repeated and the purer alcohol of greater alcohol content than the pot-still one is produced. Spirit from a Coffey, or column-still, can produce as high as 96% ABV from the fermented mash. The only way to gain a greater percentage of alcohol is by azeotropic distillation or a method that extracts water from the 96% ABV liquid. The mutual ingredient of every alcohol is ethyl alcohol. Alcohol signifies an old Arab word which translates to "finally separated". A spirit should contain at least 30% of alcohol in order to be termed as such and should not have subsequently added sugar.

Spirit maturing

The simplest way to understand how a spirit matures is to perceive the cask as an object of high content of aromas and flavors. It is very important what type of wood the cask is made of because the type of wood will define aromas of the matured alcohol. Casks used in maturing bourbon are made of white oak (*Quercus alba)* which contains a great amount of sweet aromas, spices and vanilla. Apart from that, it is important to note that every spirit that leaves the still is as clean as water, that is, that the cask is responsible for the color it gets from maturing in it. Limousin oak is also very popular for alcohol maturing, especially brandy. It is an oak from France that secures an easier flow of oxygen therefore giving different aromas and relatively high tannin concentration. Besides aromatization which happens in a spirit alcohol also evaporates from the cask and that is called "angels share." The climate in which the spirit matures plays an equally important role in the final outcome. For example, one year of maturing a spirit in a barrel in the Caribbean Islands will be equal to three years maturing in Scotland. Why? Increased humidity means the rum penetrates the wood's pores better but also that the evaporation loss is grater (up to 6% per year) in the Caribbean than in Europe. Cask used in maturing multiple times loses its aroma. Experienced master distillers, depending on the aroma they want, precisely know the age of the wood to use. Maturing in stainless steel containers has its advantages because oxygen slowly permeates its surface so the alcohol loses unwanted aromas. In stainless steel, alcohol settles down and gets its final form.

Age indications

It is very important to understand age indications on the bottle. Two year old spirits are labeled with the year of the youngest spirit in the bottle. Blending means mixing spirits of different ages. A bottle labeled with two years of age can contain an older spirit but the label ought to show the youngest spirit age. The reason for blending spirits of different ages is to use older spirits to gain depth and complexity of aroma. The master blender is the one who decides what spirits to mix and in what quantity.

Bottling with water

A standard process in alcohol production is to add distilled (neutral) water to the final product in order to reduce alcohol content. Using neutral water makes the aroma of alcohol come to the fore. In case that water used is not neutral, there is a risk of calcium reacting with crystals in alcohol which will lead to a change in the spirits's state.

Grain used in production

Wheat – One of the youngest types of grain cultivated in Europe. Wheat became popular in the 19th century in America, especially in Kentucky, Ohio, Indiana and Kansas. In Scotland, wheat replaced corn in whisky production in time. Although wheat is not used in bourbon production a lot, it possesses characteristics that provide spirits with light sweetness.

Rye – Rye proved to be extremely resistant because it could be cultivated on land where other grain could not. Rye possesses certain spicy flavors as well as a full, fruity aroma. German settlers were the ones that brought rye cultivation and production to American soil. American rye whiskey contains at least 51% of rye. Rye proved to be one of the more important ingredients in vodka production in Russia and Poland.

Barley – Barley is one of the primary used types of grain grown on Scottish and Irish soil. It greatly improved the flavor of Scotch whisky. Barley has an intensity sweet flavor and aroma with creamy notes.

Corn – American Indians showed the settlers how to cultivate this noble grain. Corn possesses high content of starch and protein and as such is perfect for fermenting. Bourbon is made of a minimum of 51% corn whereas the rest can be rye, wheat or barley malt.

Part thirteen

VODKA

"Fiery water which became the symbol of a region, its character and spirit. Popularly known as Zhizenennia voda or water of life."

- Danilo Božović, Andrija Ristić -

VODKA

The word vodka derives from the Slavic "voda", meaning water, etymologically linking the term with whisky (which comes from the Gaelic "uisge beatha", the Scandinavian term Akvavit from the Latin "aqua vitae" and French "eau-de-vie") - all meaning water of life. During the Middle Ages, distilled liquor was used mainly for medicinal purposes, as well as being an ingredient in the production of gunpowder. In the 14th century a British emissary to Moscow first described vodka as the Russian national drink. Vodka was in the mid-16th century established as the national drink in Poland and Finland. Even so, the historians and scholars till this day are having trouble pinpointing the exact origin of vodka. Since early production methods were crude, vodka often contained impurities, so to mask these the distillers flavored their spirits with fruit, herbs or spices. The mid-15th century saw the first appearance of pot distillation in Russia. Prior to that, seasoning, aging and freezing were all used to remove impurities, as was precipitation using isinglass ('karluk') from the air bladders of sturgeons. Around this time (1450) vodka started to be produced in large quantities and the first recorded exports of Russian vodka were to Sweden in 1505. Polish vodka exports started a century later, exporting their vodka from major production centers in Posnan and Krakow. In 1716, owning distilleries became the exclusive right of the nobility.

The system production that was present in the 18th century was inclined towards the wealthier class that, due to its strong economic and political connections, could acquire the needed liquor licenses for vodka production. The laws that required the manufacturer to own the grain fields used in producing vodka made things even harder for the common people. On the other hand, it secured a high standard and quality. At the beginning of the 20th century manufacturers and distilleries accepted the conditions and work norms that the committee placed with a goal of maintaining the quality of vodka as its national drink. That is the time when the best and most renowned vodkas in the world were made. It was not a cheap product and it still had not attained really large-scale production. The spread of awareness of vodka continued throughout the 19th century, helped by the presence in many parts of Europe of Russian soldiers during the Napoleonic Wars. Increasing popularity led to escalating demand and to meet this demand, lower grade products were produced based largely on distilled potato mash. Earlier attempts to control production by reducing the number of distilleries from 5,000 to 2,050 between the years 1860 and 1890 failed, resulting in a law enacted in 1894 to make the production and distribution of vodka in Russia a state monopoly. This was both for fiscal reasons and to control the epidemic of drunkenness, which was due to the availability of the cheap, mass-produced 'vodkas' imported and home-produced. It is only at the end of the 19th century, with all state distilleries adopting a standard production technique and hence a guarantee of quality, that the name vodka was officially and formally recognized. After the Russian Revolution, the Bolsheviks confiscated all private distilleries in Moscow. As a result, a number of Russian vodka-makers emigrated, taking their skills and recipes with them. One such exile revived his brand in Paris, using the French version of his family name - Smirnoff. Thence, having met a Russian émigré from the USA, they set up the first vodka distillery there in 1934. From this small start, vodka began in the 1940s to achieve its wide popularity in the Western World. However, following the Russian Revolution in 1917, a number of Russian refugees took their skills and their love of vodka, to many parts of the world. In the 1930s one such exile emigrated from Russia via France to the United States bringing with him the formula to one of the leading Russian makes of vodka. Through his dealings with another Russian émigré the first vodka distillery in the United States was set up in the 1930s. Although not particularly successful at first, this enterprise was sold on again to an entrepreneur who eventually made a hit in the 1950s with a vodka-based cocktail the Moscow Mule. Realistically though vodka did not see a great boom in popularity in the West until the 1960s and 1970s when many more brands were launched in the USA and the UK. The timing coincided with the cultural revolution in these countries, the 'swinging sixties'. With a more affluent younger generation and a generally more relaxed lifestyle and the emphasis on adventure and experimentation, vodka's 'mixability' (plus the appeal of some witty and clever advertising) led to its huge and ever rising popularity, which continues today. Vodka cocktails are almost as numerous as those of gin and are seen in the same exclusive circles and stylish bars the world over. Till this day vodka is best-selling spirit in the world and the Russians are still the largest consumers of vodka in the world.

Vodka production process

Neutral spirit of at least 96% alcohol by volume (ABV), having been checked that it is of the appropriate quality is either re-distilled to produce a pure and flavorless spirit or filtered through activated charcoal which removes any residual impurities and odors. The definition of activated charcoal is that which has been treated either by steam or chemicals to make it more absorbent. Birch charcoal was traditionally a very common and popular source of filtration in Russian vodkas. The coal should be changed from time to time in order for the producers to maintain the level of neutrality they want. Filtering is a separate process and can be repeated several times. In the filtration process (carbon filters, charcoal, silver, sand, birch charcoal, paper, cloth, crushed diamonds, crystals, etc.) remove unwanted fusel oils and other impurities. This process like all the others (fermentation, purification, still, material the still is made from, water, grain, etc.) has an effect on the final taste of the vodka brand. Filtration is done by either pumping the vodka through several consecutive columns of charcoal or, in the case of cheaper vodkas simply seeping it into tanks containing charcoal. Rectification is a process when 'rectification' columns remove any unpleasant taste from the spirit. Vodka was traditionally made of potato, rye, grain, barley, corn and wheat. Grain or potato is firstly crushed and mixed with water, then heated in order to turn starch into sugar, and with the use of yeast turned into the product known as wash. The fermentation process needs to be carefully watched due to the heat rising. If the temperature goes above 35 C or 77 F, the yeast will die and the fermentation will stop. After the fermentation is done (period unique to each brand), the result is 'wash' or similar to beer liquid. Distiller actually keep only the middle part (the heart) of the spirit and distills it up to four times. This makes it easier for yeast to ferment because of the breakdown of starch. Wash distilling in vodka production is usually done in column stills for its "purer" result than the pot still. The pot still distillation results in a 70% ABV where the use of the column still results in 96% ABV. Even so, pot stills are still used in vodka production of certain brands. The spirit should settle down before being bottled at the strength of 80% ABV. Water is a very important factor in the vodka production since it makes about 70% of its total content. Water and vodka in some cases are let to rest with one another and slowly become the vodka that we have in our glass. Before the vodka makes it to the back bar and the speed rail, it undergoes quality control testing where it is decided if the produce is of the highest quality. Distilled water is now added to the spirit to give the legal EU minimum ABV strength of at least 37.5% ABV; it is not unusual to have vodkas of up to 50% ABV. This pure spirit drink does not legally require anything added to it although some producers include additives to improve the characteristics while others introduce flavoring by either adding natural essences or by steeping fruits or herbs in the vodka for several days. No maturation period is required for vodka. Unquestionably a supremely popular spirit, vodka is enjoyed around the globe thanks to its incredible versatility and, surprisingly, even its variation of flavor.

Part fourteen

◆—▮—◆

GIN

"All we need is good old juniper."

- Andrija Ristić, Danilo Božović -

Gin

The ever innovative Dutch perfected the art of distilling the sophisticated grape juice which they called "brandewijn." This drink complemented juniper aroma and was called "genever" from the French word that meant juniper. English soldiers and sailors, fighting during the second European war in the 17th century, discovered that genever gave special strength and courage to Dutch soldiers in battle and called it "Dutch courage." The gin brought from the Netherlands by the English was of full flavor, stronger aroma, harsh and different from gin from Great Britain. Still, genever or gin, as we know it today, was taboo in England where there was no culture of consuming that kind of beverage. In 1650, London became the home of more than six thousand Dutch and therefore the center of illegal juniper trade. Juniper berries were precious as medicine for various kidney illnesses and certain kinds of arthritis. Later, juniper was considered to be almost a magical remedy and it was believed it protected from plague (Black Death) that ravaged Europe during middle ages. People did not just consume juniper but put its berries into masks worn on their faces in order to inhale its healing aromas. Everything changed in 1688 when William ascended the throne. Namely, he started a chain of changes that would transform the overall British culture. King William banned the import of French brandy which turned the people of Great Britain towards gin. The gin brought from the Netherlands by the English was of full flavor, stronger aroma, harsh and different from gin from Great Britain. London became the center of a great distilling industry which produced the English national drink – gin. Among the first moves of the British government was a restriction of importation of French wines and brandies, therefore encouraging domestic production and consumption. As a result of this law soon everybody could get a distilling license and the conquering of market started by issuing new taxes on beer in 1694 which made gin cheaper and all the more desirable. Almost overnight, gin became the favorite alcohol in England. At the beginning of 17th century, great amounts of gin were easily available which resulted in catastrophic outcomes, especially in London. The poor parts like St Giles (near today's Oxford) were the center of gin mania. This area was represented by the famous graphics of William Hogarth, Gin Lane, where the effect of gin mania overtaking London was depicted. This work of art became a powerful advertising material in fighting the contemporary happenings but the truth about gin mania, justified by shocking statistical data and the devastating effects it caused, started to come to light. Hospitals reported an increasing number of people intoxicated with this drink and numerous pamphlets and magazines classified gin as drink that had a devastating effect on family life. Because most people produced gin on their own before the raising of taxes on gin, the quality of gin was low since there was no quality regulation and sugar was added because of strong and unpleasant aroma. This kind of gin was called Old Tom Gin. In 1743, gin consumption reached the point where every man, woman and child drank more than one liter of gin a week, proportionally. Finally in 1751, the Parliament ratified a law known as the Tippling Act which brought about the first efficient control of gin production and trade (in the same year when 9 thousand children died in London from alcohol poisoning). London remained the center of gin trade and in 1790 produced 90% of English gin. London became the natural home to lots of warehouse hangars alongside the river Thames where all kinds of goods arrived from the sea into the heart of London. With the reorganization of liquor industry in 1790 lots of distilleries moved from London. Gin gained quality with the coming of dry gin which was mainly distilled in column stills and after losing its strong aroma became more elegant, mellower and nicer to consume.

Legal definition of gin

Gin is defined by the European law on alcoholic drinks (*Counsil Regulation EC No.* Introduced in 1989 and restore in 2007) as well as by the law in the US (*United States Bureau of Alcohol, Tabacco and Firearms –BATF)* and similar laws in other countries such as Canada, Australia, etc. In EU gin is, as an aromatized alcoholic drink, defined by special legislation. Distilled gin signifies gin which was made of re-distilled neutral alcohol with the presence of herbs and spices because it gets its aromas and flavor that way. In the US, under the chapter "Identity standards" it says that gin is a product distilled from the mash of plants and alcohol or re-distilled from neutral alcohol or a mixed neutral alcohol with juniper and other aromatics and/or extracted from infusion, percolation or maceration including the mix of gin with neutral alcohol. The main character of gin should come from juniper berries and it has to be bottled with at least 40% ABV. Gin produced exclusively by distillation or redistilling can be classified as distilled, with dry gin (London Dry gin), Genever gin (Holland gin) and Old Tom gin all being types of gin which are mostly produced using this kind of distillation.

How is gin made?

1 – The easiest and cheapest way is leaving all the ingredients in the base alcohol which absorbs their flavors. The result is, most often, a low quality gin.

2 – The recommended way is the one where neutral alcohol is distilled along with certain ingredients. With this type of production, stills play the most important part, along with their shape and material and ingredients used in process of distillation, maceration, percolation and so on.

Stills used in gin production are traditionally pot stills. Later, column stills became more popular. Neutral alcohol used in gin making is mostly made from wheat. The manifestation of aroma in gin depends on when the distillation begins and ends. Citrus notes are one of the first to be felt in young gin. Gin's character is grounded in the aroma of juniper and Italy is famous for the quality of its juniper. In Spain, gin producers mostly buy oranges, sour and sweet.

Types of gin

Compound gin

The process of gin production determines its classification. In order for a spirit to have the right to be called gin the production process should be the following: plant aromas are added to neutral spirit where the dominant aroma has to be juniper. Compound gin is not legally regulated so its quality is inferior. Juniper aroma is added to most of compound gins, so they, from a certain point of view, can be called "juniper flavored vodka." This way of producing is cheaper than the rest but is of inferior quality.

Distilled gin

According to the European legislation, distilled gin is repeatedly distilled from ethyl alcohol (of agricultural origin) with aromatics (herbs, spices, peels). Distilled gin is almost identical to London dry differing only in that the aromas may be added after distillation. The alcoholic content of spirit can be as high as 96% ABV.

London dry gin

Dry, pure style of gin, originally made in London, was introduced shortly after invention of Coffey still in 1831. Distillation in this still enabled the production of high percentage of alcohol, removing the unwanted flavors that manifested in the previous versions of gin. This gin was sold unsweetened or "dry" from where it got its name. In spite of the name London Dry Gin, it can be sold anywhere in the world, representing a specific style rather than origin. According to EU law (PGI) from 2008, London Dry Gin is made by re-distilling with the presence of natural herbs and spices defined as botanicals. Ethyl alcohol used in distillation of London dry ought to be of high quality and the level of methanol has to be below the maximum of 5g/hl of 100% ABV. All aromatics have to be of natural origin and it is not allowed to add aromatics after distillation or add artificial color and aromas. The final spirit should be at the minimum of 70% ABV. London gin should not be colored and only water can be added to the final product in order to regulate the wanted strength according to the specific market needs. Although London Dry Gin dominates the global market there are a few different styles of gin.

Old Tom Gin

Sweet or "Cordial" style gin was unbelievably popular in 18th and 19th century when it was of strong taste due to the limited ratification (purification) of the base spirit, probably from pot stills of the age. The harsh flavor was commonly masked with lemon, anise and sweetened with sweet herbs such as licorice and later in the 19th century with sugar. This sweetened gin is also known as Old Tom. Old Tom was traditionally made in a pot still with grain spirit and juniper berries as dominant plants in the recipe. Although there are various stories about the etymology of the name Old tom, we believe that it stems from the first version of a vending machine in England. On the outer walls of pubs there was a wooden plate in the shape of a black cat (Old Tom cat). The passers-by would, if they wanted gin, place a coin into the cat's mouth and the pipe between the cat's leg would dispense the gin. Other versions talk about the cat that fell into the still in an unnamed distillery giving gin a special aroma. The creation of this style of gin was connected to Thomas Chamberlain, one of the old gin producers. In the second half of the 19th century, unsweetened or dry gin was becoming more and more popular and started to take precedence on the market, partly owing to the popularity of dry champagne. In time, the quality of base spirit was increased thanks to Coffey continuous stills and that is when dry gin known as London dry was made. In the 20th century this type of gin with 2 – 6% of sugar practically disappeared from the market and was still produced in small quantities in England and mostly exported to Finland, Japan and US. Finally in 2007, several producers in England and US restarted the production of Old Tom gin. Compared to dry gin, good Old Tom provides a deeper, more complete taste and is an outstanding ingredient for making Martinez, Tom Collins or Ramos Gin Fizz.

Plymouth gin

Plymouth gin is protected by law with a geographic status which meant that only gin produced in a southwestern English city of Plymouth with a minimum of 37.5% ABV and a predominant flavor of juniper can be called Plymouth gin. Plymouth gin was and remains a registered and protected trademark which prevents any gin made in Plymouth to bear that name. Original Strength is made with 41.2% ABV in a copper still over 150 years old.

Cold compound gin

Cold compound gin is aromatized with juniper oil extract and other aromatic ingredients without distillation. Aromatics are simply mixed with neutral alcohol. This kind of gin was famous during prohibition as "bathtub gin" and today we can find it in numerous variants of cheap low quality gin.

Other types of gin

Gin de Mahon is another gin protected by EU legislation (PGI) and is produced in the capitol of Majorca, after which it got its name, and the only brand familiar to us is Xoriguer. Vilnius Gin, produced in Vilnius, Latvia, is also protected by PGI but, as Plymouth, is a registered trademark so it is hard to understand how this will be regulated by these strange European laws. New Western Dry is an unspecified name established by the American consultant Ryan Magarian and refers to types of gin produced following all standards except the lower concentration of juniper in the mix. This name was developed in the last nine years as a result of great brands and regional distillers both in Europe and US. By adhering to today's regulation of dry gin, these distillers took the opportunity to distance themselves from the focus on juniper in order to support other herbs and spices allowing them to take the central place in production along with juniper. While juniper has to dominate all dry gins by law, these kinds of gins are not defined by juniper flavor but the careful inclusion and balance of other ingredients, creating one completely new version of gin.

Dutch gin or Genever

All types of gin stem from the Dutch gin. There are three kinds of Dutch gin:

Oude – Dutch Old Tom gin.

Jonge – lighter body gin which came about with the invention of column stills.

Korenwijn – gin often matured in wooden casks.

The differences between English and Dutch gin are clearly visible because Genever traditionally has a stronger and heavier aroma which is the result of distillation of barley malt, grain and rye in pot stills. Genever does not use solely juniper in creating its aroma but the combination of herbs and spices very similar to English gin. A lot of Dutch gins are distilled three times, with juniper added during second distillation whereas the rest of plants and spices are added during the third distillation.

Part fifteen

WHISKY

"The pride and joy of an island"

- Andrija Ristić, Danilo Božović -

Whisky

The first written records about whisky were found in Ireland in 1405 where monks were making whisky (written records were found in Scotland also but later, around 1494). Although it is known that whisky has been around for six centuries, perhaps there will never be an adequate answer as to where and when it was first distilled. Some experts believe that distillation was firstly done between 8th and 14th century, somewhere in the Middle East, from where the art of distilling was brought to Ireland by missionary monks. All types of whisky are created by distilling grain after which they are placed into wooden casks for maturing. Generally speaking, whiskies are divided into four main categories:

Scotch whisky

Irish whiskey

Canadian whisky

American whiskey and Bourbon

Whisky has a long history, and its quality and flavor depend on lots of factors: mixture of grain, production manner, yeast used, casks in which it matures, types of blended whiskies that make up the final product. Every whisky has its own charisma, determined by the distillation boilers, types of casks, vegetation where the new make spirit ages.

Scotch whisky

The first record of whisky production in Scotland from 1494 mentions eight bales of malt that the government gave to friar John Cor to make the "water of life". That was enough malt to produce 1500 bottles of whisky and clearly shows that distillation was already established and well-practiced in Scotland. Primitive equipment and lack of knowledge meant that the first whiskies were very strong and sometimes bad, however, as years passed, distillation improved and reasonable progress was made. The word whisky was developed from the Gaelic term *uisge beatha* which means water of life. Gaelic is a branch of Celtic spoken in Scottish hills and is still in use today in many parts of Scottish plateaus. In time *uisge beatha* developed phonetically into whisky which soon became an important part of life in Scotland and was frequently used both in medicinal and other purposes. Whisky's rise to popularity among people was noticed by Scottish authorities so in 1664 Scottish parliament established the first alcohol tax. After the unification of England and Scotland in 1707, London authorities recognized the potential of taxing whisky and raised the tax by one half, which belonged to England, which led to the flourishing of black market in production and selling of whisky. Until the discovery of column still in 1831 all whisky in Scotland was malt whisky. Today, two versions are produced – malt and grain. Malt is mostly used in combination with grain whisky to produce blended Scotch whisky and only a small percentage of malt whisky is bottled and sold as single malt. The art of distilling and maturing Scotch whisky was developed over a thousand years. Scotch whisky is distilled twice, and in order to have Scotch whisky written on the label, by international law, it has to be made in Scotland and matured in oak casks for at least three years and one day. If the whisky is a blend of several casks, by law the label must state the age of the youngest whisky in that blend. Scotch whisky is much appreciated. Whisky is a complex spirit which contains a refined aroma: grain, hop, smoke, fruit, vanilla, spices, etc. Scotsmen are true artists when it comes to distilling and they are very proud of their national product. Scotch whisky mostly distilled twice although there are ones that are distilled three times. In order to understand whisky, a bartender is expected to know something about its history, regions where it is made and types that are produced in those regions.

How is Scotch whisky made?

Barley is put in water, for two to three days and then is spread across the floor where germination starts. Sprouting is stopped by drying in the kiln. Partly spouted barley is moved to the roaster where it is dried for the next seven days over fire or some alternative means of heating. The peak of drying is designated by the cell walls being almost broken. This is where the drying process stops in order to stop the grain from using its own starch and diminish its amount and therefore the quantity of alcohol. Dried barley or grist is mixed with hot water and becomes wort. The yeast is added to wort and it becomes wash. Wash is distilled two to three times. Fermentation lasts for at least 48 hours and the final result contains 8% ABV. If the fermentation lasted for less than 48 hours the result of "beer" would be a dominant spicy flavor. Longer period of fermentation creates complex flavors. The result of the first distillation is low wine with 21% ABV, which continues its road to the second still and is developed into whisky. During this process the master distiller wants to get the most out of the distilled liquid. That is its middle, the richest aroma and purity that the distiller seeks. It is called the "heart" of the spirit and the rest which is discarded is the beginning of the spirit or "foreshots" and the finish of the spirit, or the "end". In the process of distilling the length of the still's pipes is important because the longer the pipe the lighter the spirit. Commercial malting is the approach which is used in mass production of whiskies where most of the process is done by machines and computers. Although less romantic than the previous one, this approach is more efficient and therefore more profitable. There are of course manufacturers that are not fans of commercial malting but advocates of the traditional way of producing whisky.

What is peat exactly?

Peat is an old, partly carbonated, dead vegetation which is usually found in swamp country. If the peat was heated and pressurized it would become coal. Peat soil makes up 12% of the Scottish area so it could be said that Scottish use it in noble purposes. The function of peat is, apart from providing a smoky aroma, to enrich whisky with flavor and aroma of earth. Lowlands' whiskies possess the least smoky aroma out of all Scotch whiskies. Highlands' whiskies possess a distinctive smoky characteristic whereas islands like Islay and Orkney have the greatest smokiness in their whiskies. Peat digging is hard labor. Some brands use machines to dig. The peat has to dry out in order to lose its moist feature, after which a furnace is put in it and lit up and the smoke is conducted through pipes to the room where the barley is drying and in that way speeding the making of barley malt.

Triple distillation

Irish whiskey is distilled three times, some Scotch as well. Whisky distilled so contains three times more alcohol at the end of production but alcohol content is lowered to a level similar to one that is achieved by double distillation. Whisky distilled three times possesses lighter body and a richer fruit/herb aroma.

Types of Scotch whisky

Vatted malt/Blended malt whisky is blended malt from different distilleries.

Single malt whisky is malt whisky from one distillery.

Single cask whisky is single malt from one specific cask.

Blended whisky is a mixture of different malt and grain whiskies.

Regions of Scotch whisky

Scotch single malt is grouped into regions. Traditionally, there are four main whisky regions and these regions have more to do with old regulations and taxes than with anything else.

Campbeltown

Today, Scotland's southwestern region sports only three functional distilleries: Glengyle, Glen Scotia i Springbank. Campbeltowna wkiskies are of full body and flavor. They are famous for their depth of flavor and mildly salty finish. Examples of Campbeltown whiskies are: Glen Scotia, Longrow, Hazelbur, etc.

Islay

An island with just seven distilleries produces whisky famous for its smoky aroma, full of phenol and iodine aroma which make up their unique flavor. Examples of Islay region whiskies are: Ardbeg, Lagavulin, Laphroaig, etc.

Lowlands

Lowlands whiskies mostly have a dry finish which makes them some of the favorite aperitifs. The dryness comes from the malt itself and not from the peat. Lowlands whiskies mostly do not use peat, therefore they sport a more fruity flavor. They have herbal and flowery notes and present an excellent partner in blended whiskies. Examples of Lowlands región whiskes are: Auchentoshan, Glenkinchie, etc.

Highlands

Highlands make up the most of central and northern part of Scottish part of the island. Southern Highlands mostly do not incorporate peat, and are defined by honey notes and medium smokiness. Oban distillery is close in style to western islands, therefore their whiskies contain aromas of sea and salt. In the northern part of Highlands, Glenmorangie produces several whiskies that that mature in different types of casks (madeira, sherry or burgundy). Examples of Highlands region whiskies are: Dalwhinnie, Oban, Glenmorangie,Clynelish, etc.

Speyside and Islands are generally accepted as parts of Highlands.

Jura, Skye, Mull, Orkney are a group of island on the western coast of Scotland speckled with distilleries and there is no one unique description or style of their whiskies keeping in mind that the quantity of peat that they use to dry the barley varies from distillery to distillery. Orkney's Highland Park is famous for its heather notes, and not only does the heather present most of their peat, but they use dried heather during the malting process. The result is the balance between the honeyed sweetness and the peat smoke. Talisker Skye Island brings up the notes dried flowers, peat and smoke in Islay style. Examples of Islands whiskies are: Highland Park, Scapa, Talisker, etc.

Outside influences on whisky

There are a lot of outside factors that influence whisky and make the production process extremely complicated, attractive and exciting. Weather conditions have a great effect on the production of every spirit. A greater number of sunny days in a year can lead to the increase in photosynthesis which will in turn lead to the increase of starch in vegetation. The temperature of the water used in malting process has an effect on the final whisky product (grain takes longer in colder water to soak).

Water – Water is an important factor in whisky production. Softer stone will give off more minerals to whisky than a harder one. Spring water is key to malting and distilling whisky. With every sip of whisky we drink 500 million years of evolution of earth, its plates, volcanic activities and the change in vegetation (dead and alive).

Barley – Ancient Egyptians recognized barley's importance and its nutritive value which is resembled in the fact that they gave beer to their slaves in order to make them endure harsh physical labor. Ancient Greeks believed that barley gives great strength and supported its use in athlete's diets. Barley is an outstanding ingredient for whisky making because it contains high levels of starch. In 1968, a new sort of barley, called Golden Promise, was made and it replaced 90% of barley malt in Scotland. Its domination lasted until the appearance of new and better sorts in 1980. Certain brands like Belvenie and Glenmorangie use their own barley.

Types of barley that are best suitable for malting are: Two-row barley, six-row barley and Bere. The numeric parts of their names refer to the number of seeds a row possesses.

Two-row barley – Typical sort of barley mostly cultivated in Europe and some parts of America.

Six-row barley - This sort is cultivated on American soil mostly, and is produced in Chicago and Milwaukee.

Bere – One of the traditional barley sorts cultivated in Northern Scotland.

Malting

Malting is process of soaking barley in water and allowing it to germinate, there by starting the production of sugar. Typically, this process is done at a commercial malting facility and the distillery is receiving malted barley (vs. just barley). Of course, if the distillery is hand turning any portion of their barley, then they will malt it on site.

Mashing

This process starts by grinding barley in the malt mill which is placed into huge sifters after smoking and then scolding hot spring water is poured over it. Starch turns into sugar and thick syrupy liquid called barley malt goes through all sifters and is ready for fermentation. The barley left after this process is taken back to farmers to become cattle food (this is perhaps one of the reasons that beef is so good and tasty in Scotland). This process takes about six hours during which 10 thousand tons of malt are made into 50 thousand liters of barley malt. The resulting liquid is called wort.

Fermentation

The process of fermentation starts with transporting of wort, which contains 65% of sugar, to fermentation containers or washbacks. For 50 thousand liters of barley malt you get 200 liters of yeast. Yeast interacts with sugar quickly and turns it into alcohol. During fermentation, attention should be paid to measuring and controlling the quantity of sugar, alcohol and other compounds that emerge during the process of fermentation. Fermentation usually takes up to two and a half days and after that liquid called wash is created and sent to distillation.

Distillation

During this process double distillation is done in pot stills. The first distillation is done in wash stills and the second in spirit stills. In wash stills, liquid is heated at the temperature of 80 C or 176 F during which alcohol is turned into steam and starts his journey to the condenser where it is cooled and turned into liquid state called low wines. It then undergoes certain checks and goes to the second still to the second distillation. The second distillation lasts for around ten hours, despite the first one which lasts for about five hours because the distillers are doing something called the "middle cut". That is carefully chosen first spirit which will undergo second distillation after which it is left in a wooden cask where the maturing process starts.

Cask

Some people say that 60% of flavor comes from the cask in which the young whisky matured in. European casks are rich in color and tannins which enrich the flavor. American casks are rich in aromas such as vanilla, spices, honey and chocolate. Preparing casks for maturing is one of the most dynamic jobs in a distillery. Considering the fact that most whiskies use previously used casks, in order to use them again, the old casks need to be restored and brought back into function. Casks are usually around 50 liter in volume and mostly made of American or European oak. European casks are mainly used for sherry or port maturing and provide alcohol with fruity aromas, whereas American casks are used for maturing bourbons and provide vanilla aromas. By combining these two types of casks (double wood) very interesting whisky is produced. Liquid made in second distillation, more precisely its "middle cut", is poured into casks where it ought to mature for at least three years in order to, by law regulations, be called whisky. What happens in the casks is gradual evaporation of liquid by which 1.5 to 2 % of whisky volume is lost every year. So, after twelve years that is 15 – 20 % of input volume. The part that evaporates into the atmosphere is called "angel's share".

Blended whisky

The best-selling Scotch whisky is precisely blended whisky. Blended whisky is an art form and every house in Scotland that produces it has its own secret recipe. Usually, different whiskies are blended and in a blend there is 20 – 50% of single malt whisky (this differs from blender to blender). The quality can depend on the volume of malt used in the mixture but also the period of maturing of the final blend.

Malt whisky

Malt whisky is made of barley malt, water and yeast. Barley sprouts are dried and mixed with hot water, fermented and then distilled (mainly in pot stills). The product, New Make Spirit, is then matured in used casks (of American whisky, French barrels, sherry or port barrels) for a minimum of three years.

Whiskey or whisky?

Spelled with an "e" it represents whiskey coming from Ireland or America whereas whisky without "e" signifies whisky coming from Scotland, Canada and Japan. The letter "e" was added to Irish and American whiskeys so that their fans could distinguish them more easily, and to make this whiskey a symbol of status.

Irish whiskey

Whiskey production in Ireland is a few centuries old. Historical records are unclear but most whiskey experts believe that Irish missionary monks discovered the knowledge somewhere else in the Middle East over a thousand years ago. What remains unclear is if they brought this knowledge to Scotland also or the knowledge of distillation was bought to Ireland through Europe, Scandinavia or Russia. What can be said with certainty is that in 1608 Bushmills distillery from today's Northern Ireland received the license to distill whiskey from the British crown and because of that they claim that this document makes them the oldest whiskey distillery in the world today. At the beginning of the 20th century, Irish whiskey industry was blooming and Irish whiskey was the main spirit in Great Britain. Irish whiskey was supported by London traders who exported it all across the globe. The situation is different today and Irish whiskey has been overwhelmed by Scotch whiskey and bourbon. The fall of Irish whiskey industry starts in 1916 when Irish republicans protested in Dublin against the British crown, demanding that Ireland becomes an independent republic. All of this resulted in the Declaration of independence in 1919 followed by a two-year war. As part of Ireland's penalties England closed its market to their products. Scotch whisky still enjoyed protection with London exporters who transported it to Canada from where it found a way across the border into the American black market. But those doors were soon closed to Irish whiskey too. When Prohibition finally ended in 1933 lethal effects on Irish whiskey industry were noticeable. Whiskey which is distilled three times is not the only feature that distinguishes Irish whiskey from Scottish. Using malt whiskey in combination with unmalted is one of those features. Tradition of using pot still method in production of Irish whiskies faded with the beginning of column distillation use. According to Irish law, in order for a whiskey to be Irish it needs to be produced in Ireland and it has to spend at least three years in wooden casks. Unpeated malt or malt whiskey which still has not been peat dried is mostly used. Irish whiskey is divided into the following categories: single malt, single grain, blended whiskey, pure pot whiskey (category which is characteristic solely of Irish whiskeys).

American whiskey

At the end of 18th and the beginning of 19th century, European settlers brought the art of raising grain, its distillation and whiskey production to America. Germans, Irish and English soon realized the advantage of fertile lands such as Kentucky, Nashville, Tennessee, Pennsylvania and Virginia so they decided to develop these methods in these parts of America.

American whiskey is divided into the following categories:

Bourbon whiskey (primarily made from corn) – has to be made from at least 51% of corn

Rye whiskey – has to be made from at least 51% of rye

Corn whiskey – has to be made from at least 80% of corn

Tennessee whiskey – has to have a least 51% of corn in its contents

American whiskeys have to be distilled to 160 prof (80 ABV) and have to mature in brand new charred American oak casks. Corn whiskey does not have to be matured but it is done nonetheless; the casks have to be new and charred or old and used with a maturation period of six months. If certain types of American whiskey have been matured for two or more years they can be called straight, for example Straight Rye whiskey. If they are classified only as straight without the type of grain it means that they were matured for two or more years in new charred casks and were distilled to 80% ABV but that they possess less than 51% of grain. American blended whiskeys combine straight whiskey with non-matured whiskey (grain neutral spirit without color and taste). An important factor on the market is Tennessee whiskey with Jack Daniels whiskey as the most famous brand. Basically, it does not differ much from the standard bourbon except that Tennessee whiskey is filtered through sweet maple coal which gives him a characteristic flavor and aroma. American government branded the whiskey in 1941. Bourbon's predecessor in Colonial America was none other than the rye whiskey, made by farmers such as Thomas Jefferson and George Washington. Soil and climate of Virginia, Maryland and Pennsylvania suited rye splendidly. Each of these regions has its own specific style of rye whiskey.

Bourbon

The United States Congress declared bourbon as `America's Native Spirit' in 1964, making it to be the only spirit distinctive to the United States. Production of bourbon starts with mixing grains that will form its base (mash bill). That mash should contain at least 51% of corn but in practice mashes of 60-80% of corn are usually used with the rest being rye, wheat of barley. Most distillers usually use up to two types of grains. Bourbon that uses wheat instead of rye is known as wheat bourbon. That kind of whiskey is mellower and sweeter than rye bourbon. Ground grain is mixed with water and then most producers add a bit of the previous mash in order to create a sour mash where new yeast is added in order for the mash to ferment before it is placed into the column stills. By law, bourbon should not be distilled to more than 160 proof (80% ABV) so most are distilled to 130 – 160 proof (65 – 80% ABV). Bourbon is distilled twice with the second distillation in a pot still or a column still. Alcohol coming out of the still is colorless and bourbon get its color and most of the taste and aroma after it has matured in new charred oak casks. Charring the casks from the inside opens up the grains, allowing the whiskey to penetrate the wood which provides whiskey with aroma and flavor. While whiskey matures in casks a lot of things affect its final character. Climate plays the main role because as the temperature rises, whiskey in casks is expanded and wood soaks up some of its volume. Cold days make the whiskey contract back from the wood. This movement inside the wood and out frees the tannins, color and flavor of the wood.

During warmer days whiskey spends more time absorbed in wood, therefore picking up more tannins, color and flavor.

Sour mash

Sour mash represents sour liquid which remains in the still after the last distillation. By adding it to the fermented mash it helps with bacteria removal, balancing pH value of water and keeps the fermentation clean. Catherine Carpenter, from Casey County, continued the work of her family distillery after the passing of her husband and was the first to write down her recipe for sour and sweet mash in 1818. Sour mash is the most famous method used in bourbon and Tennessee whiskey production and it entails adding small doses of previously fermented mash (which contains live yeast) to the new fermentation, therefore creating a constant pH value and a standard quality and flavor of whiskey.

Sweet mash

Sweet mash uses fresh yeast in every fermentation done in open containers after which the mash is distilled which provides whiskey with fresh and sweet taste. Most people think that bourbon is made exclusively in Kentucky but this is not correct because, according to American law, bourbon can be made anywhere on US soil. Although it is correct that 95% of bourbon on today's market does come from Kentucky there are bourbons coming from Massachusetts, Virginia, Ohio, Indiana, etc. Kentucky is the center of bourbon distillation for three reasons. The first one is corn which is abundant in Kentucky. The second one is limestone which is plentiful in Kentucky, which helps the water going through it get rid of metals which give off bad flavors and influence the appearance of the whiskey.

The third is the climate, because hot summers and cold winters of Kentucky are ideal for maturing bourbon. Bourbon's roots go back to the immigrants west of original colonies in 18th and 19th century. The immigrants were mostly Scottish or Irish dissidents who already knew everything about Scotch and Irish whiskey production. There were English, Welsh, German and French immigrants who brought the first distillation stills in 1774. Before it became commercial and an industrial product, bourbon was an agricultural product and the first bourbons were made by farmers in autumn and winter when corn was dry enough to be ground. Grain was hard to transport and even harder to sell, so it became very practical to make whiskey out of it which farmers sold in great markets which in turn sold it to saloons and bars. Whiskey was transported by barges from Kentucky across Mississippi all the way to New Orleans. The first mention of a charred cask was found in a letter from 1826 which a merchant from Lexington sent to John Corlis. In the letter, he orders a new batch of whiskey and writes: "If the casks are charred from the inside, whiskey will be of much better flavor". After that, in 1880 in Galt House in Louisville, Kentucky Distillers Association was founded whose main role was to organize the producers and protect bourbon from the obstructive laws and regulations. It is interesting that before prohibition in Kentucky there were around two thousand distillers while there are only about ten today.

Corn whiskey

It has to contain 80% of corn and contrary to the stereotypical Moonshine, corn whiskey uses the standard mash process, distilled to a maximum of 160 proof. Corn whiskey is different than the rest of American whiskeys because it is not matured, and if it is, it is matured for six months (or less) in new, un-charred or used oak casks. Maximum of 125 proof can be left to mature. As for bourbon, if the producer wants to put straight on the label the whiskey ought to be matured for two years. The greatest popularity of the corn whiskey was during prohibition because, due to its simplicity, it was available almost to anybody so it nearly overran the black market. Unfortunately, as illegal distillation was not controlled most of the produced whiskey caused health problems for its consumers.

Tennessee whiskey

Tennessee whiskey is a special category of whiskey which, due to its filtering (must be filtered through charcoal), is characterized by mellow flavor, sweet note and a recognizable and unique aroma. Besides the fact that Tennessee is almost a "dry" region, which means that alcohol sales and consumption is illegal, its production of alcohol maintains a high level. In Tennessee, alcohol can be produced in the following regions: Mor, Kofi and Lincoln. When Tennessee whiskey is mentioned, two of its greatest brands spring to mind: George Dickel and Jack Daniels, but although they stem from the same region these two are different. Jack Daniels is a heavier whiskey of a more oily character while George Dickel is lighter and very aromatic. The first distillery was opened in 1825 in the Tennessee region. Five years after the Prohibition ended, Tennessee was able to produce whiskey once more. Tennessee whiskey was recognized as a separate category of American whiskey in 1941 when it started its new life, same as bourbon, with minimal 51% of corn content. After distillation is done whiskey is filtered through maple's coal.

Similar technique of filtering can be found in vodka production process. After the filtration whiskey is matured in new American white oak barrels.

Canadian whisky

Canadian whisky (spelt without "e") was the best-selling whisky in the US for decades. In 1875 the government specified that Canadian whisky must be made in Canada, using patented method, that is, a continuous distillation. The regulation also stated that Canadian whisky should be matured for a minimum of 3 and maximum of 18 years in charred oak casks. It is made of wide range of grain. So, there are no specified and strict rules as in Scotch and Bourbon. Blending is the key to Canadian whisky. Although it is made of different types of grain, corn is still the most used as well as rye, which is crucial to Canadian whisky's flavor.

The rule says that the more different spice notes you can taste in a Canadian whisky the more rye there is in it. The proportion of grains differs from brand to brand as well as the length of distillation and the type of still. Finally, maturing casks can differ a lot, starting with charred ones and the ones used to mature bourbon, sherry, port, rum or some other whisky. It is usual to distill grain three times in order to get a pure, neutral basic whisky to which a second whisky is added during the process called "flavoring" and that second whisky is usually rich in rye. The result is a whisky of generally mellow character but full flavor. It is a practice in Canada to ferment, distill and mature each grain separately. Blending is done at the very end; therefore we get a varied specter of different styles of Canadian whiskies. Barley was not common so the producers added corn, wheat and rye. Although it is believed that Canadian whisky bloomed during Prohibition when Canada became the main supplier of speakeasies that sprouted across the US, it did not bring any progress to the distillers that intended to work legally.

Japanese whisky

Outstanding geographic location and passion towards good whisky are just some of the virtues of Japanese whisky. On the northernmost point of Japan, Hokkaido is located, a place often compared to Scotland, whereas the island of Honshu is extremely mountainous and suitable for whisky production. Masataka Taketsuru was the man responsible for the advancement of production, development and uniqueness of Japanese whisky. Masataka comes from a family of sake makers. He graduated from the University in Glasgow and earned his experience by working for Hazelburn distillery in Campbeltown and Longmore distillery in Speyside. Towards the end of 19th century the production of Japanese whisky started to soar. After the First World War, Masataka helped the Suntory Company to open their first distillery, after which he opened his own distillery named Nikka Yoichi. A lot of time was needed for Japanese to gain the popularity of Scotch whiskies. Pot stills are dominant in Japanese whisky production (Yamazaki, Hakushu, Yoichi) and the combination of column and pot stills can also be found in production processes of Sendei, Gotemba, Karuizawa and Toa Shuzo. The producers of Japanese whisky take much care about the location where they grow their grain but about the grain also.

Japanese whisky uses grain from Japan, Scotland and the rest of the world. Japanese whiskies have a very important element which distinguishes them from Scotch. Japanese Single Malt is not malty, which means that they do not have grainy character. In order to achieve that, Japanese distillers try to keep the tiniest parts of grain out of the wash still. Wide mix of yeasts affects the uniqueness of flavor, while using long fermentation helps in creating complexity and aromatic elements while simultaneously reducing grainy elements. The roots of Japanese whisky are not well known. The first Japanese Shirofuda (white label) was presented to public in 1929 and in the next decade Jamazaki whiskies started to be exported. Japanese whisky bloomed and new distilleries were opened, and in the 1980's industry expanded and bought distilleries in Scotland. Nikka bought Ben Nevis, Takara took over Tomatin, and Suntory bought Morrison Bowmore and a part of Macallan. Soon, Japanese whisky started winning awards for the best whisky in different categories at the most prestigious world competitions and kept that trend until today.

Part sixteen

◆—◆—▮—◆—◆

RUM

"The drink of sailors, pirates, slaves and kings."

- Danilo Božović, Andrija Ristić -

Rum

Rum had a long journey, going from the slave plantations to royal halls. It is one of the reasons of war between America and England, as well as various criminal activities and plantation estates' businesses. In the 14th century, Marco Polo wrote on his journeys that, somewhere on the territory of today's Iran, he was welcomed with a very good wine made of sugar. Sugar cane underwent an expansion in the 4th century when it was brought to Egypt from Asia. Arabs were the first to distill fermented sugar cane juice. Arab influence brought the culture of consuming this beverage made from sugar cane as well as sugar production to Venice, Europe in the middle of the 15th century.

Rum can be made from molasses (byproduct in sugar production) or directly from juice pressed from sugar cane (guarapo). The colorless spirit is usually matured in casks that can be American Oak, French Oak and Sherry among others. The greatest rum producers are in the Caribbean region, with countries like Puerto Rico, Cuba, Dominican Republic, Jamaica, Barbados and Martinica to name a few. Central and South America also produce great rums, Venezuela, Guyana, Panama, Guatemala and Nicaragua are a few examples of quality rum producers. The first distillation of rum was done on the Caribbean sugarcane plantations sometimes in the 17th century. Slaves discovered that molasses, a thick syrupy liquid left after the crystallization of sugar from the heated sugar cane juice, can be turned into alcohol and legend has it that it was the slaves that first consumed this strong drink. The records of father Jean Baptista Labata speak of how the slaves' spirit became more cheerful after consuming a strong drink made from sugar cane. Later, all impurities in this drink were cleared by distillation and the first rums were made. Christopher Columbus brought sugar cane to the Caribbean and planted the first sugar cane during his long voyage. He planted the first sugar cane in La Hispanola, a territory that today is Cuba, Dominican Republic and Haiti. After the first successful harvests of sugar cane Columbus notified the King of Spain of the good news, and sugar became a valuable ingredient which led to the increase of the number of plantations and, sadly, slaves.

Rum made of sugar cane was named rum in 1667. The origin of the word rum varies and it is possible it stemmed from the following words:

Roemer or rummer - big drinking glass used by Dutch sailors.

Rummage - English term for space below deck where rum was stored.

Brum - name of Malaysian alcoholic drink, probably an abbreviation used by Dutch sailors during their journeys to Malaysia

Saccharum - Latin word for sugar, probably abbreviated to rum

Rumbullion - an old term for rum. It is supposed that it was made by amalgamation of words "Rheum" which means stem in the dialect of Seville and "Bouillon" which means cooking in French.

Whatever the true origin of the word rum is, English term kill-devil is the best way to describe the taste of these first, primitively distilled, rums. Sugar was not only a drink sweetener but an important culinary and even medical good. Portuguese and Spaniards establish colonies on Canary Islands, Madeira and Sao Tome in order to supply Europe with sugar. Sugar was not the only preoccupation of colonizers but also gold and other valuable metals. Competing to make profit the English, French and Spanish realized that they could make considerably greater profits in rum trade, whose production cost two times less than other spirits (i.e. French cognac). In 1640, Wilhelm Kieft, governor of New Amsterdam, built the first gin distillery in the New World. During the English occupation of New Amsterdam, the newly built distillery started to produce rum due to the proximity of sugar and the potential profit. In the 17th century, English held a complete monopoly on rum trade so in 1763 in New England, there were over 150 different distilleries. Almost 200 years after the first distillery was built in the New World, the battle for rum trade domination still roared between England and America.

Molasses

After harvesting sugar cane (usually between February and June), it is transported to the processing place where it is cut into smaller pieces which provide juice when pressed which is used in sugar production. When sugar cane juice is heated and stirred, after some time crystallized sugar starts to appear on the surface of the mixture. When this process is completed, what remains is molasses. It is a syrupy liquid which remains below the crystals that became sugar. After the sugar is removed, the mixture is heated, water and yeast are added, then fermented and distilled into rum. Rum can be categorized according to the area it comes from or style of its production. Rum possesses complexity, history and a lot of interesting stories. Earlier rums did not possess the quality of today's rums. Master distillers were inexperienced and distillation was done according to general sense, and fast production was paramount in order to maximize profit. That kind of rum could not easily defeat its competition. Brandy and Madeira, for example, were aristocratic drinks and it took a long time for rum to be on a par with other alcoholic beverages. Towards the end of 17th and the beginning of 18th century, rum consumption in England rose from 207 gallons to 2 million gallons per year. Rum slowly became a product that people traded and made fortunes off in England and Europe. Various cities in Europe grew thanks to rum profit. A great turnover in overall rum production happened in 1831 when Aeneas Coffey invented his continuous still which is still in use today. The advantage of this kind of still is that it produces more alcohol of lighter character. In 1862, Don Facundo Bacardi bought a distillery in Santiago and produced lighter style rum for the first time. During this time period, world rums could be divided into: Jamaican, French, Demerara and Cuban. During the prohibition in New York, alcohol could be bought in more places than before. After the Bacardi family left Cuba, wanting to keep their family business private, they left behind a factory that became the home of Havana Club rum.

How is rum produced?

Questions like: is rum made from sugar cane juice or molasses, whether to use laboratory yeast or a domestic one, what still to use, is it filtered and what casks to use to mature it, are just some of the questions that everybody who wants to make rum requires answers to. Climate and air influence the sweetness of rum. After the harvest, a sugar mill cuts, grinds and presses the juice out of sugar cane after which it is boiled in vacuum. Sugar crystals start to form after the liquid is cooled and are separated by a centrifuge. This process is done twice in order to separate all the crystals. After that, what remains in the pot is a thick black liquid called molasses. The greatest exporters of molasses are Brazil Venezuela and Guyana. Demerara sugar comes from Demerara region called Guyana Brown sugar coming from this region is highly valued due to its rich aroma, high quality and standard. Rums made in this region are highly regarded. Like a cocktail, rum should not be only sweet. It has to be balanced properly, like a good Manhattan. Carta Blanca is a unique method of rum production used by the traditional Cuban master blenders where after only three years of maturing young rum, or aguardiente, it can be called rum.

Territories

Spanish-speaking territories: Cuba, Panama, Dominican Republic, Puerto Rico Colombia, Venezuela.

English-speaking territories: Barbados, Belize, Bermuda, Saint Kitts, Jamaica.

French-speaking territories: Haiti, Guadalupe, Martinique.

Types of rum

Caribbean – island style of rum is produced using sugar cane, molasses or their combination This kind of rum is made using pot still or column still. Characteristics of these rums are dark color, herbal flavor with strong aromas. There is no standard method of rum distilling because some manufacturers use pot stills (darker rum of heavier body) and most use column stills. To earn the right to be called rum a spirit has to be matured for at least a year Maturing is mostly done in bourbon casks but can also be done in stainless steel or some other wood casks. Bourbon casks are the core of rum's flavor. Aging process determines the color (rum matured in oak goes darker in time whereas rum in stainless steel casks remains colorless). Owing to tropical climate of most regions where rum is produced, it matures faster than whisky in Scotland or brandy in France. Indicative of this is the angels share or loss of product due to evaporation. While products in Scotland lose about 2% per year, rum producers can lose up to 10%. Cask used in maturing is constantly replenished in order for rum to fully manifest the casks flavor. After maturing, rum is blended in order to secure a harmonic flavor, after which technologists analyze the rum composition. Blending is the final step in rum production and as a part of the process colorless rum can be filtered to remove color gained from casks during maturing process. Rums of same age can have different flavors which depend on the casks in which they were matured. It is up to master distiller to unite the aromas in order for rum to be the same every time.

French or Agricole rums - The French take pride in rum from the category of Rhum Agricole, which literally translates to "agricultural rum". The development of technology and the reduction of sugar in molasses resulted in creation of French rum which is produced using sugar cane juice instead of molasses. Rhum Agricole is distilled in pot stills and the result is rum with 65 – 70% ABV. This type of rum is distilled to 70% ABV or 140 proof, after which it is reduced to 40 – 55% ABV. French rums are usually matured from 3 months to several years, and after three years in oak casks they can be called "rhum vieux" or old rum. Characteristic flavor of French rums is strong character, herbal aromas with a lot of spices.

Cuban style - Cuban style of rum is, contrary to some kinds, purer and gentler. Cuban style rum is made exclusively from molasses, distilled using column still and matured in used American oak bourbon casks.

Typical rum categories

White rum (light rum) – light body without harsh aromas and with a presence of molasses sweetness. It serves as a good base for cocktails that do not need a strong character. Spanish territories boast of light rum of high quality.

Gold rum – possesses medium body, and most of them are matured in casks that provide them with color, aroma and other characteristics. It is outstanding in cocktails that need an extra aroma like vanilla, caramel, chocolate and cinnamon.

Spiced rum – category of rum with spices and flavors in order to boost the aroma. Examples of spiced rum: Captain Morgan, Sailor Jerry.

Dark rum – rum that spent a longer period of time in a cask, possesses a strong aroma, heavy body and presence of spices. Most of dark rums come from English and French speaking territories.

Overproof rum – rum whose alcohol percentage is considerably higher than the usual 40% ABV; most of them are over 75% ABV, usually around 151 and 160 proof.

Navy rum – love between the Royal Navy and rum started around 1655 with the occupation of Jamaica. Navy officers switched their brandy rations with Jamaican rum supplies. At first they gave pure rum to sailors but then mixed it with lime juice, sugar and water. Royal Navy continued to ration rum to its sailors until 1970, and the Royal Navy of New Zealand is the only military force that still provides their sailors with rum. Overproof rum/navy strength categories are rums with a higher alcoholic content – more than 75.5% ABV. Pour a glass of rum and leave it overnight in the open and if the rum leaves a dark, caramel colored ring on the glass it means it is of inferior quality and that is contains great amounts of caramel. This is the advice from a dear friend and a rum connoisseur, Carlos Esquivel.

Cachaca

Cachaca is known as heart opener (abre coracao), holy water (agua benta), tiger's breath (bafo de tigre). Cachaca is a globally known Brazilian spirit and people usually compare it to rum, agricole rhum and brandy. The greatest difference between rum and cachaca is that rum is made from molasses whereas cashaca is made from sugar cane juice which makes it similar to the Brazilian category of agricole rum and even brandy. Chicca is a drink similar to rum, produced in Brazil. Cachaca is distilled directly from sugar cane juice and there are over 4000 brands of cachaca in Brazil. It became popular thanks to the Caipirinha cocktail. The trend of popularizing alcohol through cocktails can be seen in examples of the Moscow Mule, Cuba Libre, Margarita, Pisco Sour, Batidasi and others. In the 16th century, the Portuguese brought sugar cane and distilling culture to Brazil. Most of cachaca that is matured is left in European, Brazilian or American casks. Brazilian law states that cachaca should be matured for at least one year in order to be marked as aged. Cachaca is divided into silver (non-aged) and gold (aged). Seco from Panama is similar to rum but also vodka, bearing in mind that it is distilled three times.

Part seventeen

———◆◆◈◆◆———

TEQUILA

"Mystical plant, beneath the starry sky, gives off nectar equal to Gods."

- Andrija Ristić, Danilo Božović -

Tequila

Folk tales explain the origin of tequila through the legend of Mayahuel and Quetzalcoatl, the savior God. Mayahuel was an ordinary woman who became an Aztec Goddess when she discovered an agave plant. Evil Goddess Tzitzimitl could not allow their love. After the stars swallowed Mayahuel, out of the remains of her body sprouted an agave. A lightning from the skies struck the plant as a final form of punishment. When the lightning struck, leaves fell off the plant leaving just the heart and its sweet juice which represented the blood of Mayahuel, that is, tequila. This is a very interesting legend that conjures up the mystic origin of tequila. Aztecs consumed the fermented sweet juice of blue agave "pulque" long before the Spanish came. It cannot be said with certainty that people of Latin America knew how to distill before they came into contact with the Spanish conquistadors. The natives of Mexico started producing Mezcal wine immediately after the arrival of Spanish conquerors in 1521. Tequila went through great rises in exportation, especially during the prohibition in America when tequila was imported illegally and sold, and also during the Second World Was when European drinks were hard to come by. Apart from 136 sorts of agave that exist, tequila is produced solely from blue agave which, contrary to many opinions, belongs to the family of lily. City of Tequila is 65 km away from Guadalajara in the highlands of Los Altos in a state of Jalisco. This region is rich in volcanic soil which is extremely fertile for agave growing. Period of complete maturation is 8 – 10 years and tequila has to be made of at least 51% of blue agave and this kind of tequila is known as mixto tequila. Residents of Mexico did not have the right to make tequila until the middle of 18th century when Don Jose Antonio Cuervo merited permission from the King of Spain, Charles IV. This act of the King will encourage the production of Mezcal wine in La Rojena distillery. In the early 1990's tequila started to conquer the rest of the world. Don Cenobio Sauza, the mayor of the city of Tequila (1884 – 1885) was the first exporter of tequila to American soil. Mexican laws dictate that tequila can only be produced in Jalisco region and in limited amounts in regions Guanajuato, Nayarit, Michoacan and Tamaulipas. Jalisco owns two dominant regions in tequila production process: Amatitan valley and Arandas city plateau. There is a difference between tequilas from Amatitan valley and Arandas – the first is decorated with fruity, herbal, flowery and relatively light aromas whereas the second are distinguished by earthy, heavier aromas. Tequila is a spirit that was created from boiled, fermented agave juice, a Mexican plant that looks similar to cacti. Many distillers today make tequila traditionally using traditional equipment and hand work but, of course, as in other parts of industry, technology sped up the whole process and made it less strenuous.

Agave

Tequila is made from agave, a Mexican plant, whose name originates from the Greek word meaning noble or delightful, delicious. In Mexico, this plant is sometimes called maguey and although it resembles a cactus physically, this plant is botanically classified in the category with sansevieria, yucca and amaryllis, in the great family of *Agavaceae*. The simplest and most widely accepted definition is that agave is the part of the lily family. There are over 300 variations of agave, out of which 200 were discovered in Mexico and grow in a wide spectrum of colors and sizes, but legally only one can be used to make tequila, Agave Tequilana, Agave Weber azul. Originally named after the European botanist, Weber, the reference blue was added later, due to the blue sheen on the green leaves which is quite noticeable when a whole field in Jalisco is observed. The rest of Mexican spirits such as mezcal and sotol are made out of other variations of agave. Blue agave is basically a big sphere from which great blue-green, silvery, prickly leaves sprout (pencas), one meter long which end in a sharp, brown thorn giving an adult plant a 2.1 – 3.6 m in diameter. Agave grows in volcanic soil, rich in minerals, in Jalisco and the surrounding Mexican states. Agave is planted before rain season (June – September) in order for it not to suffer water deficiency in the first year of growing. The best picking period is from January to May when it gives the greatest harvest.

Harvest

Agave usually reaches adulthood after 5 – 8 years when it is ready for harvesting. Agave growing in the hills needs a lot longer to reach maturity (around 12 years). It is a standard practice to fertilize soil in order to maximize the harvest. There is no legal regulation about when the agave can be harvested and plants are hand picket according to their ripeness, usually the whole field. Adult agave reaches around 1.8 m in height but ripe agaves are lower because during ripening their leaves increase in width. One more indication of the ripeness is the loss of lower leaves (pencas). Ripe piña of adult agave has more sugar, therefore produces more tequila. Pickers, called "jimadors", use tools that have a long wooden shaft and a rounded knife on its end (coa) which they use to remove long leaves in order to get to piña, the head of the plant that looks like a big pineapple. The tool used to cut agave got its name from the sound it makes when a jimador slices through the air. When the plant becomes ripe, reddish and brownish dots appear due to plant juice on piña after the leaves are cut off. Four to six dots of this color on a piña indicate that it is ripe for harvest, and more than that that it is overripe and starts to decay, similar to the brown dots on a banana that indicate its age. When the plant reaches full ripeness, tequileros have 6 -12 months to harvest it or else it starts to die out and fall apart. Some distillers prefer overripe agaves while other prefer not ripe, all depending on the character they want to give tequila they are making. Unripe agaves tend to provide less complex tequilas with herbal notes while overripe agaves usually give off sweeter, heavier flavors. Late harvest agaves called sobre maduro can start to produce sourness which influences the flavor and complexity of tequila and often gives off vinegary notes. Jimadors work from sunrise to little after noon in order to avoid the afternoon heats and a skilled worker is expected to pick around 100 piñas a day. This job demands great skill and is traditionally passed on from father to son. Even very experienced jimadors sometimes lose a finger to coas blade. Snakes and tarantulas also hide in plants' shades. Premium tequila brands often point out that agave was grown on their property which enables distillers to control the way plants are treated, that is, that they have their jimadors which will secure that the leaves are cut all the way to the piña. When third-rate growers sell their piñas, they are paid by the kilogram and it often happens that they do not cut the leaves all the way to the pine in order to enhance profits. The result is that the remaining leaves have a kind of wax on their surface which makes tequila bitter.

Boiling agave

Depending on the size, piñas are cut into two or four parts in order to be boiled evenly. Parts are left in the oven where they cook on steam in order for their juice full of starch to turn into sugar. Traditionally, steam heats the agave and it cooks for 24 – 48 hours. After that, boiled piñas are left to cool for 16 – 48 hours when the cooking process is complete. Each distillery boils piñas at a different temperature and in a time period they consider best, and the cooling is sometimes sped up by opening the oven doors or by fans. Many distilleries use automatic ovens instead of traditional jornos. These are big, chrome ovens that function like pressure cookers in which agaves are boiled very quickly (around 7 hours at the temperature of 121 C or 250 F) and the cooling period is shortened greatly. Too quick a boil increases the risk of burning out sugar and creating a bitter, caramel flavor whereas the slower boiling provides a lot sweeter and fruity flavor. Agaves naturally contain inulin which is hydrolyzed into fructose during boiling. Traditional and modern ovens transform inulin into fermentable sugar using temperature, but if the traditional approach is not used the same effect can be achieved by adding special enzymes (active proteins).

Extraction

After cooking, piña has to be pressed in order to release juice and that was traditionally done in a mill called tahona. Tahona wheel made from volcanic stone is turned in a round pool (originally it was moved by mules) while boiled piñas are put into the pool by hand where the stone grinds them and presses the sugar juice. Today, lots of producers use modern machines for this where everything is automatic.

Fermentation

Fermentable sugar in agave juice (aguamiel) is converted into alcohol using yeast. Before the fermentation, aguamiel is analyzed in order to establish the level of sugar and to, if necessary, dilute it with water in order to get it to 8 – 16%. Mosto (wort) is usually based on experience rather that scientific methods. If the tequila is going to be sold as a mix then corn sugar is added or sugar cane sugar up to 49% of the overall fermentable sugar. For a spirit to be named tequila there needs to be a minimum of 51% agave sugar. In the 100% agave tequilas only blue agave aguamiel is fermented without the addition of sugar. The type of yeast used during fermentation will determine the flavor and the characteristics of the final product. Traditionally, spontaneous fermentation with natural yeasts is conducted. Fermented juice from the previous fermentation is mixed with the new in order to secure the continuity of flavor (as in sour mash bourbon). Fermentation can be done in open wooden stills or chrome constructs and usually lasts for 24 – 96 hours depending on the type of process and gives off mosto similar to beer with 3.8 – 6% ABV.

Distillation

In order to get tequila, fermented juice has to be distilled at least twice and the combination of stills or a traditional method can be used, where the whole distillation is done in pot stills. Stills can be copper or chrome steel but it is very important for the spirit to be in contact with copper during the process of distillation so even steel stills have certain parts made of copper (base or condensing pipes). The product of the first distillation is known as ordinario and only after the second distillation the spirit can be called tequila. Although it is uncommon, some distillers opt to distill it a third time. The first distillation results in 20 – 25% ABV whereas the second distillation usually gives off 55 – 75% ABV. As with other spirits the important part is to find the balance between art and science and choose the best middle cut. Different parts of the spirit vaporize at different temperatures and it is up to the distiller to find the best balance. The first part of the spirit known as head and the last known as tail are usually put back to re-distill. It is interesting that there is no legal maximum of ABV so it is technically possible to distill tequila of neutral taste.

Maturing

Clear tequila as a product of second distillation can be bottled and sold as blanco tequila, in contrast to reposado and añejo tequila that are matured in oak casks where wood provides them with tannins, softens the alcohol and gives character. Legally, tequila can be matured with the maximum of 55% ABV. Casks used can be new or already used where tequila or some other spirit (most often American whiskey) matured. Casks can be charred which provides color and flavor. Type of wood, degree of drying, previous maturation, temperature, humidity and alcoholic content of the spirit will certainly affect the maturing process of tequila. Reposado tequila can also be matured in casks. The law states that the container where tequila is stored is sealed and the paper is placed over that only Compliance Assessment Agency can remove.

Mixing and additives

Additive such as caramel, glycerin, sugar syrup, older tequila, oak extract flavoring components (approved by the Mexican Ministry of Health) can be added to all types of tequila up to 75g/l for sugar and 85g/l for other additives, but the total of dry matter should be less than 1% of the total volume.

Filtering and diluting

Belief that tequila ought to have at least 38% ABV is canonized but the rule says that the strength of tequila should be between 35 – 55% ABV. Distilled or demineralized water is used to dilute tequila to the wanted strength and before bottling tequila ought to be filtered through active coal at room temperature or cold filtered.

Bottling and packaging

Mixto tequila for distribution outside Mexico is sold and exported in tanks with high level of alcohol and is diluted and bottled in countries where it will be sold or exported further. Whereas 100% agave tequila by law has to be bottled with a geographic origin where it was made.

Tequila classification

There are two categories of tequila, mixto and 100% agave. These two categories are further classified according to whether or not tequila was aged and for how long and also there is one more category – aromatized tequilas.

100% agave – This term is used for tequilas distilled completely from agave without the addition of sugar during fermentation. It has to be bottled in the geographic area where it was produced and these are essentially the best tequilas.

Mixto – term used to denote tequilas where sugar was added during fermentation. Although the percentage changed during years, today mixto tequila has to contain at least 51% of agave's fermentable sugar and the rest can be corn or sugar cane sugar. It is important to say that the term mixto is not found on the labels of this kind of tequila but is simply labeled tequila. Therefore, if the label does not state 100% blue agave tequila we know that it is a mixto.

Joven (Gold or Oro) tequila – Joven means young and the best example is the mix of young and matured tequilas. Unfortunately, they are mostly not matured and just colored with caramel and additives which provide them with a specific flavor. Because of its color they are known as gold or oro.

Blanco (Silver) tequila (aged 0-59 days) – Blanco tequila is usually colorless, transparent tequila. Although blanco tequilas are usually not aged they can be matured in chrome stills in order to oxidize and settle (up to 60 days).

Reposado (Aged) tequila (aged for 2 months or more) – The term reposado was introduced in 1968 and it means rested. Reposado has to be matured in oak casks of undefined size or reservoirs called pipones for a minimum of 60 days. Some casks used in maturing reposado tequila are so huge that a little caramel is added to enhance the color. On the other hand, some reposados are aged in smaller casks (mostly bourbon) a lot longer than 60 days and are very close to añejo tequilas in character and age.

Añejo (Extra Aged) tequila (aged for 1 year or more) – Añejo or old is tequila matured for at least a year in oak casks. Caramel or additives can be added to enhance color or flavor.

Extra Añejo tequila (aged 3 years or more) - Extra añejo or extra old tequila is a relatively new category, established in 2006. Tequila connoisseurs compare it with the finest cognacs and are ready to pay prices similar similar.

Regions

Tequila possesses an appellation of origin and can be produced solely in the officially determined regions which include 181 municipalities in five Mexican states, including the whole region of Jalisco and specific border regions of Guanajuato, Michoacan and Nayarit. The exception is the small region of Tamaulipas which is home to Chinaco tequila and is located far from Jalisco region on the eastern shores of Mexico. When, in December 1974, tequila regions were officially determined, Tamaulipas was not included. Three years later appellation was modified and the move was judged as political. Two main production areas remain in Jalisco, Amatitan valley, where the production is centered around the city Tequila and the plateau of Los Altos in the eastern Jalisco around the city of Arandas. At 2000m above sea, Los Altos has less humidity and is colder than Tequila valley at 1200 – 1600m, so it produces agaves with higher sugar percentage thanks to the temperature difference between night and day. Agaves that grow in the high regions need more time to ripen, therefore are more expensive. The position of soil also influences ripening because the fields on the western slopes get more sun so plants ripen faster. South slopes are the sunniest after that and on the northern slopes agaves need most time to ripen. Micro climate and soil certainly affect the final profile of agave flavor. The ones that grow on volcanic soil in the tequila valley have herbal and spicy aromas whereas the ones that grow on red soil (due to iron oxidation) of lower pH in the plateau are of finer, sweeter and fruitier aromas. The producers sometimes use agaves from different regions to avoid the character of certain soil.

Traditional way of serving

In Mexico, tequila is not mixed and is usually served straight at room temperature in 2 oz or 60 ml glasses called caballito (little horse) with another same glass after it called sangrita which means little blood. Since it is red, with no alcohol and spicy, people usually think that sangrita is spicy tomato juice similar to Bloody Mary cocktail but is in fact made of tomato juice, lime, pomegranate and hot chili sauce. The finest tequilas are best drank pure, the same way that cognac is traditionally served. Tequila is used in cocktail culture extremely often and there is no good bartender who does not know how to make a good Margarita. In Mexico, Cantaritos is one of the mixed drinks with tequila which is mostly found in bars and cafes of Jalisco and is made of freshly pressed orange juice, grapefruit and lime, little salt and carbonized grapefruit soda. It is usually served in simple clay bottles.

Mezcal

Origins of mezcal take us back throughout history to an age before Europeans arrived to the American continent. Agave had been cultivated for centuries before that and used for various industrial purposes as well as for fermentation into a mild alcoholic drink, pulque, which was ritually consumed over two thousand years ago. With the arrival of Spaniards, knowledge of distillation came and the predecessor of tequila was born. The first mescal appeared around the year 1500 and spread across Mexico during the next few centuries and was probably exported to Spain. The etymology of the word "Mezcal" comes from an Aztec language Nahuatl, derived from the word *mexcalli* [meʃ'kalːi] *metl* [metɬ] and *ixcalli* [iʃ'kalːi], which means overcooked agave. Internationally, mezcal was defined since 1994 by the Appellation of Origin (AO, DO). There is also a geographical indication (G I) which is limited to the countries where mezcal is produced.

There are eight specific regions in Mezcal production:

1. **Oaxaca**; 2. **Durango**; 3. **Guanajuato**; 4. **Guerrero**; 5. **San Luis Potosi**; 6. **Tamaulipas**; 7. **Zacatecas**; 8. **Michoacan** (recently approved).

In Mexico mezcal is regulated through Norma Oficial Mexicana from 1994, legally ratified in 2003, and in 2005 certification started.

Production

Unlike tequila which is solely made from blue agave, Mezcal is pruduced using more tan thirty species and subspecies of agave, including blue agave. It should be noted that most mezcals are made from Agave Espadin which is the dominant species of agave in Oaxaca. After jimadors finish with collecting agave the same way as for tequila and pinas are brought to distillery, the differences between tequila and mezcal production start to appear.

Premium mezcals use the traditional way of production, therefore we will pay attention to them. In order for a mescal to be called Artisanal/Traditional, it has to follow certain steps:

Hand-picked and processed agave

Boiled in underground ovens

Ground using volcanic rock

Fermented using natural yeast

Distilled in copper alembic stills

The production of mezcal starts by boiling pina underground in earthen kilns of conical shape and coated with volcanic rock. Wood (usually oak) is placed at the bottom of the kiln whose fire heats the volcanic rock to the extremely high temperatures.

Pinas can be cut into pieces and put onto the hot volcanic rock and covered with a thick layer of earth and agave leaves. Now this "underground kiln" is starting to smoke, boil and caramelize the pinas in a process that last for a couple of days. This is the part of the process that provides mescal with its smoky aromas.

The process is continued by grinding boiled pinas using the traditional Tahona volcanic rock (some producers), where we get the fermentation material and finally distill it. After grinding, the pulp is mixed with water and is traditionally left to the natural yeast to do the fermentation. In the industry, cultured yeast is added which speeds up the fermentation process. After the fermentation, wash is distilled in the copper alembic stills.

It is usually distilled twice (some brands used triple distillation) and a single distillation can take up to 24 hours.

When we talk about spirits such as rum, bourbon and scotch, we know that distillers often mix distillates from different casks in order to gain the consistency of the product. On the other hand, most of mezcal producers produce significantly smaller quantities of mezcal so there is not enough of it for blending. That means that each cask has its own unique character, different from the next one. Technically, there are: Type I – 100% agave and Type II mixto – 80% agave. "Crema de Mezcal," is mezcal with aromas of fruit, stone fruit, or agave nectar. "Con Gusano," which means "with a worm." That is not a worm but a larva. There are two types of larvae you can find:

Gusano rojo (red larva) and gusano oro (Golden larva). The red one lives in the root and pina of agave while the white one lives in the leaf.

Categories

Joven – young mezcal, usually unmatured, or matured up to two months

Reposado – rested, matured in oak casks for 2 – 12 months.

Anejo – old, matured in oak casks for 1 -3 years.

Extra Anejo – extra old, matured in oak casks for over 3 years.

Part eighteen

BRANDY

"Fiery taste of fruit, war and conquest."

- Andrija Ristić, Danilo Božović -

Brandy

Brandy stems from a Dutch word brandewijn (smoked wine), brandy wine. The world was introduced to brandy thanks to wine and salt trade. Merchants sent their salt deliveries to Norway, England and the Netherlands and started to export wines. As wine was too complicated to transport due to its volume, instability and short expiration time, Dutch and local winemakers got an idea to distill wine in order to make it easier to transport. In the beginning, out of practical reasons, the liquid was stored in oak barrels but it was soon discovered that the liquid matures stored in casks so Dutch merchants started making a beverage which they called brandewijn which meant "smoked wine". At the beginning of 17th century, the demand for local wines grew and therefore the way of distillation was sped up. In the second half of the 17th century new distilleries start to open in the Cognac region, owned by clergy, nobles and farmers.

Brandy is a traditional spirit made from wine or fruit. It is believed that Christians have been distilling wine and making brandy for ages. Brandy was, however, first mentioned in the 12th century whereas it became popular in the 14th century. France and Spain are the countries which dominated the brandy market while other countries fell behind but in time the quality of world's brandies rose to the same level. Wine used to be fortified in order not to go sour during long sea voyages and it is believed that wine was distilled in order to avoid huge taxation based on weight. By transporting it in barrels people realized that the flavor changes for the better and enriches it.

Armagnac

Armagnac had to wait for the railroad in France to be built in order for it to become popular around the world. Transfer from pit stills to continuous still had a great effect on Armagnac. The period of phylloxera (wine disease) in France was ruinous to brandy production. That is when other spirits got the chance to shine. Armagnac is divided into three regions: Bas-Armagnac, Tenareze and Haut-Armagnac. Armagnac from the first two regions possesses an extraordinary quality. Bas-Armagnac possesses soil rich in sand and clay which provides an extra developed brandy whereas the region Tenareze which is surrounded by Bas-Armagnac produces brandy which has a full, fresh, fruity aroma. Most producers in Armagnac industry use grape sorts such as Folle Blanche, Ugni Blanc, etc. Due to the climate specific to this region it is recommended to do the distillation immediately after the fermentation in order to preserve all the light aromas of brandy. Most producers use alembic armagnacais or a column still. The secret to Armagnac's uniqueness is in the size of stills used in its production which is smaller than the one used in cognac production. Because of this Armagnac is characteristic of rich fruity and earthy aromas. The first Armagnacs were made in pot stills but today almost all are made using column stills.

Cognac

Cognac got its name after the town of Cognac in France. The most popular sort of grapes used in production of Cognac is Ugni Blanc or Saint-Emilion. Cognac is twice distilled in copper stills and has to be matured for at least two years in French oak casks (limousine or troncais). One should keep in mind that all cognacs are brandies but not all brandies are cognacs. Cognac is a distilled drink made from fermented white grape juice and matured for at least two years. Cognac can only be produced in the city of Cognac and the six neighboring regions. Cognac is famous for its unique quality which is the result of centuries old techniques that make its identity. The production process is extremely controlled and undergoes rigorous rules and regulations so, for example, only presses made from natural materials can be used to press grapes. Grapes are also special and it is grown on limestone under the influence of the climate altered by the Atlantic Ocean. As maturation is as important as the distilling process even the type of wooden used to make the casks is controlled and specified. Only specific oak 60 – 100 years old is good enough to be used. Grapes are grown randomly and unsystematically, vineyards sprout everywhere which led to several sort of grapes to distinguish themselves as ideal for brandy production: Folle Blanche, Ugni Blanc and Colombard. However, in 1870 virus phylloxera completely ravaged the vineyards. This crisis lasted for 10 years, during which time whiskies and gin made a comeback. In the 18th and at the beginning of 19th century, cognac was sold in casks and it was only around 1850 that it's bottling started. It was then that cognac got its name after the region it came from and a decree from 1909 states that cognac is a drink whose ingredients should undergo a complex procedure of turning grapes into wine and wine into eau de vie (water of life) and that all of that has to be done exclusively in Cognac region in France. The process starts by picking grapes which lasts from the start towards the end of October and, after picking, grapes are pressed by pneumatic presses and juice is left to ferment which turns sugar into alcohol. Adding sugar is strictly forbidden and the pressed liquid is store along with its sediment. Pressing and fermenting processes are rigorously followed because they influence the quality of drink. Wines made after three weeks of fermentation, from end of October to end of November, contain around 8% ABV. That is when the distillation in copper stills starts since copper does not change the flavor at all. Cognac is distilled twice and the whole process is named chauffes. The first distillation takes between eight and nine hours after which a murky liquid called brouillis is obtained. Then, it is distilled again and the second distillation, lasting for about 12 hours. The obtained spirit is divided into the "head", the "heart" and the "tail", out of which only the "heart", which is best in quality, is left in oak casks to mature. The "head" and the "tail" are mixed with the next batch of wine or another spirit and are sent back to distill. The obtained purified liquid with an average 70% ABV is put into oak casks and left in the cellars to mature which rounds up the whole cognac making process. During maturation cognac loses about 3% of its volume which is called, angel's share. In order for a cognac to be ready for bottling it has to be matured for at least 30 months and usually a lot longer (few decades). In order to be able to know what kind of cognac you are buying/drinking, you have to know how to interpret the signs on the label because they denote age, geographic origin and the cellar which they come from.

V.S./SELECTION/de Luxe – denotes that the youngest ingredient is at least 2 years old.

V.S.O.P./RESERVE – matured for at least 4 years.

X.O./NAPOLEON/HORS d`AGE/IMPERIAL – matured for at least 6 years.

Fine champagne means that at least 50% of the mix originates from the Champagne Grande region and the rest is from Petit Champagne. The same goes for the labels Fine Borderies, Fine Fins Bois and Fine Bons Bois. We should not forget that enjoying a cognac is not complete if it is not consumed from a glass of specific shape. In better restaurants cognac is served in a big balloon glass although the real connoisseurs maintain that the full experience demands cognac is drunk from a so called tulip glass on 4 oz or 12 cl in volume with almost 1 oz or 3 cl of cognac poured in it. There are no clear rules on when or how to drink cognac. It is usually drunk after a meal, along with a good cigar or a quality dark chocolate with a high percentage of cacao. Due to the great popularity among younger generations, this drink has been greatly commercialized lately. It is very common to mix Cognac with various drinks such as mineral water, Coca Cola and often it is consumed with ice, although that is pretty far from original tradition.

Cognac region

This region stretches along the banks of Charente and, 120 km north of Bordeaux, it reaches the shores of Atlantic Ocean and includes six regions: Grande *and* Petit Champagne, Borderies, Fins Bois, Bon Bois, Bois Ordinarie with Grande and Petit Champagne being the most famous. Cognac regions should not be mistaken for the northeastern Champagne region, wine region from where the famous sparkling wine originates, although they share the same etymology which French use to denote limestone soil. In the 3rd century BC Romans brought grapevine sort to this region, which, as it turned out, with its partly maritime and partly continental climate and soil rich in lime and salt, offered conditions for cultivation of specific sorts of grapes which were impossible to grow anywhere else.

Cognac production

Grape juice is fermented using wild yeast during a period which lasts between two and three weeks. The fermented juice contains 7 – 8 percent of alcohol. Distillation is done in the traditional copper stills called alembic. After the rigorous control of production, cognac is matured. In order for cognac to possess cru label it has to be made out of 90% of Ugni Blanc grape sort with the maximum of 10% of Folignan, Jurancon blanc or Blanc Rame.

Other types of brandy

Calvados is distilled from the fermented juice of specially grown apples of Normandy (apple cider) and the mixture can contain up to a hundred sorts of sweet (Rouge Duret), sour (Raimbault) and bitter apples. Apples are usually hand-picked and carefully selected after which the juice is fermented and made into dry cider which is then distilled once or twice depending on Calvados type the distiller wants to make. Double distillation is done in pot stills whereas single in column stills. The main argument for a single distillation is that it produces a lot more complex Calvados which can be matured longer, while double distillation produces Calvados with many flavors of fresh apples but little complexity. After it has been matured for two years in oak casks the spirit gains the right to be called Calvados. Brandy de Jerez is a brandy made in Jerez region in Andalusia and is distilled from different wines made all across Spain, mostly Palomino and Airen sorts which are used in sherry making. Two different types of distillation are used in different stills but both stills have to be copper. Single distillation is done after which the spirit matures in American oak casks where sherry wine was previously matured. Traditional maturing system known as the Solera system has to be applied. It is classified as:

Brandy de Jerez Solera – matured for a minimum of six months

Brandy de Jerez Solera Reserva – matured for a minimum of one year

Brandy de Jerez Solera Grand Reserva – matured for a minimum of three years

The Solera system is the series of great connected barrels where every barrel contains a little older brandy than the one before it. When the brandy is withdrawn from the last barrel, where no more than a third is ever withdrawn at one time, it gets refilled by the brandy from the previous barrel in the series and so on up to the first barrel where new brandy is poured in. This system speeds up the maturation process.

Grappa, Pisco and fruit brandy

Grappa is an Italian brandy which is distilled from the fermented mixture that remains after the grapes are pressed to produce wine (grapes, seeds, stems). Flavor and quality of Grappa will depend on the quality and type of pressed grapes. It is very similar to Orujo, French Marc or Marc schnapps. In Italy, Grappa is served alongside espresso. Grappa can be classified according to the geographic designation, grape sort and style.

There are eight geographic Grappa regions and they are:

1. **Grappa di Barolo**

2. **Grappa Piemontesse**

3. **Grappa Trentina**

4. **Grappa Friulana**

5. **Grappa Veneta**

6. **Sudtiroler Grappa / Grappa dell'Alto Adige**

7. **Grappa Siciliana**

8. **Grappa di Marsala**

Grappa that is bottled and labeled with one of the above geographic origins should be made from grapes from that region with a minimum of 40% ABV. Grappa which does not have a geographic origin should contain at least 37.5% ABV. Grappa can also denote the name of wine - DOCG or DOC (Chianti, Amarone, etc.)

Styles and age labels:

1. **Grappa Giovane** (non-matured) – grappa with aromas attained from wine and fermentation.

2. **Grappa Giovane Aromatica** (non-matured) – similar as the previous grappa but can contain aromatic or semi-aromatic wines such as Muller Thurgau, Traminer, Sauvignon.

3. **Grappa Affinata in Lengo** (matured in wooden casks) – grappa matured in wooden casks but for a shorter period of time than the law states is necessary to be called matured.

4. **Grappa Affinata in Lengo Aromatica** (matured in wooden casks) – similar to the previous group but can contain aromatic or semi-aromatic wines.

5. **Grappa Vecchia or Invecchia** (matured) – grappa matured for at least 12 months.

6. **Grappa Riserva or Stravecchia** (matured) – grappa matured for at least 18 months

7. **Grappa Invecchia Aromatica** (matured) – grappa made from aromatic or semi-aromatic wines and matured for at least 12 months.

8. **Grappa Aromatizzata** (aromatic) – grappa with aromas of herbs or fruit like blackberry

9. **Grappa di vitigo** (specific sorts) or **Grappa monovitigo** (made from one sort) – Grappa made from a specific and domestic sort of grape such as floral Moscato.

Non-matured Grappa should be served cold (9 -13 C or 48 – 55 F) while matured Grappa is ideal at the temperature a few degrees lower that room temperature (15 – 17 C or 59 – 62 F). It is said that it is better to serve it too cold that too hot, and is ideally served in middle sized tulip glasses, whereas serving Grappa in balloon or flute glasses should be avoided altogether. It is usual to add a little Grappa to espresso in Italy in order to create "Caffe Corretto". All traditional Italian ways of consuming Grappa with espresso taste better when the coffee is sweetened and if you prefer coffee with no sugar then it is better to pair it with Grappa liqueur. Flavors and aromas typically found in Grappa include wooden, grape/wine, cheese, floral, fruity and compote.

Pisco is a grape spirit made by the Spanish settlers in the 16th century as a cheaper version of the Orujo. The dispute between Peru and Chile over whose national drink Pisco is still goes on but both of these countries present the Pisco Sour as their own. There are differences in classification and the way of production between Chilean and Peruvian Pisco. In Chilean Pisco production, mostly Muscat, Torontel and Pedro Jimenez are used. It is classified as:

Regular - sweeter and wooden aromas, and light yellow in color.

Special - special and reserve are of very similar flavor and aroma and murky yellow in color. The flavor is more intense than regular and leaves a stronger alcoholic flavor in its finish.

Reserve - very similar to Special, both being subtly sweet and resembling color.

Great - strong dominant flavor and a pleasant murky yellow color. Not as sweet as the previous one and has a stronger wood influence in its finish.

Peruvian pisco is classified as:

Pure – made from one sort of grapes, usually *Quebranta*, *Mollar* or *Common Black*, but does not allow for mixing of these sorts.

Aromatic – made from Muscat sorts such as *Albilia*, *Italia* or *Torontel* but does not allow for mixing of these sorts.

Mosto Verde (green must) – partially made from grape juice containing seeds, stems and peel.

Acholado – blend of different grape sorts.

Aging

Pisco should be matured for at least three months in containers made of stainless steel, glass or some other material that does not affect it physically, chemically or organically without addition of any additives that would influence its color, flavor or alcohol percentage. Brandies made of fruit such as apples, pears, plums, quinces, berries, apricots and sour cherries usually contain 40 – 45% ABV of colorless alcohol and are usually consumed cooled.

Rakia

Rakia has been consumed on the territory of Serbia and the Balkans for centuries and it contains the spirit and character of our ancestors. The beginnings of alcohol consumption on Balkans are connected with our culture of drinking wine, brought by the Greeks to our lands around the 4th century BC. Although rakia arrived with the Turks in the 15th century, the tradition of rakia production in Serbian villages starts towards the end of the 19th century when, after vineyards were decimated by phylloxera, people started planting various fruit which was later used in fruit rakias production. Many families were renowned for their fruit's quality and were distinguished by rakias made from that fruit. Through time, distillation process was perfected, the recipes were improved which brought about the increase in quantities of produced rakia, so it became the most popular strong alcoholic drink served in various, more or less formal occasions. The culture of rakia production was encouraged by immense grape fields left by Greeks and Romans. As the production technique was brought by merchants from Far East, Balkan nations started to make brandy from all kinds of fruit, grapes, plum, pear, quince, raspberry, walnuts, etc. It is characteristic in rakia production in southeastern Europe that households mainly produce rakia for their own needs. It is not easy to find good rakia. As any other alcohol, rakia was used in medicinal purposes and was prepared in clay stills but the development of technology enabled its improvement which is the reason people happily consume it today. As with other alcoholic drinks the quality depends on the ingredient's quality as well as the producer's knowledge and the technology at disposal. Today's still come from primitive Mongolian stills heated on open fire. The first stills, or alembics, were made of clay in these parts, and the so called "Serbian domestic stills" are still used in some households that make rakia for their own needs, and they are made of copper and usually are from 75 to 150 liters. Their bottom is made out of thick copper sheet, and its shape is similar to a truncated cone with a lid on top. It is mostly built upon a brick base and has openings for feeding the fire and ventilation. There is also a barrel where the distillate goes, from where the distillate reaches a smaller container used for tasting. Most of the domestic stills were mobile, in order for it to be more convenient to move. In one such neighbourhood there would be a couple of these stills which would be put onto a cart and moved from village to village. Therefore, rakia distilling had a strong social context because it led to socializing in the late autumn and winter months, when villagers gathers around it, got warm, and tasted the new distillates infinitely all the while joking and singing. Due to the hassle and noise people made around stills they also called them "merry machines". It was only after the World War Two that mass production of rakia started, owing to the modernization of stills and the continuous distillation. Out of these and similar standard stills which are already a part of history, came today's modern stills which enable automatization and industrial production of rakia of steady top quality. The process of rakia production starts with picking fruit where the assessment of fruit's ripeness is crucial to schnapps' quality. After the harvest, fruit is ground and left to ferment and, in case of stone fruits, seeds have to be removed before fermentation. Duration of fermentation depends on the temperature as well as the amount of sugar the fruit possesses. After the fermentation is done, the mixture is ready for double distillation in copper stills. The produced brandy is left to age in various wood type casks (oak, mulberry, walnut, cherry, acacia). Depending on the fruit used the rakia will bear the name: plum brandy, apricot brandy, quince brandy, honey brandy, walnut brandy etc. Some of the more famous brands of rakia from home are: Stara Sokolova, Žuta Osa, Kovilj Manastir, Stara Rakija, etc.

Metaxa

Bandy originating in Greece and made from Savatiano, Sultana and red Corintha grapes combined with aged Muscat wine from the island of Samos and Lemnos. Metaxa is divided into the following categories:

3 stars – 3 years

5 stars – 5 years

7 stars – 7 years

12 stars – 12 years

12 stars Grand Olympian Reserve

Private Reserve (can be up to 30 years of age)

Part nineteen

ABSINTHE

"The fatal and attractive green fairy."

- Andrija Ristić, Danilo Božović -

Absinthe

This spirit is also known as "green fairy." Many people think that absinthe is a liqueur. That is not correct, because during distillation of absinthe, sugar is not added. The mysterious green color, as well as various rumors, contributed to its global popularity. It was believed for a long time that after a mere couple of glasses of absinthe a man becomes possessed and goes crazy. The main problem was in its abuse which could not be controlled by the state. First written records about wormwood use (*artemisia absinthium* – a type of wormwood plant) in medicinal purposes were recorded on Ebers Papyrus in ancient Egypt around 1550 BC. In ancient Greece, wormwood extract and its leaves were soaked in wine and used as a remedy for digestive illnesses and gastric problems with gas. The contemporary history of absinthe started during the French revolution (1789 – 1799) when thousands of French loyalists sought asylum in Switzerland, Alaska and other countries. One of the immigrants was Pierre Ordinaire, who escaped to a little town of Kuvet. Pertaining to the popular legend, doctor Ordinaire worked on an herbal elixir using wormwood which was famous for its healing properties. He planned to make a tonic out of herbs which would be easier to drink and tasted better. In 1792, he succeeded by using distillation in his formula which finally had 15 plants infused in a grape spirit. That included wormwood, star anise, licorice, fennel, hyssop, parsley, spinach and coriander, and the tonic was called Extract d' Absinthe.

Commercial absinthe used for drinking, rather than as an elixir, appeared around 1794 and it was made by Abram-Louis Perrenoud. What is certain is that Major Dubied commercialized absinthe. Absinthe sales rose and French society accepted it very well as a new drink and an excellent addition to the limited selection of bitter quinine tonic wines in French cafes. French doctors who prescribed absinthe to soldiers during the war in Algeria as a remedy for malaria, fever, dysentery contributed to the popularity of absinthe. In the 19th century phylloxera ravaged European vineyards and threw wine industry to its knees so cheap and easily accessible absinthe became an excellent alternative. The support of some renowned artist such as Van Gogh, Henry de Toulouse-Lautrec and Picasso, certainly helped absinthe's rise to popularity. The overuse of absinthe produced a syndrome known as absinthism which was characterized by addiction, hyper-sensitivity, irritability and hallucinations. Some of bad effects of absinthe were probably caused by bad ingredients which cheaper manufacturers used like copper-sulfate used to color it and antimony-trichloride. Stories about bad effects of absinthe grew, supported by the scientific studies of Dr. Valentin Mangana, who gave pure extract to animals and published his results as a clear evidence of his theories that this plant caused violent behavior. Modern science got the same results in regards to coffee by giving animals large quantities of pure caffeine. Therefore, doctor's work on absinthe was far from exploratory and hence, far from successful and truthful discovery. Still, he was not dissuaded so he continued to write about absinthe affecting the future generations since the effect of consuming can be transferred from parent to children.

Absinthe was considered responsible for Van Gogh's ear incident but perhaps the most appalling story about absinthe was created in 1905. The story tells of a Swiss farmer Jean Lanfray who, after numerous shots of absinthe, murdered his pregnant wife and two daughters. Nobody took into account that Lanfray was an alcoholic and that he had drunk several liters of wine that day along with a considerable amount of brandy. The bad reputation and rise anti-alcoholic lobbies brought about the ban on absinthe production, firstly in 1898 in the Republic of Congo, then in 1905 in Belgium, followed by Switzerland in 1907 and finally in 1912 in the US. In the meantime, First World War started in France and brought about new bans on absinthe on 16th August 1914 when the Secretary of the interior banned its sales. Absinthe consumption continued for a while, mostly owing to great depositories in storage. In 1932, it finally got banned in Italy by a referendum. Absinthe continued to be produced legally in Czech Republic and Spain and somewhat in Switzerland but remained almost completely forgotten until George William Rowley discovered it again. His La Fee Parisienne was the first grand wormwood absinthe distilled in France after the ban of 1915. His story of getting absinthe back to world scene is interesting but also very long, but what followed was the return of absinthe to London scene. On a great party of Czech Hill's absinthe, in December 1998 in London Groucho Club, what was once known as "absinthe madness" returned again.

Traditional ways of serving absinthe

French method: Pour absinthe slowly over a sugar cube mounted on a perforated spoon, repeat with water and stir.

Czech method: Pour absinthe slowly over a sugar cube, flame the sugar and stir.

American method: Pour sugar syrup, water and absinthe in a mixing glass and briefly shake.

Italian method: Pour sugar, maraschino, water, absinthe and absinthe liqueur in a shaker and briefly shake.

Mister Pernod could not get over the loss of market in 1920 so he launched "Pastis," liqueur with anise base, reminding of absinthe. Pastis differs from absinthe in means of production because Pastis is made by maceration and absinthe through distillation. Absinthe started to come back big time in 1990 and nowadays a great number of Absinthes can be found on the market, although not all of the same quality. Some Absinthes do not possess thujone at all, a substance which is one of the crucial ingredients of absinthe and cannabis.

The flaming technique is mostly practiced in Czech Republic. It caramelizes sugar and is one of the more interesting things one can see at a bar. Some people simply do not like the smell of fire fumes so they opt out of this. During flaming superfine sugar is easier dissolved than brown one and it is recommended that the sugar be in cubes. The style of diluting absinthe with water is a technique practiced in France during which no sugar is added. Absinthe can be consumed with clear, cold water and the proportion should be 3:1 or 5:1 in favor of water. Color is another property that makes absinthe special. Green absinthe gets its color from chlorophyll whereas red absinthe should get its color from hibiscus (in case of other colors absinthe is probably colored by additives). Louche or louching is "whitening" of absinthe by adding water and since anetol (anise's main oil) is not soluble in water it creates an emulsion which gives absinthe white color.

Part twenty

LIQUEURS

"Herbal elixirs."

- Danilo Božović, Andrija Ristić -

Liqueurs

Liqueurs are herbal/fruit beverages that were used in medicinal purposes in the 8th century. They mostly contain around 15% ABV. Some may have more which, of course, depends on the manufacturer. Leaving liqueurs to mature has become very popular in the last few years. People often mistake these for one another (cordial and liqueur). Traditionally the word cordial signifies liqueurs made solely from fruit whereas liqueurs were made from spices and plants.

Bitter liqueurs – they have a dominant aroma of herbs, roots or teas. They are liqueurs with a long and primarily medicinal use: Chartreuse, Benedictine, Galliano are but some of the brand names.

Amaro – Italian adjective for bitter. This category includes: Campari, Fernet Branca, Ramazzoti, Averna Amaro, Cynar.

Emulsion liqueurs - mostly made of eggs, milk coffee or chocolate. More popular brands are: Baileys, Kahlua, Amarula, Sheridans.

Crème liqueurs – they possess considerably higher amounts of sugar that the rest: Crème de banana, Crème de Cassis.

Berry liqueurs – liqueurs made of berry fruits and some of the examples are: Chambord, Crème de Cassis, Cherry Heering and Maraschino.

Fruit liqueurs – they are made by maceration of fruit: Cointreau, Grand Marnier, Curacao, Limoncello.

Whiskey liqueurs – they are liqueurs that have a whiskey base. The representatives are: Drambuie, Southern Comfort, Evan Williams Honey Reserve.

Herbal liqueurs – they possess characteristics of Crème category and are made by maceration of herbs in alcohol. The representatives are: Crème de violette, Crème Yvette, St-Germain.

Stone fruit liqueurs – made of stone fruits. This category includes brands like: Amaretto, Frangelico, Nocello.

How are liqueurs made: process of maceration, percolation and infusion.

Maceration – Maceration is a process where the product (fruit, vegetable, herbs) is left in liquid (water or alcohol) which absorbs its aroma after a period of time and later sugar is added and the level of alcohol raised to the desired level.

Infusion – Infusion is the process similar to maceration during which the product is left in the desired liquid (water or alcohol) in order to absorb the aroma of the product (fruit, herbs or something else). The only difference is that during the process of infusion heat is used, that is, the liquid is heated in order to release the desired aroma. Later, sugar and alcohol levels are regulated.

Percolation – This process uses steam to derive the aroma from spices, fruits etc. Liquid is heated to a boiling point and a sieve with fruit or spices is placed above the container.

The steam coming through the sieve absorbs the aroma and is then condensed and turned into liquid using cooling.

Distillation – Process of distillation usually means distilling alcohol with specific ingredients.

Traditional liqueurs

Benedictine – liqueur made by Benedictine monks from Normandy in 1510. They used 27 different herbal ingredients in the production of this liqueur and it remains one of the most renowned and oldest in the world. Monk who produced this liqueur was called Dom Bernando Vincelli. It is believed that Benedictine liqueur possesses plants from all around the world and legend says that the correct recipe of this liqueur is known to just three people in the whole world. Label D.O.M. on this kind of liqueur means Deus Optimus Maximus which translates to "God, the best, the greatest."

Grand Marnier – liqueur with cognac base which gets its aroma from Haitian bitter oranges. It was made by Alexandre Marnier Lapostolle in 1880. Cordon Rouge and Cordon Jaune are brands that Grand Marnier owns. Cordon Jaune's Yellow Ribbon (of neutral alcohol base) is of lower category than Red Ribbon (cognac based).

Chartreuse – Monks from Massig de la Chartreuse are the ones responsible for the creation of this herbal elixir which was created 300 years ago. Chartreuse consists of 130 different herbs, roots and other ingredients. It is extremely complex and refined with 40 – 55% ABV. Green Chartreuse (55% ABV) consists of 130 ingredients and is of green color (chlorophyll). Yellow Chartreuse (40 – 43% ABV) is a little lighter and sweeter than its green brother.

Campari – is an aperitif consisting of plants, spices, fruits, alcohol, water and sugar. It is of dark red color and bitter taste. In the beginning it was made for medicinal purposes and had the right to be sold during prohibition in America. Campari was made in Italy in 1960 by Gaspare Campari who later founded the first factory in Sesto San Giovanni, near Milan. Besides its bitterness, Campari possesses nice aroma which works well with other drinks.

Cointreau – type of triple sec liqueur made from orange which changed its name to Cointreau in order to be more recognizable than its cousins. The original name of this liqueur was Curacao Bianco Triple Sec Cointreau and was made by brothers Adolphe Cointreau and Edouard-Jean Cointreau in 1849. The key to its success are mixing two types of sweet and bitter oranges.

Chambord – a very popular French liqueur made from black raspberries (from Denmark), blackberries, honey, spices, vanilla and cognac. It is liqueur which dates back to 1685.

Fernet Branca – Italian liqueur of strong herbal aroma, created in 1845 in Milan by Mario Scala. Its ingredients remain a secret but it is suspected that it possesses around 40 ingredients. Fernet Branca is a digestive which is consumed after meals in order to stimulate metabolism and make food absorption easier. It is very famous in bar circles.

Suze – Very popular liqueur among the cocktail lovers and an interesting cocktail ingredient. Suze, a French bitter liqueur that possesses a dominant aroma of the plant gentian, was created in 1885 in Paris thanks to Fernand Moureaux.

Galliano – although it falls under the old liqueurs category it almost belongs to modern liqueurs. It was created in 1896 by Italian distiller, Arturo Vacari from Tuscany. Galliano possesses a strong aroma of vanilla, spices and anise.

Curacao liqueurs – made from dry peels of bitter oranges, this liqueur possess an intense aroma of bitter and sweet.

Part twenty-one

HOUSE-MADE SYRUPS
AND INFUSIONS

"House made ingredients are a true necessity in our craft lineage."

- Ulysses Vidal -

House-made syrups and infusions

Along the journey of becoming a bartender it will become necessary, at some point, to understand how to create house-made ingredients. The idea of bartenders making their own syrups, cordials and infusions is nothing new. Looking back at Jerry Thomas' bar manual one can see the importance of knowing how to produce certain ingredients. This was, more than anything, born out of necessity; a typical bartender in the nineteenth century could not count on buying things like ready-made orgeat or grenadine. The rebirth of the cocktail in the twenty-first century saw bartenders being subjected to learning this aspect of the craft as numerous people and their modern, ready-made products slowly filled gaps in the market. In the United States, a barkeep now has the option of purchasing ingredients which are ready to serve, complete with nutrition facts, stabilizing agents and other safety standards thanks to the passage of the Food and Drug Act—something that was not in place in the nineteenth century. Bartenders of today can source things like grenadine, orgeat, bloody mary mix, and syrups and bitters of all sorts of colors and flavors. This is just the beginning. The convenience of all this is that it opens up the ability to explore new flavors and essences to be captured. A barkeep who has taken the time to make his or her own basic ingredients will ultimately be able to capitalize on the abundance of fresh produce, herbs and spices the world has to offer, thus providing a creative edge in the execution of new ideas.

Syrups

One of the most basic components in a well-balanced drink comes in the form of sweetness—the go-to being simple syrup. The quintessential simple syrup, part of every bartender's operation, is comprised of white sugar and water. The ratio of sugar to water used is entirely dependent on what the bartender desires in his or her syrup. A ratio of 1:1 is commonly used to achieve a basic syrup; its consistency and sweetness are just enough to make execution of recipes easy. Most bartenders will find that a sugar-to-water ratio of 2:1 has superb advantages in making cocktails. This ratio is commonly known as "rich" simple syrup. The end result is that cocktails can be sweetened while minimizing the amount of water and thus, dilution in the final product. Another thing to take into consideration is the texture that this will give the cocktail. In addition to these aesthetic advantages a bartender will find the "rich" syrup less likely to spoil as fast as the basic syrup since more sugar is present to keep microbial growth at a minimum.

Of course, one would hope business is good enough to not have to even take this into consideration. Simple syrups should be kept in a cool, refrigerated environment to maintain their freshness. Because the density of sugar and water are not the same, measuring each one individually will achieve a more accurate ratio. Furthermore, knowing more about the types of sugar being used is pivotal. The sugars used to make syrups are various. White sugar, having already been mentioned, comes in various forms. The most common is ordinary table sugar, which is most likely what bartenders will come across. This sugar dissolves well into a syrup, though it does require a good amount of agitation and heat. Super-fine sugar features much smaller crystals which will dissolve rather easily, often without any heat required. Even more fine than this is "powdered" sugar although it is not a good candidate due to the inclusion of starch, usually around 3%, to prevent caking. White table sugar and super-fine are both acceptable types of sugar to use in making syrups and cordials, although super-fine is easier to work with. Brown sugars are another category to take into consideration. These are typically more flavorful than their white counterparts. The two most common used in bartending are demerara and turbinado. Demerara is the result of early crystallization of cane juice. Its golden color and rich aromas of vanilla and butter make it a prime candidate for "rich" simple syrups. It is, however, much more coarse than the above-mentioned white sugars and as a result, requires substantial agitation (a good whisk is useful here) along with high heat. A syrup made from brown sugars will give a cocktail more depth, as is the case for Old-Fashioneds. Making flavored syrups will give a bartender a particular edge and flexibility when making cocktails. There is no shortage of liqueurs and fruit based eaux-de-vies available on the market which can be used to give a cocktail the desired flavor but the advantage to using a syrup is that the freshness of the ingredients can make it superbly potent. A good example might be raspberry syrup, essential to making great drinks such as the Clover Club. Sure, one could use a framboise liqueuer or eaux-de-vie to give it the raspberry flavor but a proper syrup is what truly makes the drink shine. It is important to note fruit-flavored syrups will spoil much sooner than simple syrups. When cooking your own syrups, take time to consider the fruit you are using. For raspberry or pineapple, white sugar is perfectly sufficient. For something like banana, you might find that brown sugars are even better. Aside from white and brown sugars there are other sweeteners such as agave nectar, honey, molasses, cane syrups and even coconut sugar. Each of these has its own flavor profiles and consistencies, and like the white and brown sugars can be infused with different flavors. Agave nectar can be infused with different types of chiles or honey can be given orange peel and vanilla bean to give it more complexity. Date molasses can be diluted with hot water to make it less viscous and then used in cocktails for a nice date flavor that might otherwise be especially difficult to capture. Nut syrups are an especially enticing ingredient to master. Orgeat syrup, made out of almonds, water, and sugar is another product whose authenticity was lost for a long time. Almond-flavored syrups have been, for a long time, easy to find. Just about any coffee shop will feature one or two. These, however, pale in comparison to what can be accomplished by a savvy bartender in the kitchen. Using two parts almond milk to one part white sugar and infusing the mix with orange-flower water will yield a suitable orgeat syrup. However, the potent almond flavor so many of us enjoy is not really present in the almonds that are safe for consumption. Almond flavoring is usually derived from bitter almonds—which are actually poisonous and must undergo a process to separate the flavor from the toxic chemicals—or it may also be found in the pits of apricots.

Whatever the source, adding some almond extract to the orgeat will complete it and now the bartender can make anything from an outstanding Mai-Tai to a Japanese Cocktail. Almond milk itself is an easy item to purchase but is also feasible—though time consuming—to make from scratch. Other nut milks might not be available in the grocery store so if the bartender wishes to have say a pistachio or hazelnut syrup, they should learn to make a milk out of those nuts and then they may be able to experiment from there with the addition of sugar, extracts and other accents.

Infusions

Finding ways to incorporate desired flavors and aromas into alcohol is one of the oldest methods for consuming alcohol in the first place. Ancient civilizations, no doubt explored ways to give their beers and wine some edge by adding flowers and herbs—long before the creation of vermouths we all know and love today. And in the age of distillation it was the perfume-making process that inspired people to throw wine or beer into the still to see what would come out. Shortly after realizing the isolation of spirits, there was no hesitation to infuse these products with herbs, spices and fruit.

The most helpful thing in learning how to infuse is understanding the relationship between the proof of what you want to infuse and the medium of the item with which you wish to infuse it with. A higher-proof spirit will do a much better job of absorbing flavors than a lower-proof spirit or wine. Furthermore, the manner in which items are introduced will have an impact on both the potency and time it takes to achieve desired results. Dried fruits herbs and peels will infuse into a high-proof spirit much faster and with more potency than fresh fruit or wet herbs might in a low-proof wine. The former setup is how bitters get made and explains their potency whereas vermouth is somewhat mellower. The amount of time needed to achieve an infusion is dependent not only on the proof and form in which ingredients are being added but also on the method for bringing the two together. The most rudimentary method a typical bartender can employ with great ease is to simply combine everything and let it sit for days or weeks. This has its drawbacks since the business need to continue with or without the infusions being available. An especially high-volume establishment might benefit from "cooking" the mixtures and then letting them cool to room temperature. Combining the spirit or wine with the infusion ingredients in a small pot and then heating the mixture up just enough to make a sort of "tea" can accomplish this. To prevent alcohol from evaporating, the bartender should place a metal mixing bowl filled with ice water, over the top of the pot so that it covers the edges. The cold mixing bowl will cause alcohol to condensate and recollect. Heating the infusion should be done just long enough to get hot and should be removed immediately from the stove top. Setting the pot in an ice bath while still keeping the iced-down mixing bowl in place will bring the infusion back an acceptable temperature while also recapturing any alcohol that could have otherwise been lost.

Other methods for infusing can be applied with ease by a barkeep assuming he or she has access to some equipment and materials. Vacuum sealing the contents of an infusion can bring about some excellent results in a short period of time but using nitrous oxide has gained great popularity. This method is executed using a cream whipper and nitrous oxide charge to create an infusion almost instantly and with great results.

Cordials

Now that the bartender has learned to make syrups and infusions, he or she may move on to the next step of creating an entire cordial from scratch. Cordials are a great way to bring flavors, accents, sugar and alcohol together in a complete product that is not only shelf-stable but also extraordinarily flexible in multiple cocktail concepts. The great reward in learning how to execute syrups and infusions is that it sets the bartender up to create something which is patently his or her own creation. In the same way that Benedictine or Cynar are near axiomatic products—complete and with little to no worthy competition—speaks volumes of how the cordial or liqueur making process can make a bartender's stock of ingredients highly coveted and maybe someday, profitable outside his or her own bar. Mastering the ability to make your own creative cordial based on whatever you can think of will allow you to execute new cocktail creations and hopefully, modern classics future generations of bartenders will want to learn. If you wish to make something like a bell pepper or chamomile or even a coriander cordial, go for it. The first thing to take into consideration is the nature of the focal ingredient you are using. For a chamomile or hibiscus cordial, try cooking a "tea" of dried leaves and water, adding sugar for sweetness to create a syrup. Next, add alcohol to stabilize and add more flavor. The tea can be enhanced as well by adding other herbs, spices or citrus peels. There are plenty of resources that can help guide the bartender in creating full-flavored and well-balanced cordials. Knowing what herbs and spices work with certain fruits, for example, will give the liqueur an edge. Adding alcohol for fortification based on its own flavor profile will also contribute to the overall product.

Part twenty-two

CLASSIC COCKTAILS

"Classic cocktail, the foundation of all drinks."

- Danilo Božović -

Americano

1 ¼ oz. Campari

1 ¼ oz. sweet vermouth

slice of orange

Top up with club soda

Method: Pour Campari and vermouth into a Collins glass, add ice and a slice of orange. Cap shake and add club soda.

History: Americano comes from Turin and was created in 1861. It used to be called Milano-Turino but due to great popularity among the American tourists visiting Italy the name was changed to Americano.

Dominant aromas: biter fruit and spices

Body: light

Dryness: dry

Complexity: medium

Finish: bitter sweet with a refreshing finish

Aviation

2 oz. gin

1 oz. lemon juice

¾ oz. Maraschino liqueur

¼ oz. sugar syrup (2:1 sugar to water)

Splash of Creme de viollete

2 dashes of Angostura bitters

Method: Shake all the ingredients with ice. Strain the cocktail into a chilled cocktail glass and garnish with a brandied cherry.

History: This cocktail is first mentioned in 1916 in Recipes for Mixed Drinks written by Hugo Ensslin, head bartender of Wallick Hotel, New York City. Aviation is a cocktail dedicated to Wright brothers for successfully creating an aircraft on 17th December, 1903. Aviation reminds of sky in color which it gets from Creme de viollete or Creme de yvette. Creme de viollete was the original ingredient of Aviation but in time lost popularity and simply disappeared.

Dominant aromas: herbal and citrus.

Body: light

Dryness: medium to dry

Complexity: medium

Finish: citrus note with maraschino and juniper background

Bellini

2 oz. peach puree

½ oz. peach liqueur

5 oz. sparkling wine or Champagne

Method: Pour all ingredients into the mixing glass. Slowly stir and strain the cocktail into a chilled Champagne flute glass.

History: Bellini was made in 1945 in Harry's bar in Venice by Giuseppe Cipriani. The cocktail got its name after a renaissance artist Giovanni Bellini.

Dominant aromas: white peach

Body: medium

Dryness: semi-dry

Complexity: low with a distinct aroma of peach and light citrus note of the sparkling wine

Finish: short, sparkling and sweet

When stirring in the mixing glass, do not stir too vigorously in order to not make it foam and slow the service down.

Black Russian

1 ¾ oz. vodka

1 ¾ oz. coffee liqueur

Method: Pour all ingredients into an Old fashioned glass, easily stir and serve.

History: The drink was invented by Gustave Tops in Metropol hotel in Brussels.

Dominant aromas: coffee aroma

Body: medium

Dryness: semi-dry

Complexity: low with elegant coffee aroma

Finish: medium with a note of coffee

Try not make and serve the cocktail stronger than it should be because it will not taste pleasant to most guests.

Blood and Sand

1 oz. Scotch whisky

1 oz. Cherry Heering

1 oz. sweet vermouth

1 oz. orange juice

Method: Shake all ingredients with ice. Strain the cocktail into a chilled cocktail glass and garnish with a orange twist and discard.

History: Blood and Sand got its name after the silent movie from 1922 which starred Rudolf Valentino.

Dominant aromas: light smoky whisky with sour cherry

Body: medium

Dryness: low to medium

Complexity: medium

Finish: presence of smoke, refreshing touch of sour cherry and orange

Bloody Mary

1 ¾ vodka

2 dashes Worcestershire sauce

4 dashes Tabasco sauce

¼ oz. lemon juice

4 oz. tomato juice

Pinch of salt and pepper

Method: Pour all ingredients into a Collins glass, cover it with cap-shaker and mix the cocktail with easy up and down wrist movements (rolling technique). Repeat these movements a couple of times until the cocktail becomes cool, but as easily as you can, in order not to ruin the texture of tomato juice. Garnish with a lemon wedge and three olives.

History: This cocktail was created in Harry's bar in Paris in 1920.

Dominant aromas: tomato and spices

Body: medium to heavy

Dryness: low

Complexity: low to medium

Brandy Crusta

1 ¾ oz. brandy

½ oz. triple sec

½ oz. Maraschino liqueur

½ oz. lemon juice

1 dash of Orange bitters

Method: Shake all the ingredients with ice, strain the cocktail into a chilled cocktail glass with a sugar rim and garnish the cocktail with a long orange spiral peel.

History: The first recipes of Crusta family cocktail are found in Jerry Thomas' 1862 book, *How to Mix All Kinds of Plain and Fancy Drinks*. Legend has it that this cocktail was invented by Mr. Santina, a famous Spanish caterer.

Dominant aromas: whisky with citrus and maraschino notes

Body: light to medium

Dryness: low

Complexity: low to medium

Finish: presence of brandy after a light aroma of maraschino and orange

Brandy Cobbler

2 oz. brandy

¾ oz. Grand Marnier

1 pineapple wedge

1 wheel of orange

1 lemon wedge

Method: Muddle the fruit in a mixing glass, add water (to taste), Grand Marnier and brandy. Shake vigorously and strain the cocktail into an Old-fashioned glass over crushed ice. Garnish the cocktail with a slice of orange, lemon and pineapple wedge.

History: This cocktail family got its name after cobbles, shape of ice served in it. Traditional ingredients include wine (sherry) and ice.

Dominant aromas: citrus

Body: light to medium

Dryness: low

Complexity: low to medium

Finish: dry and refreshing

Caipirinha

2 oz. Cachaca

3 table spoons of superfine sugar

3 lime wedges

Method: Muddle lime and sugar in the mixing glass, add Cachaca and shake vigorously. Pour everything into an Old fashioned glass.

History: The word Caipirinha means "little village beverage" in Portuguese and represents a drink that rose to popularity on Brazil's sugar cane plantations.

Dominant aromas: citrus and sugar cane

Body: light

Dryness: low

Complexity: medium

Finish: refreshing with citrus notes

Champagne Cocktail

½ oz. brandy

¼ oz. Grand Marnier

1 sugar cube

3 dash of Angostura bitters

6 oz. Champagne

Method: Soak the sugar cube with Angostura bitters and place it on the bottom of a chilled Champagne flute glass. Add Grand Marnier and brandy into the Champagne glass. Top up the with Champagne and garnish with a orange twist and discard.

Dominant aromas: champagne with fruity aromas

Body: light

Dryness: medium

Complexity: low

Finish: sparkling and refreshing

Clover Club

1 ½ oz. gin

½ oz. raspberry liqueur

½ oz. sugar syrup (2:1 – sugar to water)

1 oz. lemon juice

1 egg white

Method: Dry-shake all ingredients, add large ice and shake vigorously. Strain the cocktail into a chilled cocktail glass.

History: The first record of this classic's recipe can be found in Albert Stevens Crocket's book, *Bar Days*, from 1931.

Dominant aromas: juniper and raspberry

Body: medium

Dryness: medium to high

Complexity: medium

Finish: dry herbals with fresh raspberry

Corpse Reviver #2

1 oz. gin

1 oz. Cointreau

1 oz. Lillet Blanc

¾ oz. lemon juice

¼ oz. Absinthe

Method: Shake vigorously all ingredients with ice. Strain the cocktail into a chilled cocktail glass.

History: Harry Craddock best described this cocktail in his book *The Savoy Cocktail Book*: "Four of those taken in swift succession will revive the corpse again."

Dominant aromas: juniper and anise

Body: light to medium

Dryness: medium

Complexity: low to medium

Finish: citrus with juniper and anise aroma

Cosmopolitan

1 ¾ oz. citrus vodka

1 oz. Cointreau

¾ oz. cranberry juice

½ oz. lime juice

Method: Shake all ingredients with ice. Strain the cocktail into a chilled cocktail glass and garnish with an orange twist.

History: There are many stories about the creation of Cosmopolitan; Sheryl Cook is one of the people credited with its creation, whereas Dale DeGroff and Toby Cecchini are credited for popularizing it.

Dominant aromas: citrus and cranberry

Body: light

Dryness: medium to low

Complexity: low

Finish: citrus fruit with a hint of cranberry

Cuba Libre

2 oz. rum

4 oz. Coca Cola

1 lime wedge

2 dashes of Angostura bitters

Method: Pour rum into a Highball glass, add ice, Coca Cola and Angostura bitters. Press the juice from one lime wedge into the glass. Place a fresh lime wedge on the rim of the glass.

History: The creation of this cocktail is linked to the appearance of Coca Cola on Cuba, at the start of 20th century, which was mixed with alcohol by American soldiers.

Dominant aromas: Cola and sugar cane

Body: light to medium

Dryness: low

Complexity: low

Finish: Coca Cola with presence of strong sugar cane spirit

The addition of Angostura bitters to a Cuba Libre was a delicious touch I saw from Jason Kosmas, while enjoying a Cana Brava rum Cuba Libre in Panama.

Daiquiri

2 oz. rum

1 oz. lime juice

½ oz. simple syrup (2:1 – sugar to water)

Method: Shake all ingredients with ice. Strain the cocktail into a chilled cocktail glass and garnish with a lime wheel.

History: It is hard to say when this cocktail was created. According to legend, Daiquiri was first made in Santiago in a bar called Venus which was located near the Daiquiri beach on Cuba. All the credit goes to Jenning Cox, general manager of the Spanish – American steel factory.

Dominant aromas: citrus

Body: light

Dryness: low to medium

Complexity: low

Finish: citrus notes with sugar cane aromas

Note: Daiquiri should be shaken vigorously for a long time in order for ingredients to better mix and provide a better cocktail.

All simple syrup recipes mentioned in this book recommend the 2:1 sugar to water ratio.

Dark 'N' Stormy

2 oz. dark rum

4 oz. ginger beer

½ oz. lime juice

1 thin slice fresh gingerroot

splash of Velvet Falernum

Method: Muddle the ginger. Shake Velvet Falernum, muddled ginger and lime juice vigorously. Add ginger beer. Strain the cocktail with a Julep strainer into a Collins glass over ice and slowly top up with dark rum. Garnish with a lime wheel.

History: Dark 'n' Stormy is the national drink of Bermuda which is traditionally made in the Naval Officer's club. On Bermuda, the residents consume it without lime juice.

Dominant aromas: ginger

Body: light

Dryness: low

Complexity: low

Finish: ginger with full rum aroma

French 75

1 ½ oz. gin

1 oz. lemon juice

¾ oz. simple syrup (2:1 – sugar to water)

4 oz. sparkling wine or Champagne

Method: Shake all ingredients except sparkling wine or Champagne. Strain the cocktail into a chilled Champagne flute glass. Add sparkling wine or Champagne and garnish the cocktail with a brandied cherry.

History: Harry Craddock wrote about this cocktail in his book *The Savoy Cocktail Book* written in 1930. Cocktail got its name after the cannon which French and Americans use in the First World War.

Dominant aromas: citrus and juniper

Body: light

Dryness: high

Complexity: low

Finish: refreshing and sparkling with herbal aromas

Gin Gimlet

2 oz. gin

1 oz. lime juice

½ oz. simple syrup (2:1 – sugar to water)

Method: Shake all ingredients with ice. Strain the cocktail into an Old fashioned glass over fresh ice and garnish with a lime wheel.

History: Legend has it that Sir Thomas D. Gimlet, surgeon of the British Royal Navy, created the first gimlet in order to prevent scurvy on the ship. True lovers of this cocktail ask for rose's lime syrup in their gimlet and most bars today make this cocktail with fresh lime juice.

Dominant aromas: lime and juniper

Body: medium

Dryness: semi-dry

Complexity: low

Finish: juniper pleasantly joined with lime and sugar

Hemingway Daiquiri

1 ¾ oz. rum

¾ oz. grapefruit juice

½ oz. maraschino liqueur

½ oz. lime juice

¼ oz. simple syrup (2:1 – sugar to water)

Method: Shake all the ingredients with ice. Strain the cocktail into a chilled cocktail glass and garnish with a lime flag.

History: This cocktail got its name after one of the most famous American writers, Earnest Hemingway. The cocktail also bears the name Papa Doble, since Hemingway used to order a double cocktail in El Floridita bar in Cuba.

Dominant aromas: citrus with maraschino background

Body: light to medium

Dryness: low to medium

Complexity: medium to high

Finish: dry citrus notes with fleeting aromas of maraschino and sugar cane.

By adding dry rum to Hemingway Daiquiri the charm of this cocktail are amplified.

Hot Toddy

1 ¾ oz. whiskey or rum

½ oz. lemon juice

¾ oz. agave or honey syrup

4 oz. hot water

Method: Pour all ingredients into a mug glass. Garnish with a cinnamon stick and a lemon wheel.

History: Toddy is a cocktail served hot.

Dominant aromas: whiskey with citrus

Body: light

Dryness: semi-dry

Complexity: low

Finish: whiskey softened with citrus and honey

Agave or honey are perfect sweeteners for this cocktail

Irish Coffee

1 ¾ oz. Irish whiskey

2 table spoons of sugar

4 oz. espresso

Top up with whipped cream

Method: Flame Irish whiskey and sugar in a mug glass, let the flame die out, add fresh coffee and top up the rest of the cocktail with whipped cream. Garnish with three coffee beans.

History: This drink was made by cook Joseph Sheridan from Ireland in order to welcome his guest during winter as best as he could.

Dominant aromas: whiskey and coffee

Body: light

Dryness: semi-dry Complexity: low

Finish: whiskey in coffee and cream background

Kir Royale

½ oz. creme de cassis

6 oz. sparkling wine or Champagne

Method: Slowly pour sparkling wine or Champagne and liqueur into a chilled Champagne flute glass. Garnish with a lemon twist and discard.

History: Kir Royale was a cocktail which celebrated the popular cassis liqueur from Dijon in France. All the credits to popularization of this cocktail belong to former mayor of Dijon, Canon Felix.

Dominant aromas: black currant and Champagne

Body: light

Dryness: semi-dry

Complexity: low

Finish: sparkling with a sweet note of black currant

Last word

1 oz. gin

1 oz. maraschino liqueur

1 oz. green Chartreuse liqueur

1 oz. lime juice

Method: Shake all ingredients with ice. Strain the cocktail into a chilled cocktail glass.

Dominant aromas: juniper, maraschino and herbals

Body: light

Dryness: semi-dry

Complexity: low to medium

Finish: juniper in a perfect balance with maraschino and herbals

Mai Tai

2 oz. rum

½ oz. almond syrup

½ oz. Orange Curacao liqueur

½ oz. lime juice

Top up with Angostura bitters and aged rum

Method: Shake all ingredients except Angostura bitters and the aged rum, strain the cocktail into an Old fashioned glass over fresh ice. Top up the rest of the cocktail with Angostura bitters (3 dashes) and aged rum (1 drizzle). Garnish with a lime wheel and a mint top.

History: This cocktail, whose name means "the best" in Tahitian, was made by Victor Bergeron. Victor, or Trader Vic as he was called, would serve this cocktail to his friends who would exclaim "Roa re" while drinking it which means "The best."

Dominant aromas: citrus with a note of sugar cane and almond

Body: light

Dryness: semi-dry

Complexity: medium to high

Finish: outstanding flavor of citrus, almond and rum

Manhattan

1 ½ oz. 100 proof rye whiskey

1 ¾ oz. sweet vermouth

¼ oz. Grand Marnier

3 dashes of Angostura bitters

Method: Stir all ingredients in a mixing glass. Strain the cocktail into a chilled cocktail glass and garnish with a lemon twist.

History: The first article about Manhattan was published in 1882 in *NY Democrat* magazine.

Dominant aromas: rye and floral aromas

Body: light

Dryness: semi-dry

Complexity: high

Finish: spicy rye whiskey with floral and herbal vermouth aromas and citrus notes.

During the free pour, it is easier to make a Manhattan if one starts with vermouth first.

Margarita

2 oz. tequila 100% blue agave

1 oz. lime juice

¾ oz. Cointreau

½ oz. agave nectar

Method: Shake all ingredients with ice. Strain the cocktail into an Old fashioned glass over fresh ice and garnish with a lime wheel (salted rim optional).

History: Margarita is part of Daisy cocktail family (alcohol, orange liqueur and citrus). America has been drinking tequila Daisies since 1936, and legend has it that this cocktail was made by Margarita Sames in 1948.

Dominant aromas: citrus note with floral note of tequila

Body: medium

Dryness: semi-dry

Complexity: medium

Finish: medium

A good Margarita needs a slightly longer and vigorous shake.

Martinez

2 ¼ oz. gin (57% ABV)

1 oz. sweet vermouth

½ oz. Maraschino liqueur

¼ oz. Absinthe

Method: Stir all ingredients with ice. Strain the cocktail into a chilled cocktail glass (half sugar rim optional) and garnish with a lemon twist.

History: Legend has it that this cocktail was the predecessor to Martini. Martinez was first mentioned in Jerry Thomas' book, *Bartender's Guide*, and the recipe in this book was created by Jason Kosmas and Dushan Zaric, owners of Employees Only and Macao Trading Co.

Dominant aromas: juniper with background of anise and citrus

Body: light

Dryness: semi-dry

Complexity: high

Finish: juniper in herbal aroma of vermouth and maraschino

Martini

3 oz. gin

¾ oz. dry vermouth

1 dash of orange bitters

Method: Stir all ingredients in a mixing glass. Strain the cocktail into a chilled cocktail glass and garnish with a lemon twist.

History: The Martini is the king of cocktails and it is the peak of cocktail culture. It was first mentioned in Harry Johnson's book, *New and Improved Bartender's Manual,* from 1888.

Dominant aromas: juniper

Body: light

Dryness: high

Complexity: high

Finish: dry with elegant presence of juniper, herbals and citrus notes of orange and lemon.

Martini should be extremely cold with an oily texture and in case of vodka-martini vigorously shaken. It is not advised to have lumps of ice on top (during straining leave a minimal space between Hawthorne strainer and the shaker). Dirty Martini should have ½ oz. of vermouth in order for olive juice to better merge with vodka or gin.

Mint Julep

2 oz. bourbon whiskey

3 dashes of Angostura bitters

3 tablespoons of superfine sugar

Splash of soda or carbonated water

Spray peach liqueur

Pinch of mint

Method: Add mint, sugar and bitters into an Old fashioned glass or a Julep Cup. Spray the glass with peach liqueur. Easily muddle the ingredients in the glass. Add bourbon, crushed ice and slowly top up the glass with soda or carbonated water. Garnish with a bouquet of mint tops.

History: This southern delicacy became popular in the beginning of 20th century. The author of *The Mint Julep* book, Richard Barksdale Harwell, claims that this cocktail was first written about in 1803.

Dominant aromas: whiskey with mint and spices

Body: medium

Dryness: semi-dry

Complexity: medium

Finish: refreshing mint with full flavor of spices and whiskey

Mojito

1 ¾ oz. rum

3 tablespoons of superfine sugar

1 oz. lime juice

½ oz. simple syrup (2:1 – sugar to water)

Pinch of mint

Top up with club soda

2 dashes of Angostura bitters

Method: Add mint and sugar into Collins glass and muddle slowly, add lime juice, simple syrup, rum and cap shake. Add crushed ice and top up the rest with club soda. Add Angostura bitters and garnish with a mint top.

History: Mojito is a very popular drink in the world, especially among the Cuban worker's class. At the start of 19th century Mojito became the trademark of Bodeguita del Medio bar in Cube which was frequented by Earnest Hemingway. Legend has it that famous pirate, Francis Drake, consumed a beverage made from rum, sugar, lime and mint called Drake which resembled today's Mojito.

Dominant aromas: rum and mint

Body: light

Dryness: semi-dry

Complexity: low

Finish: rum followed by presence of mint, citrus and herbal note of Angostura bitters.

Moscow Mule

2 oz. vodka

½ oz. lime juice

4 ½ oz. ginger beer

1 thin slice fresh gingerroot

Method: Muddle the ginger. Shake vodka, muddled ginger and lime juice vigorously. Strain the cocktail with a Julep strainer into a copper mug over ice. Add ginger beer and garnish with a lime wedge.

History: Moscow Mule was the cocktail responsible for spreading vodka popularity in the US and it was made by John Martin, representative of Hublein Company, the American distributor of Smirnoff vodka, and Jack Morgan, owner of Cock 'n' Bull restaurant chain

Dominant aromas: ginger and citrus

Body: light

Dryness: high

Complexity: low

Finish: presence of citrus and ginger vodka character

Negroni

1 ¼ oz. gin

1 ¼ oz. Campari

1 ¼ oz. sweet vermouth

Method: Stir all ingredients in a mixing glass. Strain the cocktail into an Old fashioned glass over fresh ice and garnish with a slice of orange and an orange twist. Discard the twist.

History: In 1920, bartender Fosco Scarselli got the inspiration to , after the request of his guest, Count Camillo Negroni, make a stronger Americano, because of which Fosco added gin instead of soda and made a first Negroni.

Dominant aromas: herbal and liqueur bitterness

Body: medium

Dryness: medium to low

Complexity: high

Finish: herbals with a subtle bittersweet presence

f ice is dry and large, Negroni is recommended to be stirred a little longer. In case of free pour, one should use both hands to pour Campari and vermouth. This way the bartender makes it easier on him self to balance properly this great classic. A good Negroni should give off a refreshing sensation.

Old Fashioned

2 oz. 100 proof rye or bourbon whiskey

3 dashes of Angostura bitters

2 dash of Orange bitters

2 dash of Peychaud's bitters

1 cube of brown sugar

1 tablespoon of superfine sugar

3 splashes of water

Method: Place the sugar, bitters and water in an Old fashioned glass, muddle the ingredients and add whiskey. Add ice and stir all ingredients. Top up the cocktail with one or two ice cubes. Garnish with a lemon and orange twist.

History: Old Fashioned was known as Whiskey Cocktail before. Legend has it that it was created by Colonel James E. Pepper, a distiller of bourbon who worked as a bartender in Pendennis club in Kentucky.

Dominant aromas: whiskey and bitters

Body: medium

Dryness: semi-dry

Complexity: high

Finish: whiskey followed by aromatic bitters and subtle herbal texture

One should try to always place superfine sugar in the cocktail firstly in order to make it easier to measure the amount of sugar in the cocktail.

Old Pal

1 oz. 100 proof rye whiskey

1 ¼ oz. dry vermouth

1 ¼ oz. Campari

Method: Stir all ingredients in a mixing glass. Strain the cocktail into a chilled cocktail glass and garnish with a lemon twist.

History: Old Pal was first mentioned in Harry MacElhone's *ABC of Mixing Cocktails* from 1922. Here, Harry maintains that this cocktail was made by Sparrow Robertson, editor of New York Herald at the time.

Dominant aromas: rye and spices

Body: medium

Dryness: semi-dry

Complexity: high

Finish: whiskey followed by aromatics of bitters and spices

Pimm's Cup

1 ¾ oz. Pimm's No. 1

¾ oz. Cointreau

¾ oz. lime juice

3 oz. ginger ale

3 slices of cucumber

Pinch of mint

Method: Pour all ingredients into a Collins glass, add mint, cucumber and ice. Cap shake and top up with ginger ale.

History: The recipe in this book was created by Jason Kosmas and Dushan Zaric, owners of Employees Only and Macao Trading Co.

Dominant aromas: spices and ginger

Body: light

Dryness: dry

Complexity: low

Finish: herbals in combination with ginger and fruit

Piña Colada

1 ¾ oz. rum

1 oz. coconut puree

½ oz. heavy cream

¼ oz. lime juice

¼ oz. coconut syrup

4 oz. pineapple juice

2 dashes of barrel aged bitters

Method: Place all ingredients into a blender except the bitters, add crushed ice and blend for 20 seconds. Pour the cocktail into a Hurricane glass and add bitters. Garnish with a pineapple and an umbrella.

History: Pina Colada comes from the Caribbean and it was first made in Beachcomber bar in Caribbean Hilton in 1954. The first records of this cocktail can be found in the book *Mixologist: The Journal of the American Bar.*

Dominant aromas: rum and coconut

Body: medium to heavy

Dryness: medium

Complexity: low

Finish: refreshing presence of coconut and pineapple

Pisco Sour

2 oz. Pisco

1 oz. lime juice

½ oz. sugar syrup (2:1 – sugar to water)

1 egg white

3 drops of Angostura bitters

grated nutmeg

Method: Dry shake, add large ice and shake vigorously. Strain the cocktail into a chilled cocktail glass. Garnish with three drops of Angostura bitters and grated nutmeg.

History: Pisco Sour rose to popularity in San Francisco in 1849 during the Gold rush.

Dominant aromas: grapes and citrus

Body: medium

Dryness: dry

Complexity: medium

Finish: dry aroma with egg white texture and a citrus background

Ramos Gin Fizz

1 ¾ oz. gin (57% ABV)

1 oz. lemon juice

¾ oz. sugar syrup (2:1 – sugar to water)

¼ oz. Green Chartreuse

1 oz. heavy cream

1 egg white

5 drops orange flower water

Top up with club soda

Method: Dry shake. Add large ice and shake vigorously until the shaker becomes very cold (frozen). Pour the cocktail into a Collins glass over two ice cubes and add soda. Garnish with orange slice and a brandied cherry.

History: This is a classic American cocktail from New Orleans made by Henry Ramos in 1800. Legend has it that cocktail were made by special men behind bar called "shaker boys" who would shake the cocktail for twelve minutes each time it was ordered which secured the balanced texture from top to bottom. It is very hard to whip sweet cream, egg white and other ingredients in order for them to be constant from the first to the last sip

Dominant aromas: juniper, creamy aroma and citrus

Body: medium

Dryness: dry

Complexity: high

Finish: juniper in the background of creamy and refreshing body with mildly present citrus note

Rob Roy

1 ¾ oz. blended Scotch whisky

1 ½ oz. sweet vermouth

¼ oz. Benedictine liqueur

3 dashes of Angostura bitters

Method: Stir all ingredients. Strain the cocktail into a chilled cocktail glass and garnish with a orange twist.

History: Rob Roy was created in 1987 in New York and it represents an impressive variation of Manhattan with Scotch whisky.

Dominant aromas: whisky and smoke

Body: medium

Dryness: dry

Complexity: high

Finish: presence of whisky smoke with tender tones of vermouth and orange

Sazerac

2 oz. cognac

¼ oz. absinthe

1 cube of brown sugar

1 tablespoon of superfine sugar

2 dashes of Angostura bitters

3 dashes of Peychaud's bitters

Method: Pour absinthe on the bottom of a glass. Add crushed ice and leave it to cool and louche. Add sugar and bitters into a mixing glass, muddle the ingredients and add cognac. Stir the cocktail and strain into an empty chilled glass. Garnish with a lemon twist and discard.

History: Sazerac was made by a French pharmacist Antoine Amedie Peychaud. The integral parts of the cocktail are its bitters without which this cocktail would not be what it is and legend has it that throwing a glass of absinthe in the air and saying "Sazerac" brings good luck.

Dominant aromas: cognac and bitters

Body: medium

Dryness: semi-dry

Complexity: high

Finish: cognac perfectly balanced with anise, wormwood and spices.

Firstly one should pour superfine sugar in order to easier measure its amount in the cocktail.

Sidecar

2 oz. cognac

1 oz. Cointreau

½ oz. lemon juice

Method: Shake all ingredients. Strain into a chilled cocktail glass with a sugar coated rim and garnish with an orange twist and discard.

History: This cocktail was presented for the first time in Robert Verneire's book *Cocktails: How to Mix Them*, written in 1922.

Dominant aromas: cognac and orange

Body: light

Dryness: dry

Complexity: low to medium

Finish: elegant aroma of cognac with citrus notes

Gin Singapore Sling

1 ½ oz. gin

½ oz. Cointreau

½ oz. Benedictine

3 oz. pineapple juice

½ oz. lime juice

¼ oz. grenadine

1 dash of Angostura bitters

Method: Shake all ingredients. Strain the cocktail into a collins glass over fresh ice and garnish with an orange slice.

History: Bartender Ngiam Tong Boon from Raffles Hotel in Singapore invented this cocktail in 1913.

Dominant aromas: juniper and pineapple

Body: light to medium

Dryness: semi-dry

Complexity: low to medium

Finish: juniper with presence of pineapple, spices and fruit

Tom Collins

2 oz. gin

1 oz. lemon juice

¾ oz. simple syrup (2:1- sugar to water)

Top up with club soda

Method: Shake all ingredients except soda. Strain the cocktail into a Collins glass over fresh ice. Top up with soda and garnish with a lemon flag.

History: The cocktail was created in the beginning of 19th century in London. The original Tom Collins was made with Old Tom gin to which sugar was traditionally added in order for the cocktail to have a more pleasant taste.

Dominant aromas: juniper and citrus

Body: light

Dryness: dry

Complexity: low

Finish: light citrus aroma and a light gin presence

Vesper

2 oz. gin

1 oz. vodka

¼ oz. Lillet Blanc

1 dash of orange bitters

Method: Shake all ingredients. Strain into a chilled cocktail glass and garnish with a lemon twist.

History: The cocktail was made by Gillbert Preti in 1951 for Ian Fleming and his first book about James Bond, *Casino Royale*, and here is the famous line Bond says: "Just a moment. Three measures of Gordon's, one of vodka, half a measure of Kina Lillet. Shake it very well until it's ice-cold, then add a large slice of lemon-peel. Got it?"

Dominant aromas: juniper and herbals

Body: light

Dryness: dry

Complexity: medium to high

Finish: elegant presence of alcohol with background of juniper and citrus notes

Vieux Carre

1 oz. 100 rye whiskey

1 oz. cognac

1 oz. sweet vermouth

½ oz. Benedictine

1 dash of Peychaud's bitters

1 dash of Angostura bitters

Method: Stir all ingredients in a mixing glass. Strain the cocktail into an Old fashioned glass over fresh ice.

History: Vieux Carre was made in 1938 by Walter Bergeron in New Orleans. The litera translation of this cocktail's name would be "Old Square."

Dominant aromas: whiskey and spices

Body: light to medium

Dryness: semi-dry

Complexity: high

Finish: whiskey and cognac with a finesse of vermouth and outstanding herbal note

Whiskey Sour

1 ¾ oz. whiskey

¾ oz. lemon juice

¾ oz. simple syrup (2:1 – sugar to water)

1 egg white (optional)

Method: Dry shake. Add large ice and shake vigorously. Strain the cocktail into an Old fashioned glass over fresh ice. Garnish with an orange flag.

History: The Whiskey Sour became popular at the start of 19th century and the first Whiskey Sours were made with egg whites but that practice was dropped in time.

Dominant aromas: whiskey and citrus

Body: light

Dryness: dry

Complexity: low

Finish: whiskey followed by citrus notes

White Lady

2 oz. gin

1 oz. Cointreau

½ oz. lemon juice

1 dash of Orange bitters

1 egg white

Method: Dry shake all ingredients except orange bitters. Add large ice and shake vigorously. Strain the cocktail into a chilled cocktail glass and garnish with Orange bitters.

History: The cocktail was made by Harry MacElnohe in 1919 in London.

Dominant aromas: juniper and citrus

Body: light to medium

Dryness: dry

Complexity: medium

Finish: juniper with presence of citrus of dry body and subtle orange notes

Zombie

1 oz. rum

½ oz. spiced rum

½ oz. dark rum

½ oz. lime juice

1 oz. Velvet Falernum

1 oz. pineapple juice

1 oz. passion fruit puree

1 dash of Angostura bitters

Method: Shake all ingredients. Strain the cocktail into a Tiki glass over crushed ice and garnish with a lime flag and a mint top.

History: The most famous creation of Don the Beachcomber, Zombie was created in 1934.

Dominant aromas: rum, citrus and tropical fruit

Body: medium

Dryness: semi-dry

Complexity: medium

Finish: rum in presence of citrus notes and tropical fruit

Part twenty-three

✦━━━━━━━━━◆●◆━━━━━━━━━✦

COFFEE AND TEA

"Plants which keep the world going."

- Danilo Božović, Andrija Ristić, Nenad Stanojlović -

Coffee

Coffee is part of Rubiaceae family, a category of shrub. Its seed is the product w call coffee. It is a species of flowering plants (Maagnoliophyta) which originates from tropical parts of Africa (Ethiopia) and Asia. The Arabs are credited with first written trace about coffee which did not take long to gain global popularity. In the 16th century, coffee was still not very well-known, and the market was almost completely open to this beverage So, many world powers tried to dominate coffee trade. The Dutch East Indian Company was one of the first to engage in the coffee trade on a global level. So, owing to coffee, the Netherlands reached Far East (Indonesia, Phillipines and Japan) and later the American continent. Venice, as a center of trade between Europeans and Arabs, held the place fo center of coffee trade for a long time. Wars, trade, and travels kept introducing people to this noble plant. Apart from the Netherlands, Turkey had a big role in raising awareness about coffee. During the reign of Suleiman the Great in the 16th century, taverns became very popular and it was the intent of the Turkish ruler for traders, wayfarers, and soldiers to have a place where they could rest, drink a cup of coffee and regain their strength. With the growing popularity of coffee in the 17th century, Europeans started consuming coffee even more in everyday life. America did not fall behind Europe and Asia much. After the Boston Tea Party in 1773, Americans turned to coffee instead of tea, out of boycott. In the 18th century, coffee arrived in the Caribbean which, unfortunately, lead to an increase in slavery Coffee soon became the second article sold in the world (first one being petroleum). Today we can hardly think of a world without coffee.

Caffeine is the main stimulant of the human central nervous system. Coffee needs to be consumed in moderation, and people with heart conditions are advised against consuming it because it quickens the heart rate. The human body can easily become immune to effect of coffee, and with building up resistance you lose that „good feeling" you once had Doctors maintain that 200 mg is a recommended daily intake of caffeine which would be two cups of this beverage. Tea, on the other hand, has two times less caffeine. There is still no certain explanation as to how humans discovered the effects of coffee. There is an amusing story about Kaldi, an Ethiopian goat herder, who noticed one day that his goats were more energetic than usual. After some time, he discovered them eating re coffee beans and concluded they were responsible. There are over fifty species of coffee in the world, and two of the most commercially common species are coffee arabica and rubusta (coffee canephora). These plants originate from Ethiopia and can reach a height from five (arabica) to ten (robusta) meters. Arabica contains more complex aromas as well as a greater concentration of acids. This breed is most common in Latin America, Asia and Africa. Robusta is a lot more resistant than arabica, is more bitter and makes up around 3 % of coffee sold worldwide. Apart from that, it contains twice the amount of caffeine than arabica, which makes it more bitter. Due to its great bitterness, robusta is mostly used i blends with arabica (10 – 15 % of robusta) in order for coffee to gain texture, flavor, arom and bitterness.

How is coffee traditionally made?

After maturation of the plant, its beans are gathered and dried. During drying, the moisture of beans drops to 11%. After drying, the skin is peeled and only the seed is left. They are polished in order to remove the last bits of peel on the seed. After that, coffee undergoes checks where all the seeds that do not meet industry standards are rejected. The chosen green seeds are then roasted at a temperature of 260 C or 500 F. The seed is ready when both sides open up and get brownish color. The longer the seed is roasted the color is darker and the caffeine content lower. Roasted coffee should reach the guest in as short time as possible.

Working with coffee

Coffee is best for consumption after four to seven days after the roast. Coffee is very sensitive to the outside atmosphere (air, moisture, temperature, smells) and the bartender should be mindful of the state of coffee during his shift. The best milk for making foam is fresh, unused, cold milk with 0 – 2% of milk fat. Coffee should be served immediately after the preparation.

Introduction to espresso preparation

Barista is an Italian word for a bartender responsible for making coffee, drinks, cakes and sandwiches. In some countries, barista means to be an expert in preparing coffee, but in any case, he needs to understand the way an espresso machine and coffee grinder work and of course understand the main ingredient – coffee. A barista needs to be able to make a perfect espresso even under pressure. The paramount thing is that a true barista has to feel passion towards coffee. In many countries, you can see people fascinated with coffee, less than seldom, planning their day around a coffee break. Coffee helps wake them up and allows them to work and study longer and more efficiently. After water, coffee is the most consumed beverage in the world.

In order to make a perfect espresso the following conditions should be met:

Equipment has to be clean, dry and properly adjusted (grinder, temperature, pressure)

Coffee should be fresh.

Pressure in the espresso machine has to be 9 bars.

Temperature in the machine should be 88 – 92 C (109 – 197 F).

Machine has to be adjusted to release the specific amount of water when making coffee.

Grinder has to be adjusted to certain granulation and to release a specific amount of coffee (7-9 gram).

Properly pressed coffee in the portafilter is a technique called tamping (making a coffee cake).

Espresso

Espresso is not a sort of coffee but a beverage that is mad by hot, pressurized water seeping through pressed, finely groun coffee. Without an espresso machine it is impossible to make a espresso. The coffee used should be fresh in order for espresso have full and quality flavor. One shot of espresso uses up 7 - 9 (sometimes more) of ground coffee. Use tamper to firmly pre (around 13 kg of pressure depending on granulation of coffe coffee in the portafilter. Before putting the portafilter back into the machine, allow som hot water flow freely in order to dispose of the remains of the previously made espress The so called mouse tail, or the way coffee escapes the machine, has to be continuous an resemble a mouse's tail. The time frame for making a cup of espresso is between 23 an 30 seconds. A shot of espresso should be 1 oz. or 33.3 ml. Ristretto or short espresso is tw times smaller than the regular (1/2 oz.). Bearing in mind that 92 – 98% is water, filtere non-mineral water of 92 – 95 C or 197 – 203 F is recommended. The cream/foam depen on the coffee sort and should be around 3 mm thick. The quality and texture of coffee depends on the freshness and the amount used in preparation. Darker foam indicates that more coffee was used or that the espresso was not made in an adequate time frame. Lack of foam can be indicative of the fact that too little coffee was used or that it was ground too fine. Extraction should be compact, foam should look like velvet and most importantly, in order to make certain that an espresso is properly prepared measure the extraction time and its volume.

Espresso

Length/Volume: 25 – 30 ml

Extraction duration: 25 – 30 seconds

Foam: 2 – 4 ml thick, compact, chestnut colored

Ristretto is an Italian word for restriction and in this case, signifies an intensiv concentrated, sweet, short coffee of as little as 15 ml.

Doppio espresso is a double espresso – 60 – 70 ml with 14 – 16 g of coffee, extracted 25-30 seconds.

Macchiato is an espresso without milk, 30 -35 ml, with a little foam on top. Milk, if requested, can be served in a little pot on the side.

Cappuccino is an espresso mixed with equal part of warm milk and foam. It is usually served in a layer of 18 - 24 cl. In a traditional cappuccino all three layers should be visible.

Caffe Latte is an espresso mixed with warm milk and topped with milk foam which does not exceed 1 - 2 cm. It is served in a cup of 27 – 36 cl.

Caffe Mocca is an espresso mixed with warm milk and chocolate; can be topped with whipped cream.

Americano is a shot of espresso with hot water. Depending on the size, an Americano can vary in water – coffee proportion (1:2, 1:4).

Turkish coffee is prepared by pouring water into a coffee pot until it boils after which the pot is taken off the fire and ground coffee is added. Pot is then returned on medium fire and once it boils, fire is put out and the coffee is ready.

Espresso preparation

Removing portafilter from the machine – it is removed with one hand in one move.

Removing used coffee – clean the remaining, used coffee from portafilter, by letting water flow without the portafilter in order to clean the head on the machine.

Pouring coffee in portafilter from the grinder – dosage and whether portafilter is full of coffee

Pressing coffee in portafilter, tamping – spread ground coffee in the portafilter paying attention to the edges of the portafilter, position of hands and tamper, the level and pressure required for proper pressing.

Fixing portafilter on the machine – same as removing, place the portafilter back on in one motion.

Start of extraction – press the button for extraction the moment you place the portafilter back on in order to avoid burning of coffee on the head. Extraction commences immediately after the portafilter is back on (and do not worry, you have enough time to place the cup on).

Speed of extraction – espresso poured from head in a mouse tail should be a thin continuous stream. Dripping and too quick streams are not desirable; measure the time needed for extraction, almost 1oz or 25ml – 25 seconds.

Final result – quantity, foam, flavor, flexibility of cream. Foam should close up after you slide your teaspoon through it, flavor should resemble a syrup instead of being watery; combination of bitter, sweet and sour, depending on coffee species, has to be balanced.

Milk

Milk and foam preparation for coffees like cappuccino, caffe latte and similar demand a specific technique of creating milk texture for every espresso individually. One should start by putting the steam atomizer just below the surface of the milk. As the temperature rises, place the atomizer one mm deeper. Make sure that during warming there are as few air bubbles as possible. When the temperature reaches 65 C or 149 F, milk is ready for use. Wipe the atomizer after use. If the milk was prepared properly, it can be poured directly from the container without the use of spoon. After that, use a spoon to mix the milk in the cup in order to mix it in evenly, start pouring foam for the cappuccino by putting latiera in a horizontal position relative to the cup and then pour cream in its center. Always use fresh and cold milk. Never warm up the same milk more than twice.

Milk preparation

Milk volume in latiera – depending on what type of beverage you are making pour the exact amount of milk you need.

Position of steamer in milk – if the surface of milk forms a circle in latiera, it is necessary to split the circle into quarters and position the steamer on one of the quarters, never in the center.

Slowly position the latiera lower as the milk increases in volume – as the foam volume ncreases dip the steamer deeper into the milk.

Sound of milk turning into foam should be a constant hissing sound.

Temperature at which the steam is turned off – you do not have much time so take care about the milk temperature because it is overheats it will not form nice cream, therefore it is necessary to remain in the scope around 65 C or 149 F. The temperature is right when touching the latiera becomes uncomfortable.

Milk appearance at this phase – without visible bubbles on the surface, flexible and mobile mass of visibly creamy volume.

Steamer cleaning – should be wiped immediately after the milk heating is completed.

Foam pouring techniques – directly from latiera into the coffee without spoon, start pouring cream by bringing the latiera closer and farther from the surface of coffee and observe the difference in appearance of the overall drink; practice making a traditional cappuccino look starting from one dot.

Tea

Tea originates from China and is one of the oldest ways to heal body and mind. Te is made by boiling plants in water. This process extracts proteins, enzymes and herbal oil from plants. Tea is a plant that belongs to the species called *camellia sinesis* that include white, yellow, green, oolang, black and pu-erh tea. As other goods, tea has its expiratio date, so the longer it remains unused the more it deteriorates in regards to flavor and qualit The traditional kettle used for serving tea also stems from China, and is an excellent way t consume this beverage. Ruling Chinese dynasties respected tea as the „potion of life". Th first written mentions of tea date back to 760 AD. People of Asia used to express the dept of their respect towards tea through various techniques of consuming it. The culture of te consumption was equally strong in Turkey, India and Great Britain.

The English transferred the tea culture from China to the „Island" in order t suppress China's domination of the tea market, and at the same time, develop their own All tea leaves (except herbal and fruit) stem from the evergreen plant *Camellia sinesi.* Leaves contain bioactive substances: thein, theobromine, theophylline and essential oil Tea of the greatest quality is gathered from young plants, so bushes are pruned every yea You can get up to 4 harvests from one bush. Leaves give the best quality tea just before th harvest, and with each following harvest the quality diminishes. There are a few categorie of tea:

Golden – of greatest quality, only the youngest leaf buds are harvested.

Orange pekoe – first leaves picked after the buds open.

Pekoe – tea from second generation leaves.

Pekoe–souchong and souchong – leaves of the third and fourth generations

Congon – tea made from old, big leaves of the lowest quality.

Green tea is processed exclusively using steam, without oxidation or fermentation, and dried on air which preserves the color and other precious ingredients.

Black tea is fermented and is almost completely black due to this. Black teas mostl originate from African, Indian and Indonesian plantations, whereas green ones are mostl from the lands of far East, China and Japan. Teas with aromas enjoy great popularity ar there are over a hundred sorts (jasmine, gardenia, magnolia, chamomile, rose – the choic is great).

White tea is very rare and grows only in certain parts of China. It is made of only th finest, youngest leaves and buds covered with short white bristles. It is of light golden col and has a remarkably refreshing flavor.

Rooibos tea or "mother's miracle," which is found only in the South of Africa, is given abies because it alleviates cramps that they experience in the first few months. It does not ontain caffeine so it can be consumed throughout the whole day. It is also tasty when cold nd can be mixed with orange juice or cocktails.

Herbal and fruit teas are made of flowers, peels, and seeds as well as all kinds of fruit. hey contain no caffeine, so they are suitable for children. During preparation, herbal tea eeds to sit in boiled water and is strained after around ten minutes.

Tea preparation

Japanese method – boiled water is poured over tea and left for three minutes. If the tea is oo sour, repeat the procedure, that is, throw away the used water, pour hot water over it gain and serve after 2 minutes.

English method – one cup of tea – one small teaspoon of tea. Hot water is poured over eaves. After five minutes, tea is served.

Three fingers method – for each cup, take the amount of tea that you can grab between our thumb, index and middle finger, plus one pinch extra for the teapot. Pour hot, but not boiling water, over all of it.

Tea can be compliment in lots of ways: by adding milk, rum, lemon, vanilla, etc. is mostly sweetened with sugar or honey. In China and Japan, they drink it without weeteners and with no additions. It can also be used as a spice. Americans discovered ice ea during the First World Fair and patented it. The idea was to serve tea to visitors but due o overwhelming summer heat, no one was interested in drinking tea. Someone thought of utting a great amount of ice into the boiled tea to cool it. That is how iced tea was created nd became the absolute hit of the fair. After that, iced tea started spreading across the lobe. A few years later, an American, Thomas Sullivan, developed an idea of tea bags. e took samples of tea enveloped in gauze to various restaurants. He then realized that estaurant owners served tea without removing the gauze in order not to leave leaves of tea l over the kitchen and came up with a new product.

Part twenty-four

---◆·◆·▮·◆·◆---

CIGARS

„A toast to life."

- Danilo Božović -

Cigars

European conquerors who first visited Cuba discovered the indigenous populatic smoked folded leaves of tobacco. This ritual left a significant impression on the sailors wl brought the tradition of enjoying tobacco to Spain in the 15th century. It did not take lor for the love towards consuming cigars to develop in other European countries all than to the skill of Dutch traders. In the middle of the 18th century, the cigar industry becan a large and lucrative business. One year occupation of Cuba by Great Britain led to tl popularization of tobacco. It became so popular that at one moment, American preside Franklin Pierce offered Spain a substantial amount of money to buy Cuba. Leopold (Rothschild asked Cuban company, Hoyo de Monterrey, to make smaller cigars so that I could enjoy their rich aroma without consuming the entire cigar. Alfred Dunhill is amor the first companies that understood the importance of humidors in keeping cigars fresh. Tl first and Second World Wars, as well as the American embargo, had huge consequences (cigar production. Apart from that, this period was characterized by the industrialization (cigar production, which led to firing people and the lowering the standard of the workir class that was no longer able to afford a quality Cuban cigar. Before the American embarg on Cuba in 1962, American president, John F. Kennedy, ordered his secretary to buy thousand H. Upmann Petit Coronas cigars. Very quickly, other Caribbean countries joine the quality cigar production race. Cuban immigrants happily passed on their knowledg and passion towards cigar making in the countries they moved to. Countries such a Honduras, Nicaragua, the Dominican Republic, the Canary Islands (which made ciga for the Spanish market for years), Brasil, Mexico, etc. The times changed, and Cuba ha to maintain a high quality of tobacco which it had built for years. After the decision prevent Cuban export and production of cigars for other companies, great brands such . Dunhill and Davidoff turned to other countries.

How cigars are made

Cigar made of 100% Cuban tobacco leaves is also known as a clear ciga Traditionally, cigars were handmade and were appreciated as such. One man can make whole cigar on his own or delegate work to bunchers (the ones who bind the inner part (cigar) and rollers (who make the wrapper). Hand-craft is very demanding and requires lot of effort, concentration and experience. On the other hand, even with the productic using machines one part of the cigar has to be done manually. There are also cigars mac completely mechanically. Entubar is the name for an old Cuban technique of cigar makir where every leaf is rolled into a tube which will eventually become the filler. The fill is placed onto the leaf (binder) and rolled. The result is the bunch or cigar without tl wrapper. The bunch is then placed into the wooden frame whose main function is to secu the wanted shape and size of the cigar. The bunch spends up to 45 minutes in the frame order to get a regular shape. The unfinished cigar is taken from the frame and placed on the final leaf and wrapper, which is precisely cut and shaped with a Cuban knife (chaveta Later, the cigar is placed into a cutter where it gets its final shape. Making cigars is complex process during which an experienced manufacturer can make up to 700 cigars day. As is the case with wine, the geographic origin of tobacco defines its characteristic

Depending on the seed of the plant, tobacco will possess different size, color, texture while the country of origin and climate will determine what flavor and aroma tobacco will have. From the germination of seeds, each plant is under careful farming supervision and after 45 days, the most durable ones are moved to tobacco fields where they are strategically replanted. There are three basic types of leaves: "Volado" are the leaves on the bottom of the plant and are used to make the mildest cigars; "seco" are the leaves in the middle of the plant and give away a moderately strong aroma; "ligero" are the leaves on the top of the plant which give away the strongest flavor and aroma. After the harvest, depending on the type, leaves are left to dry for up to eight weeks. Drying is performed in special fermentation rooms where the tobacco leaves, on a strictly regulated temperature, sweat out the extra moisture. During this process, the leaf slowly changes its color and character. The fermentation process lasts for six months, sometimes more, after which the leaves are assessed individually and regrouped. After that, the tobacco is left to age for 1 – 3 years and sometimes, if required, longer. After the aging process leaves are separated into those that will be used as wrappers, ones that will serve as binders and ones that will be fillers. The filler is the heart of the cigar. The binder is the part that holds the cente filler together. The wrapper completes the cigar and gives it character. The wrapper makes 30 – 60% of the cigar.

How to properly consume a cigar?

Cigar consumption, like cocktails, depending on when and how one enjoys, will result in completely different flavor and aroma. Therefore, one can start an evening with a Martini or a Negroni and if one enjoys a casual conversation during summer, Tom Collins is a great choice. If one is somewhere next to water, there is nothing like a refreshing Mojito. Similarly, one should find the right moment for a cigar in order to enjoy it fully. Choosing a moment for enjoying a cigar is personal and depends on the mood and desire of the individual. It is important to not stress when smoking because one will not be able to enjoy the experience fully.

Cigars can be cut in three different ways

The guillotine cut involves removing the cigar's head at a right angle.

"V" cut is, like the name suggests, cutting the cigar in the shape of letter V.

Pierce cut, technically speaking, is not a cut but a hole drilled into the center of the cigar's head. In most cases, people opt for the guillotine cut and in that case it is recommended that the cut be performed above the horizontal cap-line of the cigar. Lighting of a cigar is done strictly by a match or a butane lighter. During lighting, a cigar should be held at an angle of 45 degrees and cannot touch the flame but should be slowly rotated. When the foot of the cigar is hot enough, it is placed onto the lip while the head is still over the fire. In order to light the cigar uniformly, continue drawing in the first smoke while the cigar is still above the flame. Smoke is not inhaled during use of cigars. Cigar aroma is felt in the mouth. Therefore smoke is never inhaled. A properly consumed cigar will stay straight during the entire process of smoking. A long trail of ash on the cigar is indicative that its wrapper is healthy and well-made and properly consumed. An irregular line shows that the wrapper is of inferior quality. Ash should be removed before the consumer thinks it will fall off on its own. At the end of consumption, easily put away the cigar and let it go out on its own.

Cigars characteristics from different regions

Aside from the fact that every brand possesses its own tobacco which has specific characteristics and aroma, there are regions from which cigars can originate which will give them their identities:

Dominican Republic – extraordinarily mild aroma.

Nicaragua – moderately sweet aroma; can possess aroma of meat in the back.

Honduras – fuller body than a Dominican.

Havana – moderate and full bodies.

Jamaica – slightly fuller body and flavor that a Dominican.

Ecuador – full bodies.

Cameron – slightly fuller body and spicier aroma than a Dominican.

Mexico – full aroma.

Philippines – milder aroma.

Part twenty-five

Food lexicon

"Extra knowledge never hurt"

- Živko Radojčić -

A' la carte (menu)	Free choice of dishes in the establishment based on the menu
Blanching - Blanched	Process where the vegetables, or rarely fruits, are shortly cooked in boiling, salty water and then immediately cooled (shocked) with ice.
Roasting – Roasted	Method of cooking over an open flame or in an oven, where hot air is used to cook food from all sides evenly at the temperature of at least 300 F (150 C).
Boiling - Boiled	Process ingredients in boiling water.
Braising - Braised	Thermal treatment of food on steam in a closed container with a certain amount of liquid.
Béchamel	One of five basic sauces in French cooking. Béchamel, White sauce, contains *Roux* (flour and butter) and milk.
Dicing - Diced	Cut into small cubes.
Gratin	Culinary technique where ingredients are firstly thermally treated and then covered with grated cheese or breadcrumbs and then baked in an oven or a salamander to give it brown color.
Marinate - Marinated	Process where the food is kept in a specific liquid in order to improve the taste or to soften it, which is usually the case with meat.
Poaching - Poached	Technique where the ingredients are slowly cooked in milk water or broth but differs from braising and boiling because the ingredients are thermally treated using lower temperature (71 – 82 C).
Beurre blanc	Literally means white butter; hot emulsion sauce made of reduced liquid (wine, vinegar and chives) and cold butter added gradually so as not to separate fat ad water.
Veloute	One of five basic sauces in French cooking; it is made of chicken broth and white fried flour (same amount of butter and flour).
Purée - Pureed	Process where vegetables or fruit are ground into a juicy creamy paste or thick liquid.

Sauté' - Sautéed	Culinary method where ingredients are shortly fried in the hot pan with a little oil or other fat.
Pate'	Spreadable mass made of boiled ground meat, fat with various additives such as vegetables, fresh aromatic grasses, spices and usually white wine or brandy.
Dressing	Type of sauce used for seasoning the taste of the dish, usually salads.
Vichyssoise	French term for thick soup made of leek, potato, neutral sour cream and chicken.
Breaded	Food coated in flour, whisked eggs and breadcrumbs.
Flambé'	Pour alcohol over the food in heated pan and set it on fire. It gives the dish distinctive smell and taste. Liqueurs are mostly used for Flambéed sweats whereas for the salty dished cognac, gin, vodka etc. are used.
Glazing - Glazed	Gives certain dishes sheen.
Roux	Mixture of flour and butter can be cold or hot and it is used for thickening the mass of cooked foods.
Sous vide	New method in cooking. Literally means "in vacuum". It is used for ingredients vacuumed with special plastic bags and boiled at certain temperature, which is physically able to be controlled with a machine for heating up water.
Grilling - Grilled	Roasted on a barbecue.
Hollandaise	One of five French sauces; hot emulsion of egg yolks and melted butter, boiled on steam and usually seasoned with lemon juice and white wine, salt and white pepper.
Béarnaise	In the same group as Hollandaise; emulsion of yolks and extracts (white wine, vinegar, chive, peppercorns) whisked on steam with melted butter and seasoned with tarragon.
Foie gras	Luxury product made from fattened ducks and geese.
Terrine	Similar to Pate' but always served cold and usually made of goose liver, pork and wild game.

Tartare	Finely chopped and seasoned raw meat from beefsteak, and recently from tuna, salmon or some other ingredient.
Torchon	This term is used because, traditionally in France, goose liver wa wrapped in a dishcloth and boiled in water. Liver boiled like this i similar to Terrine but is in shape of a cylinder.
Boiled	Processed in salamander using great temperature.
Jus	Sauce made from roasted bones that give him brownish colo vegetables, aromatic herbs and broth. Is reduced to desired thickness Literally means "its own juice" made of roasted meat.
Stock/Broth	Is a filtered liquid (soup) that can be made from beef, chicken, fish o vegetables. Broth is the base for soups and sauces. I.e. the differenc between soup and broth is that broth is unseasoned liquid while sou is and has additions such as sliced vegetables, noodles etc.
Consommé'	Usually made of strong chicken or beef broth; during the makin process whisked egg whites are used which separate the fat an derivatives. Lately, this term has been used in confectionery strawberry, watermelon Consommé' etc.
Au poivre	Pepper sauce, usually made of chive, cognac, mustard, butter, neutra sour cream and pepper.
Mousse	Food that has light and airy structure. Sweet taste usually come from whisked egg whites or sweet sour cream with the addition o melted chocolate or fruit puree.
Ceviche	Originates in South American countries such as Peru Colombia, Ecuador and is a chopped raw fish seasoned with Ahi paprika or peppers, lemon or lime juice. Additives suc as red onion, coriander and salt can be a part of this sauce Ceviche is also served with side dishes such as sweet potatoes corn, salad or avocado.
Crudo	In Italian language it signifies raw fish sliced thinly an seasoned with lemon juice, spices and olive oil.
Menu	The offer of food and drinks in the establishment.
Confit	Technique where an ingredient is thermally treated in fat (oil pork or duck fat) using low temperature usually around 200 I (93 C). Literally means to preserved. The ingredient is salte and therefore preserved, before being put into fat and thermall treated. This way of conserving is one of the oldest ones.

Beefsteak temperature

Black and blue - raw

Rare

Medium rare

Medium

Medium well

Well done

Acknowledgments

I feel like this book was in the making starting from the first shift working behind the bar. The road to completing Barkeep was not easy but it was well worth it. Many thoughts were awoken thanks to every minute behind the bar, every cocktail, coffee or drink made. Wanting to help out that younger me or any one like that is what the true motivation for making this book was. I am truly happy and blessed knowing that someone will be able to see, read and feel this book for what it is.

There are many people to thank for this book coming alive. I would like to start with my parents for taking up with me when I was flairing and breaking bottles in my room, making noise, spilling water on the wooden floor, damaging the wall of my room, etc. They accepted it with embrace. I bet it wasn't the most pleasant thing to listen to but thank you very much for the support! I love you and miss you both dearly, every day I spend without you.

The Night Club Magacin, Belgrade, 2009, was where I meet Dushan Zaric to whom I am most thankful for opening my eyes, believing in me and leading me into a whole different world of bartending. A huge thank you as well to Igor Hadzismajlović, since the first shift at Employees Only you have always been a great support. Thank you both greatly!

I would also like to thank everyone who has been affected in anyway, while Barkeep was taking time, focus, and energy. I would like to thank everybody at Macao Trading Co and Employees Only. You guys rock! You are one cool, hard-working, easy-going bunch which I am blessed to have met.

Thanks to everyone who was a part of the creative process behind this book: Andrija Ristić, my old friend and college, the coauthor, for contributing largely and of great importance to the Barkeep. Živko Radojcić, friend and chef, for giving a big piece of mind in the food department. Gabriel Lehner for the best possible book art and illustrations one could wish for. The illustrations are truly amazing. Thanks to my dear brother Milan for making the best decisions for the benefit of this book. Thank you Nenad Stanojlović for the coffee input. Uros Djukić for your wine expertise. Thank you Allen Katz, Ivan Papic and Philip Duff for their time, effort and the evaluation of Barkeep as well, as my friend and colleague Ulysses Vidal for proof reading Barkeep. Thank you as well Robert Kruger, Carlos Esquivel, Steph Ridgway and Osvaldo Vazquez for the contribution. Thanks to my dear friend, the graphic designer and artist, Aleksandar Najdenov (Evolve Company), for the wonderful cover and graphic design behind Barkeep.

It is a blessing to know you all.

Thank you and Godspeed!

Afterword

It is safe to assume that without the modern day professional barkeep the rise craft distilleries in the United States (and increasingly other parts of the world) wou be a muted ascent to the contemporary cocktail renaissance. In these intertwined trade precision, curiosity and a constant zest for learning are skills that can lead to innovatio distinction and pure joy.

Barkeep harkens tradition and classic aesthetic with an eye toward mode hospitality and mixology.

The link is unmistakable and Barkeep, as a comprehensive primer and indispensab reference is a one-stop source for history, practical service and expert technique.

The continued growth and passion for cocktails and spirits – both classic ar contemporary – lies firmly in the access to information. Here, in the pages of Barkee is the elemental tool of education – the willingness to share - from the point of trainin challenge and ultimately success.

Allen Kat
Founder, New York Distilling Compar
New York City, February 20

Barkeep is educational and entertaining read. Goes beyond cocktail recipes ar techniques, teaches you history, spirits and steps of service, among many others. Everythir you need as a professional bartender to make your guest happy, which is ultimate goal everyone in the service industry. A must have, weather you are seasoned bartender or ju entertaining your friends at home.

Ivan Papi
Bartend
New York City, April 20

Good bartenders put a little bit of their heart and soul in each drink that they make; so too with the book you hold in your hands. On the face of it there are many books with a similar table of contents, but Danilo's writing, like his mixology, is infused with his deep love – need, even – of ensuring that everything he does is of the highest quality, and that afterwards everyone goes home happy. To see him effortlessly orchestrate the raucous symphony that is the bar at Macao on a busy night, is to see someone at the peak of their skills, doing what they love best, and performing on the best possible stage they could occupy. "Barkeep" will equip you with knowledge of the skills needed to become a good basic bartender, but it will also inspire you to be a great host. Danilo's honesty, humility and humor infuse these pages, and this fine book both invites, and rewards, reading and frequent re-reading.

Philip Duff,
Door 74 Bar (Amsterdam), Spirits Educator (Liquid Solutions Ltd), and Director of
Education (Tales of the Cocktail)
New York, April, 2016

Cheers!

It's been a pleasure sharing the Barkeep experience with you. If you loved the book an have a moment to spare, I would really appreciate a short review. Your help in spreadir the word of Barkeep is truly appreciated.

If you wish you can stay up to date with the next books by subscribing to the mailing li at www.hollowpointpublishing.net

P.s. No junk mail will be sent out, only important information

About Danilo Božović

While bartending for more than a decade I have been competing as well as judgi mixology and flair competitions. A while after winning the first place in a Flair Competiti in Croatia 2008, Andrija Ristic and myself became the co-founders of Belgrade Bartendi Academy, a Bartending School in Belgrade. At that time in Belgrade, I was the bar manag at the night club "Magacin" and the bar manager at the cocktail bar "Crveni Petao" (R Roster). I started to work at Employees Only and Macao Trading Co. NYC in 2011 a shortly after that I became the bar manager of Macao Trading Co. After being the b manager at Macao Trading Co, I have been working on this book, a modern day bar bo and manual.

Connect with Danilo online:

facebook.com/Danilo.Dacha.Bozovic
instagram.com/danilodacha_ddb
dacha@hollowpointpublishing.net

About Andrija Ristić

Having worked my way around the Belgrade bar circuit, I have been a bartena at the most visiting city center bars and clubs including "Insomnia", "Del Mar" and "R Rooster" - where I met Dacha and together we started consulting and training staff whi result in the opening of Belgrade Bartending Academy. Shortly I became a profession consultant for Pernod-Ricard Serbia and the Hospitality School Belgrade.

Connect with Andrija online:

andrijaristic@gmail.com

Bibliography

Baker, Phil, The book of Absinthe, 2001

Don Pancho, Origenes Rum, 2011

Broom, Dave, Rum, 2003

Campana, Andy, How to make good cocktail, 2002

Carleton Hacker, Richard, *The Ultimate Cigar Book,* 2015

Gascoyne, Kevin, et al., *Tea: History terroirs varieties,* 2014

Anderson, Fred, The War that made America: A short history of the French and Indian War,2006

Falkner, James, The War of the Spanish Succession 1701-1714, 2016

Embury, David, *Fine Art of Mixing Drinks,* 1948

Haigh, Ted, *Vintage spirits and forgotten cocktails*, 2009

Jackson, Michael, Whiskey, 2005

Broom, Dave, Whiskey The Manual, 2014

Kosmas, Jason et al., Bar Manual, 2008

MacNeil, Karen, *Wine Bible*, 2001

Miller, Anistatia et al., *The Deans of Drinks*, 2013

Ristic, Andrija, *Belgrade Bartending Bar Manual*, 2008

Sinnott, Kevin, *The art and craft of coffee,* 2010

Stojanović, Rodoljub, *Kuvarstvo i poslasticarstvo,* 2000

Webb, Tim et al.,*The World Atlas of Beer: The Essential Guide to the Beers of the World*, 2012

Vanity Fair, "*A new Brand of Russian Mogul*", 2008

Diffords Guide, Vodka - How vodka is made?, 2014

Carlson, Jen, Gothamist, New York City's First Printed Liquor License, 2013

Hess, Robert et al., The Museum of the American Cocktail Recipe Guide, 2008

Dale deGroff, The Craft of the Cocktail, 2002

Kosmas, Jason et al., Speakeasy, 2010

Bellis, Marry, The History of the Blender, 2010

Hiles, Theron, The Ice Crop: How to harvest, Store, Ship and Use ice, 1893

Weightman, Gavin, The Frozen Water Trade: How Ice from New England Lakes kept the World Cool, 2003

Barker, Robert, The Process of Making Ice in the East Indies, 1775

Berger, Dan, *How can you make ice without electricity or without a fridge?*, 1999

Femme, Gaastra, The Dutch East India Company: expansion and decline, 2003

The New York Times, Company news; Judge rejects Stolichnaya trademark suit, 1992

Signorile, Michelangelo, Val Mendeleev Stoli CEO Interview, 2013

- Lewis, Richard, Aboslut Book, 1996
- Absoluted.com, The Story, 1997
- Kindersley, Dorling, Eyewitness Companions: Whisky, 2008
- Barnett, Richard, The book of Gin, 2011
- Ford, Adam, Vermouth: The Revival of the Spirit that Created America's Cocktail Culture, 2015
- Broom, Dave, New American Bartenders Handbook, 2003
- Wormwoodsociety.com
- McEvoy, John, Holly smoke! It's Mezcal, 2014
- Regan, Gary, The Joy of Mixology, 2003

Web sites

- liquor.com
- esquire.com
- diffordsguide.com
- punchdrink.com
- cognac-knowledge.com
- wormwoodsociety.com

Magazines

- Imbibe Magazine
- punchdrink.com

CPSIA information can be obtained
at www.ICGtesting.com
Printed in the USA
BVHW010107301121
622797BV00007B/181

9 780997 806